The Sacred Books of the Jews

The Sacred Books
of the Jews

HARRY GERSH

STEIN AND DAY / *Publishers* / New York

First STEIN AND DAY PAPERBACK edition 1972

Copyright © 1968 Harry Gersh

Library of Congress Catalog Card No. 68-17320

Published simultaneously in Canada by Saunders of Toronto, Ltd.

Designed by Bernard Schleifer

Printed in the United States of America

Stein and Day/*Publishers*/7 East 48 Street, New York, N.Y. 10017

ISBN 0-8128-1528-9

for Iz and Rose,
   Miriam and Bud,
   Jonathon, Deborah, David
   those who went before and those who come after

in appreciation:
   to Rabbi Emanuel Green, who started all this, for a scholar's eye
   and a friend's heart;
   to Rabbi Ludwig Nadelmann, who counseled, corrected, and
   urged;
   to Ernestine Burrow, who always ends up knowing these manuscripts better than the author.

Contents

Foreword

JUDAISM BEGAN IN writings and became the most literate, the most book-intoxicated, of the world's great faiths. Judaism bars worship of any physical thing—animate or inanimate—and so the Jews did not worship their books. But study of the sacred books is a form of worship and is required of Jews.

So deeply did the Jews respect their books that they were not destroyed when they became frayed and torn. When books of importance (and for two thousand years there were no other books for the Jews) were too worn for use, they were given honorable burial in a vault beneath the synagogue. In the Jewish hierarchy of values, a *Beth haMidrash* (a house of study: thus, a house of books) takes precedence over a *Beth haKnesset* (a house of assembly: a synagogue). Therefore, ruled the Rabbis, it is proper to change a synagogue into a house of study, which would be moving it upward in importance, but improper to change a house of study into a synagogue, which would be moving it downward. In all these ways Jews expressed reverence for the unique capacity of man to give permanent form to his greatest power: to provide through the written word a permanent record of his most exalted thoughts.

This Jewish intoxication with the written word comes out of the Jews' earliest history. The most ancient books of the Jews are full of the idea of books. The Commandments were not only told to Moses; they were *written* on tablets of stone. "And Moses *wrote* all the words of the Lord . . . he took the *book* of the covenant. . . ." The marshal's staff in the Song of Deborah was a writer's implement, not a sword.

The major Eastern religions also have many scriptural books. The religion of the Hindus is based on the Vedas and the Brahmana writings, on the Upanishads, the Mahabharata, the Puranas. The three Pitakas and the Avadanas are sacred to the followers of Buddha. The Confucian follows the Analects, the Doctrine of the Mean, and the works of Mencius. Taoists hold in reverence Lao-Tze's Tao-teh-ching. These books are all revered, but the religions which revere them are not literate bookish faiths. These are religions of non-literate cultures; the great mass of believers could not read the books; writings had little effect upon the development of thought or practice in the faith.

In the West, the two major faiths each had one book: the Bible for the Christians, the Koran for the Muslims. Except for some minor sects—the Book of Mormon for the Mormons, *Science and Health* for the Christian Scientists, for example—religious development was not structured on books, nor were religious books known and studied by the mass of the faithful. Even the Reformation was preached rather than written. And the Muslim schism between Shiite and Sunnite, although theoretically based on a book, the Sunna, developed along dynastic rather than literary lines.

For the Jews, however, every change in belief and practice grew out of a piece of writing; every quarrel was tied to a chapter or a book; many a martyrdom was for a scroll. Over a period of three thousand years, the Jews added book to book to book. The Torah (the first five books of the Bible) was extended by the books of the Prophets and explicated by the Writings. The Law of the Bible was extended by the Oral Law, broadened by the Mishnah, which was in turn interpreted by the Gemarah, and retold in analogy in the Midrash. These were explained in the Responsa, amplified by the Commentaries, ordered by the Codes, given depth in philosophical works, made ritual in the Siddur, and made magic in the Zohar.

Nor were these later books of extension and interpretation read only by priests and rabbis and scholars. They were read by the congregation of Israel in Babylon and Alexandria and Tiberias; in Rome and Athens and Córdoba; in Prague and Frankfort and Warsaw; in London and New York and Buenos Aires. And as they were read, they transformed the religion and the modes of religious expression of the Jews.

In some areas one book had primacy after the Torah, in other areas another book. There were centuries when the Talmud was studied more than the Bible; there were places where the books of Maimonides were treasured and places where they were outlawed; there were times and places where the Zohar was of greater import than the Talmud.

Perhaps if the Jews had had a stable national life, they would have rested with a single book, as did the Christians and the Muslims, or with a number of fixed, ancient texts, as did the Eastern religions. But in their more than three thousand year history, the Jews were politically independent for only a few centuries; they lived in their geographical homeland for only a third of their existence. From the time of the Judges, they were under continual pressure to assimilate into larger cultures, to accept more powerful religions. They lived under ever-changing social and political and physical conditions, in constant need to reformulate their laws, their concepts, and their social patterns—without violating the core concept of a unique monotheism. They did this by developing an impregnable country of the mind and spirit, independent of geography or political power. The books of the Jews defined the expanding boundaries of that country.

Every aspect of Jewish life—from worship to manner of paying wages, from business methods to care of slaves, from marital relations to martial response, from mathematics to medicine—was regulated by these books. And because the Jews were trans-national, their books profoundly influenced the development of the Western world. The early books were taken as canon by Christian and Muslim; the later books were a bridge between world cultures. Perhaps more important in their effect upon the development of the Western world, the books kept the Jews alive. Without these books the Jews would have disappeared at the time of Nebuchadnezzar, or Antiochus, or Titus, or Mohammed, or the Crusades, or the Inquisition, or a hundred times between and since. And without the Jews the history of the world would have been quite different.

These books of the Jews—the books that kept them alive and constant and vital—number many score. Some were lost and are known only by reference. Some were considered uninspired and were disregarded. Some were not read after their time and disappeared. The books discussed in this volume were chosen from among many more, some of which may have equal claim to inclusion. Those that are included were chosen because they were and are read wherever Jews are permitted to function as Jews, because they changed the ways in which Jews thought, expressed themselves, and reacted, and because they were important to the much wider world in which Jews lived.

The Bible is the most revered and the most studied book in Western man's great library. The other books discussed in this volume have been given almost as much respect and study, although by a much smaller group of students. They are, therefore, books whose inner meanings have been in the deepest contention for centuries. The interpretations given in this volume are, in the main, acceptable to a scholarly consensus. But not all the interpretations are so acceptable—and even those that are, are disputed by some scholars and interpreters. So a caveat must be entered: the datings, meanings, interpretations, and surmises of what the original authors meant are this writer's arguable conceptions based on reading a great many works of greater scholars.

Where Biblical quotations are used, they are taken from the English translation made from the Masoretic text, published by the Jewish Publication Society, 1917.

ONE

The Bible:
Sources and Authors

THE BIBLE OF THE JEWS is a national literature rather than a book. Written over a period of a thousand years, this book had many authors, even more editors and redactors. It includes books of poetry and drama, of history and fiction, of law and philosophy. By structure and content the Bible would appear to be the literature of a single people called variously Hebrews, Israelites, by the names of the tribes (Danites, Ephraimites, Gadites, etc.), Judeans, and finally Jews. But its essence is supra-national; its message is trans-cultural.

The Jewish Bible, the Old Testament of the Christians, differs from Protestant Bibles mainly in the order and number of books; it differs from the Catholic Bible not only in order and number of books, but more importantly in excluding the twelve books of the Apocrypha included in the Catholic canon.

Jews divide the Bible into three main sections comprising twenty-four books. The first section, called the Torah in Hebrew, the Law in English, contains the five books of Moses or the Pentateuch: Genesis, Exodus, Leviticus, Numbers, Deuteronomy.[1]

The second major section is the Prophets. It includes four historical books—Joshua, Judges, Samuel I and II, Kings I and II [2]; the three

---

[1] These titles are inventions of the Latin translators of the Bible. The Jews call these books by the major opening word in each book. Thus the first book, Genesis in English, is *Bereshit*, Hebrew for In The Beginning; the second book is *Shemot*, Names; the third book is *Vayikrah*, And He Called; the fourth, *Bamidbar*, In The Wilderness; the fifth, *D'varim*, Words.

major prophets—Isaiah, Jeremiah, and Ezekiel; and the twelve minor prophets—Hosea, Nahum, Joel, Habakkuk, Amos, Zephaniah, Obadiah, Haggai, Jonah, Zechariah, Micah, and Malachi. There are neither religious nor literary nor historical reasons for the separation between the three major and the twelve minor prophets; the designations major and minor refer only to the lengths of the books. Jeremiah, for example, has fifty-two chapters; Habakkuk has only three and Obadiah, one.

The third section of the Bible of the Jews is the Writings, or Hagiographa. It has two books of history—Ezra-Nehemiah, Chronicles I and II [2]; a book of prophecy—Daniel; two works of fiction—Ruth and Esther; three books of wisdom literature—Proverbs, Job, and Ecclesiastes; plus Lamentations, Psalms, and the Song of Songs.

To the ancient Jews, to the early Christians, and to fundamentalists of both faiths to this day, the Jewish Torah is quite literally the revealed Word of God put into the speech of man through the agency of prophets and sages. To these undoubting and uncritical people, God is the Author; the physical authors functioned as amanuenses.

The Rabbis of the Talmud ascribe the physical authorship of the Bible thus: "And who wrote them [the books of the Bible]? Moses wrote his own book [The Torah] and the section concerning Balaam and Job. Joshua wrote his own book and eight verses of the Law [Deuteronomy 34:5-12, telling of the death of Moses]. Samuel wrote his own book and Judges and Ruth. David wrote the Psalms, at the direction of the ten elders [Adam, Abraham, etc., who gave David inspiration]. Jeremiah wrote his own book and the book of Kings and Lamentations. Hezekiah and his college wrote Isaiah, Proverbs, the Song of Songs, and Ecclesiastes. The men of the great synagogue wrote Ezekiel and the Twelve [Minor Prophets], Daniel and Esther. Ezra wrote his own book and the genealogies of the Book of Chronicles as far as himself." [3]

By ascribing the last eight verses of Deuteronomy to Joshua rather than to Moses, the revealer of the entire Torah, the creators of the Talmud had already entered into Biblical criticism. But Christian scholars had begun this process even earlier, in the second century. And in the fifth century, St. Jerome placed the writing of the book of Deuteronomy in the seventh century B.C., thus denying the Mosaic authorship of at least one of the books of the Torah. But the growth of the power of the Church, requiring unquestioning and uncritical acceptance of the Word of God, and the loss of the tools of scholarship in the Middle Ages

---

[2] Samuel I and II, Kings I and II, Chronicles I and II, and Ezra-Nehemiah were each single books in the original Hebrew Bible.

[3] Tractate Baba Bathra 14b (see explanation of Talmudic divisions, pages 112 and 118.)

ended critical investigation of the Bible by Christian scholars for many centuries.

The Talmud, which had a force of law and tradition among Jews second only to the Torah itself, was not easily questioned, particularly about the sources of the most sacred Book of the Jews. So it wasn't until the eleventh century that Jewish scholars hinted at doubts about the Talmudic statement of the writers of the Bible. The great upsurge in scholarship in the Jewish communities in Spain, France, and the Rhineland inevitably led to critical examination of the central Book. In the twelfth century Abraham ibn Ezra suggested that there might have been additions to the Torah after the death of Moses—to whom the Talmud ascribed the entire five books with the exception of the last eight verses. And Moses ibn Gikatilla suggested that the author of the first thirty-nine chapters of Isaiah was not the author of chapters 40–66. In the fifteenth century Isaac Abravanel attempted the first scientific study of the Bible, to be continued two hundred years later by Baruch Spinoza.

Modern critical study of the Bible did not begin until the Age of Reason had led men to question the laws of nature and of God. In 1753 Jean Astruc, professor at the University of Paris, published "Conjectures as to the Original Memoirs Which, as it Appears, Moses used in Composing the Book of Genesis." The caution evident in Astruc's title—the use of such temporizing terms as "conjectures" and "as it appears"—was necessary even in the enlightened eighteenth century, if the divine authorship of the Bible was to be put into question.

The bases of Astruc's conjectures are still valid after two centuries of scholarly Biblical criticism. They have been extended and refined, but they are still most universally accepted. The French scholar suggested that there were two narrative streams in Genesis, and that they could be differentiated according to the names used for God. One narrative stream uses the Tetragrammaton JHVH, supposedly pronounced Yahveh, from which came Jehovah, translated Lord God or the Lord.[4] The author of this narrative is called by scholars the Jahvist, or J. The second narrative stream uses *Elohim,* the generic Hebrew word for Divine Being, translated God. This author is the Elohist, or E.

Early in the nineteenth century, a German scholar pointed out that the unique style, purpose, and philosophy of the last of the Mosaic books, Deuteronomy, indicated a third author. This is the Deuteronomic source, or D. And fifty years later, another scholar showed that the E writings were themselves a combination of early and later sources. The later writings emphasized ritual and religious observance, begettings and

---

[4] This is the personal name of God, never written or pronounced by observant Jews. To avoid writing His unpronounceable Name, Jewish scribes use a two-letter symbol, somewhat similar to "ii," pronounced Adonai.

genealogies and accounts. In it God is frequently referred to as *El Shad-dai,* God Almighty. This source was designated Priestly, or P. And some later scholars find within P a subsource, labeled Holiness, or H. The process of scholarly subdivision continues, after the manner of scholars. Today, authorities claim to have identified at least three J authors, three E's, two D's, and two P's.

Thus the Pentateuch and the Book of Joshua, which has the same sources (scholars lump the six books together as the Hexateuch), are ascribed to five major sources: J, E, D, P, H.[5] The earliest writers, J and E, were probably authors in the contemporary meaning of the word: each was an individual who composed a national history out of earlier legends and writings. But D, P, and H were not individuals; most likely they were colleges of scribes and schools of priests. It was proba-bly the collective Deuteronomist who first combined J and E into a single JE narrative.

The Bible opens with the P narrative; J begins at Genesis 2:4b; and E does not enter until Abraham, Genesis 15. This is also the order of length of contribution to the total Pentateuch. P contributed the largest share of the Torah, then J, then E, then the fused JE, then D; H con-tributed the smallest part.

The J and E documents, which were developed separately as a result of the division in Hebrew dynastic and political life, tell essentially the same story. During their first two centuries in the land of Canaan (Palestine), the Jews were a loose confederation of independent tribes headed by Judges, who were probably chosen by election from among the elders of the tribe. The Jews distrusted kings and other hereditary rulers with great power; in time of war the tribes came together or not, according to how each individual tribe felt threatened. They were thus prey to the stronger kingdoms around them.

Under the leadership of the prophet Samuel, the Jews accepted a king, Saul. The united kingdom was enlarged under David and made an empire under Solomon. But on Solomon's death in the middle of the tenth century B.C., the quarreling tribes divided. Two kingdoms were established: the Northern Kingdom, Israel, and the Southern Kingdom, Judah. The two kingdoms of the Jews sometimes warred against each other, sometimes joined together to war against another nation. But even in peace they were jealous of each other.

Nations must have histories, and literate nations must have written histories. Out of this need came the J and E documents. J told the story

---

[5] Some great scholars have identified other sources, or labeled the established sources with other designations. Professor Robert H. Pfeiffer of Harvard ascribes important portions of the J document to a source he designates Seir (South), or S.

of the Jews from the Creation to the conquest of Canaan from the viewpoint of a citizen of Judah. E's story is told from the viewpoint of a patriot of the Northern Kingdom, Israel. E's history probably paralleled J's—except for the national and tribal bias—but the earlier portions were lost.

Both documents were written when the kingdoms of the respective authors were at a peak of power and authority. J may have been written during Solomon's reign or during the early years of the Judean kingdom, when prosperity made the future look bright. In either case it was in existence by 900 B.C. E may have been written during the reign of Jeroboam II, shortly before 800 B.C., when Israel overshadowed the Southern Kingdom and was a respected threat to nations east and north.

The northern Kingdom fell to the Assyrians late in the eighth century B.C. Its capital Samaria, was destroyed by Sargon in 722 B.C., and its people were carried away into captivity. (This is the source of the legend of the Ten Lost Tribes of Israel.) Survivors of the catastrophe brought the E document to Jerusalem, capital of the Southern Kingdom, and in the century that followed, the two documents began to grow together.

The unknown author of the J document is the greatest of the Biblical authors and one of the great writers of the Western world. His history is a story of real people who react to pain and pleasure, to ambition and promise, to love and hate, much as men have in all ages since Genesis. To J, man is not a puppet controlled by God; he is a creature with free will who dares to question God, even to challenge Him. J's people have a direct and personal relationship to God, in contrast to E's characters, who speak to God only through angels and messengers. J's narrative is man-and-earth centered; E's narrative is heaven-and-God centered.

Thus, in the J story, when Adam acts like a child ("I was afraid, because I was naked; and I hid myself. . . ." [6]), God treats him as a child. When Abraham is torn between two strong women Sarah and Hagar, he reacts like a man of any century, not like a saint: he tries to wash his hands of the problem that is roiling his household. And Sarah, told she would have a child at the age of ninety, doesn't fall on her knees in wonder and thanks. She laughs and makes an earthy comment: "After I am waxed old shall I have pleasure, my lord [Abraham] being old also?" [7] And throughout the Jacob story, although it is obvious that Jacob will win out, J's sympathies are with Esau.

In E, on the other hand, Abraham and his descendants are ideal-

---

[6] Genesis 3:10
[7] Genesis 18:12

ized; they are never guilty of wrong-doing—unless they are under
Divine command to appear to do wrong. Telling the same story, J allows
the Patriarchs to have all the human frailties. In both the J and the E
documents Abraham sends Hagar away from his house. According to J,
Abraham sent Hagar away because Sarah nagged him about a second
woman in the house. This action, understandable in Abraham the man,
is unworthy of Abraham the Patriarch, so E says Abraham cast off
Hagar because he was commanded to do so by God. So, too, in the
Joseph story: J says Joseph was sold by his brothers; E could not imagine the fathers of the tribes behaving so ignobly; he says that Joseph
was kidnapped by Midianites.

J's concept of free will, in contrast to E's idea that God controls all
things and all men's actions, is shown in the differing versions of the
Jacob and Laban story. Both versions agree on the essential facts: Jacob
undertakes to serve Laban as shepherd in return for all the spotted
lambs and kids born in the flocks. Laban tries to cheat Jacob by removing all the spotted animals—who might bear spotted young—from the
flocks. At this point, J and E part. In the J story, Jacob conceives the
idea of putting spotted sticks over the watering troughs. The ewes would
look at the sticks every time they drank and through pre-natal sugges-
tion give birth to spotted young. This is a shrewd, even tricky, but very
human action. And it is Jacob's very own idea; God has nothing to do
with it. But in the E story, Jacob needs neither shrewdness, nor ingenuity, nor any other human quality. An angel appears to Jacob in a dream
and tells him that "all the he-goats which leaped upon the flock were
streaked, speckled, and grizzled."[8] Inevitably, these multi-colored rams
sire spotted young.

J, writing the history of Judah—an earthy, unsophisticated, agricul-
tural nation—tells how a people began, how the Hebrews conquered a
land and achieved nationhood. In this journey they were aided by advice
from God—which they often disregarded—and an occasional miracle.
E, writing the story of sophisticated, commercial Israel, gives a religious
history in which the end is foretold: selected and commanded by an
omnipotent God, the Hebrews win all battles and establish a theocracy.
These histories grow naturally out of their respective authors' differing
concepts of God. For J, God is almost anthropomorphic; for E, God is
a remote something. J lets the action speak; E tends to explain. E is
interested in what happened; J, in to whom it happened.

The Hebrews of both kingdoms were given to backsliding from the
stern monotheism of Moses. They were wooed away by the easier and
more sensual religions of their neighbors. So prophets arose to call the

[8] Genesis 31:10

Jews to account, sometimes with bitter, sometimes with beautiful denunciations. For a time the Jews would return to the God of Moses and abjure the pleasures of Baal and Ashtoreth. Then they would relax again.

One of the worst periods was the middle of the seventh century B.C. Jews worshiped strange gods, made sacrifices to idols brought into the local shrines, and practiced the "abominations" of the heathens. A school of social, religious, and political reformers developed who sought to cleanse the nation by limiting the power of the king, by establishing social justice, by abolishing local sanctuaries, and by concentrating all worship in the Temple at Jerusalem—where it could be controlled more easily. To this end they drew up a new code of law based on the ancient codes. To give the code authority they ascribed it to Moses. During the reign of the reformer king Josiah, the new code was brought forward. According to the Biblical story this code was discovered in the Temple in "the eighteenth year of king Josiah" (622 B.C.):

> And Shaphan the scribe told the king, saying: "Hilkiah the priest hath delivered me a book." And Shaphan read it before the king. And it came to pass, when the king had heard the words of the book of the Law, that he rent his clothes. And the king commanded Hilkiah the priest . . . saying: "Go ye, inquire of the Lord for me, and for the people, and for all Judah, concerning the words of this book that is found; for great is the wrath of the Lord that is kindled against us, because our fathers have not hearkened unto the words of this book, to do according unto all that is written concerning us."[9]

Josiah promulgated this code as the law of Judah, giving that nation the first written constitution. The school of reformers who created this code were the Deuteronomists—and their code was the source of the book of Deuteronomy.

Three decades later (586 B.C.), the Southern kingdom, Judah, suffered the same fate as the Northern Kingdom. The nation was destroyed by the Babylonians, the Temple was leveled, and the people led away into captivity. When Babylon was conquered in turn by Cyrus about fifty years later, that relatively enlightened emperor allowed the Jews to return to Palestine and to rebuild the Temple. But the land and its people remained vassals of Babylon.

Although the prophets of the Exile and the post-exilic period dreamed of a great new Jewish commonwealth, the scholars and priests were too hardheaded and farsighted to be carried away by dreams. They accepted the fact that Judah was a small nation in the midst of great and warring powers, that the people of Judah were comparatively few when

[9] II Kings 22:10–13

counted against the millions to the north and south and east, and that
Judah would have to accept the overlordship of this great king or that.
They set about writing the constitution of a religious nation that could
persist regardless of the mortal king to whom they had to give allegiance
and regardless of physical and political fragmentation.

Combining J and E and D and many earlier sources developed by
their own scholarship, adding their own versions of history and legend,
the priests of the school of P put together the first section of the
Bible—the Torah—the constitution of a Jewish Kingdom of God. Their
writing has been characterized as that of a notary public drawing up a
legal document. Their style was dry, monotonous, juridical rather than
literary; they paid special attention to births and deaths and exact lines
of inheritance, to measurements and dates and statistics. Lawyerlike,
they repeated commands and injunctions in every possible combination
so no loopholes would be left. For example, when they enjoined the
people against eating unleavened bread during the Passover, they
repeated the injunction five times in three sentences:

> In the first month, on the fourteenth day of the month at even, ye shall
> eat unleavened bread, until the one and twentieth day of the month at even.
> Seven days shall there be no leaven found in your houses; for whosoever
> eateth that which is leavened, that soul shall be cut off from the congrega-
> tion of Israel, whether he be a sojourner, or one that is born in the land. Ye
> shall eat nothing leavened; in all your habitations shall ye eat unleavened
> bread."[10]

The difference in style, purpose, and idea of history between the
great storyteller, J, and the lawyer-teacher-priest, P, is best exemplified
by their very different versions of the creation. P's story, told in Genesis
1:1 to 2:4a, is the one known to everyone brought up within the tradition of the Bible:

> In the beginning[11] God created the heaven and the earth. Now the earth
> was unformed and void, and darkness was upon the face of the deep; and
> the spirit of God hovered over the face of the waters. And God said: "Let
> there be light. . . ."

In this version, P's, the order of creation was light and darkness on
the first day, firmament and heaven on the second day, earth and sea
and growing things on the third day, sun and moon and stars on the
fourth day, creatures of the sea and of the air on the fifth day, creatures

---

[10] Exodus 12:18–20

[11] Rashi (Rabbi Solomon ben Isaac), in the eleventh century, suggested that
the opening sentence should be read: "In the beginning of God's creating the
heaven and the earth . . ." The most recent scholarly translation, by E. A. Speiser
in *The Anchor Bible* (Doubleday, 1965), gives this opening phrase much the
same reading as Rashi did.

of the land—including man—on the sixth day. And according to P, woman was created right along with man: "And God created man in His own image, in the image of God created He him; male and female created He them."

J was a storyteller, not a teacher, and so was not interested in the recitation of a pre-Darwinian order of evolution. He forgoes specifics for color and sense and a romantic conceit about the creation of woman:

. . . in the day that the Lord God made earth and heaven. No shrub of the field was yet in the earth, and no herb of the field had yet sprung up; for the Lord God had not caused it to rain upon the earth, and there was no man to till the ground; but there went up a mist from the earth, and watered the whole face of the ground. Then the Lord God formed man of the dust of the ground, and breathed into his nostrils the breath of life; and man became a living soul. And the Lord God planted a garden eastward, in Eden; and there He put the man whom He had formed. And out of the ground made the Lord God to grow every tree that is pleasant to the sight, and good for food; the tree of life also in the midst of the garden, and the tree of the knowledge of good and evil. And a river went out of Eden to water the garden; and from thence it was parted, and became four heads. . . . And the Lord God took the man, and put him into the garden of Eden to dress it and to keep it. And the Lord God commanded the man, saying: "Of every tree of the garden thou mayest freely eat; but of the tree of the knowledge of good and evil, thou shalt not eat of it; for the day thou eatest thereof thou shalt surely die."

And the Lord God said: "It is not good that the man should be alone; I will make him a help meet for him." And out of the ground the Lord God formed every beast of the field, and every fowl of the air; and brought them unto the man to see what he would call them; and whatsoever the man would call every living creature, that was to be the name thereof. And the man gave names to all cattle, and to the fowl of the air, and to every beast of the field; but for Adam there was not found a help meet for him. And the Lord God caused a deep sleep to fall upon the man, and he slept; and He took one of his ribs, and closed up the place with flesh instead thereof. And the rib, which the Lord God had taken from the man, made He a woman and brought her unto the man. And the man said: "This is now bone of my bones, and flesh of my flesh; she shall be called Woman, because she was taken out of Man." Therefore shall a man leave his father and his mother, and shall cleave unto his wife, and they shall be one flesh. And they were both naked, the man and his wife, and were not ashamed.[12]

The difference in the J and P concepts of God are illustrated by the roles they assign to Him in the Flood story. P's God, seeing the evil of the world, makes an unemotional, purely juridical judgment: "And God saw the earth, and behold, it was corrupt; for all flesh had corrupted their way upon the earth. And God said unto Noah: 'The end of all

[12] Genesis 2:4b–25

flesh is come before Me; for the earth is filled with violence through them; and, behold, I will destroy them with the earth.' "[13]

But J's God, seeing the same evil, is full of sorrow and regret that He must destroy man, His own handiwork: "And the Lord saw that the wickedness of man was great in the earth, and that every imagination of the thoughts of his heart was only evil continually. And it repented the Lord that He had made man on the earth, and it grieved Him at His heart."[14]

In the century between the fall of Israel and the promulgation of Deuteronomy, the J and E histories had grown together almost as a natural process. In the next two centuries, first in Judah, then in Babylonia during the Exile, and again in post-exilic Palestine, the schools produced the D and P narratives and shaped the document that was to be the Torah. It might have made more sense for the final redactors of the Pentateuch to iron out the discrepancies among the several authors and sources, to combine the differing versions so that they did not appear to contradict each other. But the ancient editors did little rewriting and very little cutting. They accepted the divine origin of the works they were dealing with and seldom exercised their editorial authority. Their method was to piece together chapters, verses, sentences, even phrases, from original sources, adding only bridges and transitional forms—if they were absolutely necessary.

The completed Torah was canonized[15] in the fifth century B.C.—the Bible places it in the year 444 B.C., but modern scholars give 400 or 420 as more likely dates. The ceremony in which the Five Books of Moses were accepted by the Jews is assumed to be described in this episode from Nehemiah:

> And when the seventh month was come, and the children of Israel were in their cities, all the people gathered themselves together as one man into the broad place that was before the water gate; and they spoke unto Ezra the scribe to bring the book of the Law of Moses, which the Lord had commanded to Israel. And Ezra the priest brought the Law before the congregation, both men and women, and all that could hear with understanding, upon the first day of the seventh month. And he read therein . . . from early morning until midday, in the presence of the men and women, and of those who could understand; and the ears of all the people were attentive unto the book of the Law. And Ezra the scribe stood upon a pulpit of wood. . . . And Ezra opened the book in the sight of all the people . . . [and the Levites] caused the people to understand the Law; and the people stood in

[13] Genesis 6:12–13
[14] Genesis 6:5–6
[15] The word canon meant originally a carpenter's rule, thus a standard of measurement. In Alexandria, the classic Greek authors were called *Kanones*, or models of excellence. Greek Christians applied this term to the Jewish books of recognized authority. The Jews themselves had no such word.

their place. And they [the Levites] read in the book, in the Law of God, distinctly; and they gave the sense, and caused them [the people] to understand the reading. . . .

And on the second day were gathered together the heads of fathers' houses of all the people, the priests, and the Levites, unto Ezra the scribe, even to give attention to the words of the Law. . . .

Now in the twenty and fourth day . . . the children of Israel were assembled . . . and [they] cried with a loud voice unto the Lord their God. . . . And yet for all this we make a sure covenant, and subscribe it; and our princes, our Levites, and our priests, set their seal unto it.[16]

Joshua, the first book of the second section of the Bible, belongs properly with the Pentateuch and has the same sources—mainly J and E. It probably was part of the original manuscript that became the Torah. However, since the Torah was ascribed to Moses, and Joshua tells of what happened after Moses' death, it could not be included in the Books of Moses and so did not become part of the canonical Torah.

Judges, the story of the presiding officers of the tribal courts and of the heroes of the Jews during the thirteenth and twelfth centuries B.C., is also largely J and E, edited by D. Most of the work is straight history, and as with all the early books of the Bible, sometimes includes two versions of the same event and characters. J, for example, tells the story of a man called Gideon; midway in the story, Gideon is called Jerubbaal, probably a P retelling. The one story in Judges for which there is no evidence in history is that of Samson; this is a folk tale pure and simple.

Judges ends with the words: "In those days there was no king in Israel; every man did that which was right in his own eyes." This statement fittingly precedes the book of Samuel, which introduces the history of the Jewish monarchy.

Samuel I and II were originally a single book. It was divided for mechanical, rather than religious or literary reasons: the Greek translation in codex took twice as much space as the more compressed Hebrew. This book, too, is a compilation of several authors. Its earliest and major contributor, a superb writer, appears to have been an eyewitness of some of the events he describes—particularly the tragic father-son quarrel between David and Absalom.[17]

Like J, the first author of Samuel wrote about individuals rather than events—in his case, the individual was David. Thus his history of the war with the Ammonites is told as the personal story of a man and a woman, David and Bathsheba, rather than as the story of a military

---

[16] Nehemiah 8:1 to 10:1

[17] Pfeiffer ascribes this writing to Ahimaaz, son of Zadok, about 1000–950 B.C. Professor Pfeiffer calls Ahimaaz the father of history, antedating Herodotus by some five centuries.

campaign of an expanding nation. And in this history the reader gets a novelist's picture of the king rather than a picture drawn by a self-conscious writer of Scripture; David is a weak father and a lustful lover, not a saint.

The later contributor to the book of Samuel, who wrote in a different time and with a different bias, was not the equal of the earlier writer either as historian or novelist. He took as his protagonist the prophet Samuel rather than King David. The earlier author says that Saul was named king because the people needed deliverance from the Philistines:

Now the Lord had revealed unto Samuel a day before Saul came, saying: "Tomorrow about this time I will send thee a man out of the land [tribe] of Benjamin, and thou shalt anoint him to be prince over My people Israel, and he shall save My people out of the hand of the Philistines; for I have looked upon My people, because their cry is come unto Me."[18]

The later writer probably lived in a period of false or foreign kings. He distrusted monarchs and the institution of monarchy—in part because mortal kings assume some of the powers of the heavenly King. This writer begins his story of the anointing of Saul with an episode in which the prophet Samuel appoints his own sons as judges in Beersheba. But the sons were bad judges; they "walked not in his [Samuel's] ways, but turned aside after lucre, and took bribes, and perverted justice." Whereupon the elders of the tribe asked Samuel to appoint them a king who would "judge [rule] us like all the nations."

Samuel asks the Lord's guidance and is told, as legend says Moses was told, to "hearken unto the [people's] voice." This Samuel does—but first he recites a doleful prediction of the evils kings do to their people:

This will be the manner of the king that shall reign over you: he will take your sons, and appoint them unto him, for his chariots, and to be his horsemen; and they shall run before his chariots. And he will appoint them unto him for captains of thousands and captains of fifties; and to plow his ground, and to reap his harvest, and to make his instruments of war, and the instruments of his chariots. And he will take your daughters to be perfumers, and to be cooks, and to be bakers. And he will take your fields, and your vineyards, and your oliveyards, even the best of them, and give them to his servants. And he will take the tenth of your seed, and of your vineyards and give to his officers, and to his servants. And he will take your men-servants, and your maid-servants, and your goodliest young men, and your asses, and put them to his work. He will take the tenth of your flocks; and ye shall be his servants. And ye shall cry out in that day because of your

[18] I Samuel 9:15–16

king whom ye shall have chosen you; and the Lord will not answer you in that day.[19]

Like the book of Samuel, the books now designated Kings I and II were also a single document in the original Hebrew and were divided when translated into Greek. Kings carries the story of the Jews from the end of David's reign to about 560 B.C., to the present for the authors of the book. The JE history, plus the history in Samuel, carried the story of the Jews from Abraham to Solomon; Kings completed the journey from Solomon to Josiah and a bit beyond. The author of Kings was D, the same school of scribes and priests that produced the book of Deuteromy. D did not write to tell a great story or as a scholarly work of history, but for more practical purposes—in the case of Kings, to demonstrate the truth of the Deuteronomic religion through historical illustration; it is, in effect, a long sermon with historical examples. The kings who were not important religiously are mentioned only briefly; the kings, good or bad, who were important in the religious development of the Jews are covered at length.

Although Kings was written some four hundred years after the events described in the opening of the book, it was not an exercise in invention. The writers used authentic sources; they had access to the annals of Solomon's court, to diaries and laws and petitions and judgments written during Solomon's reign. Two stories in the book are rather remote from history, those of Elijah (I Kings 17–19) and Elisha (II Kings 2–8, 13).

The books of the later prophets, major and minor, are mainly direct quotes from the speeches, oracles, and writings of Isaiah, Jeremiah, Ezekiel, and the Twelve. Most of the material is contemporaneous with prophets to whom the books are ascribed, from about 750 to 400 B.C. There are two major exceptions: the first thirty-nine chapters of the book of Isaiah are correctly ascribed to the Isaiah who was the son of Amoz and lived in the eighth century B.C.; but the succeeding chapters are mainly the work of an unknown writer, called Deutero-Isaiah by scholars, who lived during the Babylonian exile. Zechariah, too, can be credited only with the first eight chapters of his book; the rest belongs to an anonymous author.

The date of the canonization of the Prophets is much less certain than the date of the canonization of the Torah. However, these books must have been accepted as canon well before the Maccabean revolt established the Hasmonean dynasty—probably about 200 B.C.

The books of the prophets were made canon in this period mainly as a rejection of the contemporary prophets. The ancient prophets included

[19] I Samuel 8:3–18

in the canon spoke directly rather than in symbols, and so were easily understood by the people; they denounced ritual and pomp, and so pleased the people; they insisted on social justice and the reality of action, and so were beloved (though sometimes persecuted) by the people. The prophets of the period of the exile in Babylon and after the return to Palestine were prophets of the apocalypse: they spoke in symbols and allegories of an eventual heaven on earth, of the end of days, of the coming of the Messiah; they did not denounce the evils of the day. In the relative stability of the period, the people often stopped listening to their prophets, although new prophets—or men who called themselves prophets—kept appearing. So the priests canonized the ancient Prophets, thus effectively ending prophecy.

The third section of the Bible, the Writings, was written mainly in the fourth and third centuries B.C. But like so much of the Bible, the books of the Hagiographa have sources going back to the beginnings of Jewish history. Psalms, for example, includes hymns written over a period of a thousand years, from well before David, to whom they are ascribed, to about 150 B.C. Ruth, written about 400 B.C., is said by the author to have taken place about seven hundred years earlier, in the time of the Judges.

Ruth is pure fiction—with a purpose: after the return from the Exile, when the nation was weak and there was great danger of assimilation into stronger cultures, Ezra and Nehemiah promulgated very strict laws against intermarriage with non-Jews. As always, such laws caused many personal tragedies. Ruth was a literary revolt against this xenophobia. By telling of the foreigner, the Moabite woman who became David's progenetrix, thus the ancestress of the royal house of Israel, Ruth rejected the idea that evil consequences necessarily follow marriage outside the nation.

The book of Esther, on the other hand, is pure fiction without any apparent religious or moral motive. Even the Jews in Esther are strangely nonreligious: they fast when they are in trouble, but they do not pray; they feast when they have won a victory, but they do not utter a blessing. Such actions are contrary to the spirit of the rest of the Bible. Scholars surmise that if Esther did have a purpose, it was written as a patriotic exercise and to create a mechanism for survival, to provide a religious-historical background for the comparatively new holiday of Purim.

Proverbs, like Psalms, is also a collection of writings that go back a thousand years before the book was compiled about 250 B.C. The Song of Songs, about which the Rabbis had many doubts, is a collection of love poems ascribed to Solomon. And the book does include songs that

Solomon sang—or at least heard sung. The inclusion of The Song of Songs in the canon was made possible only when the Rabbis interpreted the poems as being symbolic of the love between God and Israel rather than between a man and a woman.

Lamentations is a collection of poems ascribed to Jeremiah—early sixth century B.C.—and appears to have been written about that time.

Ecclesiastes is so obviously influenced by the cynicism of the Hellenistic period that it could not have been written before the division of Alexander's empire made Judah a vassal of the Hellenic Seleucid kings; 250 B.C. is a probable date.

Job, the most philosophical book of the Bible, was written about 400 B.C., when the Jewish nation was still in process of composing itself, of binding itself together after the return from Babylon—a period when men naturally questioned the nature of good and evil.

Daniel is properly a book of prophecy but was written too late to be included in that canon. Probably composed during the Maccabean revolt against the Syrian-Greek Antiochus (168–165 B.C.), Daniel was written partially in Aramaic, the language of the Jews during that era. Some passages were translated into Hebrew and the whole book placed in the time of the Exile. This made it eligible for inclusion in the later canon.

The Writings also include three books of history: Ezra, Nehemiah, and Chronicles. Ezra and Chronicles are the work of a single author or school of priestly scribes. The Chronicler retells the story of the Jews from Genesis to Cyrus of Babylon. It is a sequel to the P history, but it is retold to prove the Chronicler's theory of history: human agency is unimportant in deciding events; the outcome of all wars is known in advance—God's side wins; man does exactly what God tells him to do and prospers, or man rejects God's commands and dies.

About half the material in Chronicles is taken from earlier works; the other half was composed by the Chronicler, a writer with a very vivid imagination, great originality, and unshakable convictions. If history, as written until his day, did not say what the Chronicler thought it ought to say, he rewrote history to demonstrate that Israel is God's Holy Congregation and that the Priestly tradition is pure, ancient, and unbroken. The Chronicler's thesis, for example, could not encompass a David who desired and took another man's wife, or the opulent, many-wived Solomon. So in his chronicle these two very human kings become models of piety—and dullness.

Nehemiah, on the other hand, is the honest, straightforward diary of this stern general of the Jews for the years 444 to 432 B.C.

This third section of the Bible, the Writings, was made canon at a formal convocation of priests and scholars of Israel at Jabneh in the year 90, after the destruction of the Second Temple and the end of the last Jewish kingdom. The scholars at Jabneh had many books of a sacred character from which to choose, so they had to set up arbitrary criteria for inclusion in the canon: the Bible was the revealed word of God; therefore its books must have been written by men moved by the spirit of God—or prophets. And, said the Council, since prophecy ended with Ezra, books written after Ezra could not be included. Books written in languages other than Hebrew—Greek, for example—were obviously written after Ezra, and so could not be considered for inclusion in the canon. Thus The Song of Songs, Ecclesiastes, and Proverbs were ascribed to Solomon and included. Psalms was ascribed to David and included. The anonymous Daniel was translated into Hebrew, placed in the time of the Exile, and so became eligible. But the author of the book called The Wisdom of Ben Sirach (the apocryphal book of Ecclesiasticus) was known, and so this book was excluded.

When the canon was closed, there were fourteen religious books which had been considered by the Rabbis but rejected. All were written by Jews, some in Hebrew, some in Greek, some in Aramaic. These were the books of the Apocrypha (from the Greek word for hidden); they include Esdras I and II, Tobit, Judith, The Remainder of Esther, The Wisdom of Solomon, Ecclesiasticus or The Wisdom of Ben Sirach, Baruch, Susanna, The Song of the Three Children, Bel and the Dragon, The Prayer of Manasseh, Maccabees I and II. These books follow the main style and form of the canonical books. Maccabees and Esdras are historical; Manasseh and Baruch (Jeremiah's secretary-scribe) are prophetic; Judith, Susanna, Tobit, and The Remainder of Esther are legends; Ben Sirach and The Wisdom of Solomon are wisdom books.

But these books, rejected by the Rabbis, were included in the earliest Christian canon. The Bible including these fourteen books, was translated into Greek well before the Jewish canon was closed; the Christian canon was based on this Greek translation, and so the apocryphal books were included—not without some disputes. St. Jerome included the books of the Apocrypha in his Vulgate translation of the Bible from the original Hebrew but after the books of the Jewish canon he entered a note: "Whatever is beyond these must be reckoned as Apocrypha. Therefore these books are not in the canon. . . . The Church reads them for the edification of the people."

St. Augustine differed with Jerome and demanded the inclusion of the Apocrypha. A decision favoring Augustine was made at the Council of Hippo, and the "hidden" books have been part of the canon of the Roman Church since.

When Martin Luther translated the Bible, he, too, went back to the original. Since he could not find the apocryphal books in the Hebrew canon, he excluded them from his. He followed Jerome and said that the hidden books were not revealed Word but were "good and useful for reading." Early English translations followed Luther's practice until the King James version, which dropped the apocryphal books altogether. Reacting to the Protestant rejection of what it considered canon, the Roman Church specifically reiterated at the Council of Trent (1546) its veneration of "all books of the Old and New Testament," including the Apocrypha.

The language of the Bible is Hebrew, a virile, deep-in-the-throat language made up of twenty-two consonants and three major vowel sounds. The vowels are not written; in fact they were not even indicated by diacritical marks until about the seventh century. And as in many early tongues, prepositions, articles, relationships, and gender are shown by prefixes and suffixes rather than by separate words. Thus the opening verse of the Bible is written in twenty-eight Hebrew letters; it requires forty-four English letters in the King James version. Early Hebrew writing didn't even leave spaces between words; combined with the lack of vowels, this would make the opening verse of the Bible look something like this:

NthbgnnngGdcrtdthhvnndthrth—In the beginning God created the heaven and the earth.

Biblical Hebrew has comparatively few root words, mainly verbs. Most nouns are derived from these verbs. Thus the noun *maaseh,* meaning event, is from the verb *oseh,* meaning to do. From the verb *chahtah,* to miss (one's aim), comes the noun *chet,* sin; from the verb *shuv,* to turn, the noun *teshuvah,* repentance or answer; from the verb *daber,* to speak, comes the noun *davar,* word; from the verb *maloch,* to rule, come the nouns *melech* and *malkeh,* king and queen.

These word forms give the language a powerful sense of movement, of action, heightened by the paucity of adjectives in the language. The Bible doesn't use phrases with adjectives, like "holy man," or "beloved wife"; instead, it speaks of a "man of God," or "the wife of thy bosom." There is also a tendency to paint word pictures: the idea of morality is conveyed by the phrase "turning away from evil"; the concept of religion, for which there is no word in Hebrew, is conveyed by the phrase "fear of the Lord"; the Hebrew language is "the lip of Canaan."

This combination of sparseness of words and descriptive phrasing led to narrative writing that was direct rather than abstract, to a lyric mood rather than a pedantic one, to poetic expression rather than scholarly explanation. On the other hand, commandments, injunctions, even castigations are stated flatly; thus the social gospel of Amos comes out with great power:

> I hate, I despise your feasts,
> And I will take no delight in your solemn assemblies.
> Yea, though ye offer me burnt-offerings and your meal-offerings,
> I will not accept them;
> Neither will I regard the peace-offerings of your fat beasts.
> Take thou away from Me the noise of thy songs;
> And let me not hear the melody of thy psalteries.
> But let justice well up as waters,
> And righteousness as a mighty stream.[20]

The laws of clean and unclean animals, written two centuries after Amos, are more pedantic than Amos, yet even this lawyer's listing gains strength from the flat flow of its language:

> These are the living things which ye may eat among all the beasts that are on the earth. Whatsoever parteth the hoof, and is wholly cloven-footed, and cheweth the cud, among the beasts, that may ye eat. Nevertheless these shall ye not eat of them that only chew the cud, or of them that only part the hoof: the camel, because he cheweth the cud but parteth not the hoof, he is unclean unto you. And the rock-badger, because he cheweth the cud but parteth not the hoof, he is unclean unto you. And the hare, because she cheweth the cud but parteth not the hoof, she is unclean unto you. And the swine, because he parteth the hoof, and is cloven-footed, but cheweth not the cud, he is unclean unto you. Of their flesh ye shall not eat, and their carcasses ye shall not touch; they are unclean unto you.[21]

The Biblical writers also used assonance to give point to their statements. But assonance, the repetition of words of similar sound (for example, kith and kin), rarely lives through translation. There is no assonance in the English statement, "He looked for justice, but behold, violence."[22] But in Hebrew, the first key word, justice, is *mishpat*; the second key word, violence (spilling blood), is *mishpach*. And in the succeeding line, "[He looked] for righteousness, but behold a cry," the Hebrew *tsedakah* (righteousness) is balanced by *tsaakah* (cry).

Perhaps the most striking literary technique used in the Bible is parallel construction, repetition of ideas. This appears in both simple sentences and succeeding lines of verse. It is used in simple sentences: "He opened his mouth and spoke"; "He lifted his eyes and looked." It is even stronger in verse:

> And He commanded the skies above,
> And opened the doors of heaven;
> And He caused manna to rain upon them for food,
> And gave them of the corn of heaven.
> Man did eat the bread of the mighty;

[20] Amos 5:21–24
[21] Leviticus 11:2–8
[22] Isaiah 5:7

He sent them provisions to the full.
He caused the east wind to set forth in heaven;
    And by His power He brought on the south wind.
He caused flesh also to rain upon them as the dust,
    And winged fowl as the sand of the seas;
And He let it fall in the midst of their camp,
    Round about their dwellings.
So they did eat, and were well filled;
    And he gave them that which they craved.[23]

Such a masculine language would appear to be a weak instrument for the expression of tender love songs, yet it served magnificently for the soft evocation of loveliness in The Song of Songs.

How beautiful are thy steps in sandals,
O prince's daughter!
The roundings of thy thighs are like the links of a chain,
The work of the hands of a skilled workman.
Thy navel is like a round goblet,
Wherein no mingled wine is wanting;
Thy belly is like a heap of wheat
Set about with lilies.
Thy two breasts are like two fawns
That are twins of a gazelle.
Thy neck is as a tower of ivory;
Thine eyes as the pools in Heshbon,
By the gates of Bath-rabbim;
Thy nose is like the tower of Lebanon
Which looketh toward Damascus.
Thy head upon thee is like Carmel,
And the hair of thy head like purple;
The king is held captive in the tresses thereof.
How fair and how pleasant are thou,
O love, for delights![24]

Bible translations are unique among books because they often have more authority than the original manuscript. In fact, the source document is sometimes willfully forgotten. The Bible in Hebrew is the revealed Word of God for the Jew; in Greek it is the revealed Word of God for the Orthodox Churches; in St. Jerome's Vulgate, it is the Word of God for Roman Catholics; in the King James version, it is the Word for many Protestant sects. For these religious groups, not only is the translation assumed to be sacred, but the errors of translation are jealously guarded.

---

[23] Psalm 78:23–29
[24] The Song of Songs 7:2–7

The first translations of the Bible were made for the Jews themselves. By the third century B.C. Alexandria had become a major center of Jewish population and learning. But the language of Alexandria was Greek, not Hebrew, and many of the Jews born in that metropolis spoke only Greek. Thus a Greek version of the Bible, at least of the Torah and the Psalms, was necessary if the Jews were to worship as tradition required—with regular reading of the Torah. The translation of the Pentateuch, as it could now properly be called, into Greek was made in the period 300–250 B.C. The Prophets and the Writings were translated during the next two centuries. This first translation of the Torah was called the Septuagint (referred to as LXX in scholarly books) from the legend that the translation was made in seventy-two days by seventy-two scholars called from Jerusalem by the Ptolemy Philadelphus.

In Palestine, too, the daily language of the Jews had changed. The Jews had brought back with them from Babylon a new Semitic language, Aramaic, which remained the language of Eastern Jews until the seventh century, when Arabic became the universal language of all peoples of the East. So a translation of the Bible was necessary even in Palestine, if the traditional forms of worship were to be carried out by the ordinary Jew. The earliest of the Aramaic translations—called *targumim* (singular, *targum*)—was made by a convert to Judaism, Onkelos. The Targum Onkelos includes only the Torah, since this is the section of the Bible Jews read through every year; or this may have been the only canonized section of the Bible in Onkelos' time.

Later *targumim* include the Targum Jonathon and the Targum Yerushalmi (Jerusalem). All these translations are used as reference by Jewish scholars and for worship by some orthodox Jews. (An ancient rabbi said that proper observance of the sabbath required reading of that day's portion of the Torah at least three times—twice in the Hebrew, once in the Targum.) Targum Jonathon, a translation of the Prophets, is ascribed to Jonathon ben Uziel, a pupil of the great scholar Hillel (20 B.C.–40) and so was written in the middle of the first century. Targum Yerushalmi mentions the fall of Jerusalem—in the year 70—and must have been written well after that event.

When Arabic became the daily language of the Jews, the Gaon Saadia translated the Book into that language (ninth century). Early Christians accepted the Greek Bible, the Septuagint, as the inspired version of the Word of God. But the translation was unacceptable to scholars, and in the second century three new and differing Greek translations were made by Aquila, Symmachus, and Theodotion. Portions of these translations became fixed into the Septuagint as it was transmitted by the early Church.

The first Latin translation was made about the fourth century; this is the *Itala* or *Vetus Latina*. St. Jerome found this translation too inaccurate and made his own from the original Hebrew rather than from the Greek. This is the Vulgate, still the standard of the Roman Church. (The Gutenberg Bible is a Vulgate.)

Still another translation of the Bible used by scholars is the Peshitta, the Syriac version, which has not been dated satisfactorily. Two legends would place the Peshitta before the Bible was compiled: one legend says it was written at Solomon's request as a gift to Hiram of Tyre; another legend dates it at the fall of the Northern Kingdom in the eighth century B.C.

The first European translation of the Bible was made by Ulfilas about 450. He translated the Book into Gothic, hoping it would help convert—and civilize—the Goths. But the Church ruled that the Bible could be read only in the three languages used in the inscription on the Cross: Hebrew, Greek, and Latin. This dictum stopped translation of the Bible into European languages for a thousand years.

The first English translation was made from the Vulgate by John Wycliffe in the fourteenth century. In succeeding years, six major translations into English were made, including the Catholic Douay Version. The King James, the Authorized Version, was made in 1604–11 in an attempt to reconcile the competing translations and so that "the Scripture may speak like it selfe, as in the language of Canaan, that it may be understood."

Portions of the Bible were written—that is, physically set down on parchment or papyrus—in David's time. The prophecies of Jeremiah were dictated to the prophet's secretary-scribe, Baruch. The code in Deuteronomy, uncovered in the Temple in 621 B.C., had to be a written document. And the entire Torah was read by Ezra to the assembled Jews in the fifth century B.C. and so had to have been physically present, probably as parchment scrolls.

But these and all other ancient Jewish manuscripts are gone. Until the finding of the Dead Sea Scrolls in 1948, no Jewish Biblical manuscript earlier than the ninth century was known. Portions of early Christian Biblical manuscripts from much earlier periods do exist, however. The earliest include the Codex Vaticanus (in the Vatican), dating from about 300; the Codex Alexandrinus (in the British Museum), from about 400; the Codex Sinaiticus (in Leningrad), about 300; the Codex Ephraemi (in Paris), about 450; and the Bodleian Genesis (Oxford), about 900.

Before the invention of printing, every Bible had to be hand-copied from another Bible, and every copying was an invitation to error. Even before the destruction of the Second Temple, every Jew wanted his own copy of the Bible, or at least of the Torah, for study and worship. During the period of the Second Temple, an official copy of the canon was kept in the Temple, and copies were compared to it. But despite the fact that, once canonized, the Bible was unchangeable and error was a sin, errors did creep in, and marginal notes in previous versions were copied as textual parts of the Bible.

About the sixth century, schools of scribes grew up in Tiberias, Babylon, and Mesopotamia who established an infallible system of copying the Bible. These Masoretes—from the Hebrew word for tradition—set standards for copying that would eliminate error; they also added the diacritical vowel marks that made reading easier. The Masoretic guides to copying listed the number of letters in a book, listed the chapters by their endings, cited the large and small letters, and gave a hundred other tests for exactness. For example, the Masoretic reminder at the end of the book of Genesis reads:

The total verses of the book of Genesis is 1,534, and half of them is the verse "and by the sword thou shalt live." The weekly portions are twelve in number; the sections are forty-three; the chapters, fifty; the paragraphs whose last lines are open to the end of the column are thirty-four, and those which are closed [the next paragraph begins on the same line] number forty-eight.

Until the beginning of printing, when exact copying became relatively simple, the Masoretic texts kept the Bible of the Jews unchanged by even a letter for a thousand years. Modern scholarship continues to find proofs that the Masoretic text is as close to the original as human agency could be expected to achieve.

TWO

The Bible as History

OF THE TWENTY-FOUR BOOKS of the Bible of the Jews, nine are clearly historical: Genesis, Exodus, Numbers, Joshua, Judges, Samuel, Kings, Ezra-Nehemiah, and Chronicles. The prehistory of the Jews—and of the world—a period covering about two thousand years according to Jewish reckoning, is told in the first twelve chapters of Genesis. This rearrangement of legend and folk history by J, E, and P carries the story from the creation to Abraham. The rest of the historical books cover the period from Abraham to Cyrus, about fifteen hundred years. This history is relatively accurate, considered in the context of the times and the modes of transmission. As with any book of such great age and awesome place in the minds of the people who transmitted it, the Bible must be approached with understanding of the milieu in which it was written and the purposes of the writers. These purposes were not unlike those of most history writers until this day.

Historians tend to be ethnocentric, to magnify the deeds of their own nations and to denigrate their enemies. The histories of the American Revolution written by American historians are quite different from those written by British historians; the history of the American Civil War taught in Massachusetts is quite different from the history of the same events taught in Mississippi. So, too, the Jewish history of Palestine probably is quite different from what Philistine, Babylonian, or Egyptian histories of the period would be—if they had been written. The Bible as history is, however, remarkably free of most of the excesses of ancient historians.

An approach to the Bible as history is complicated rather than eased by the work of earlier generations of scholars: too few Biblical scholars were free of national and religious bias. Some of the earlier students of the Bible were true scholars, but some had motives beyond the search for truth—from the purest to the blackest. Some scholars willfully failed to see any evidences that tended to disprove the literal truth of every passage in the Bible; these scholars saw in the order of creation given in the first verses of Genesis a forecast of modern paleontological discoveries. Then there were scholars who sought to prove that the sole meaning and purpose of the Bible of the Jews was to foretell the coming of Jesus and to give credence to the Christian New Testament. Another group developed only those lines of exegesis that established the primitiveness of the Jewish faith and the limitations of the Jews themselves. The author of a textbook on ancient history used widely between the two World Wars by American high schools not only denied the Jewish development of monotheism, but included in his works gratuitous disparaging comments about the Jews.

Of one of these scholars, who knew exactly what he was going to prove even before he began his Biblical researches, Goethe wrote:

> Had the author known how to approach the writing of Moses [the Torah] with reverence, if only as the oldest monuments of the human spirit, as fragments of an Egyptian pyramid, he would not have drowned these representations of the poetic arts of the Orient in a flow of homilies; he would not have torn every limb from this torso and hacked it to pieces to find in it the conceptual concoctions of a German university of the eighteenth century.

The ancient Hebrews were not monument builders, although they did manage to build the pyramids while they were slaves in Egypt. When they wrote, they used papyrus and parchment rather than clay tablets. Papyrus and parchment did not survive centuries; thus little external dating of the Biblical documents is possible. But dates can be approximated by internal evidences in the Bible histories. These are, necessarily, the judgments of scholars—which differ, sometimes widely. For example, almost all scholars agree that J is the earliest writer of the Bible. But J is dated variously 800, 850, 900, and 1000 B.C., depending on the scholar. E is dated variously about 700, 750, 900, and 1000 B.C.[1]

The prehistory of the Jews as told in the Bible differs from other scriptural stories of the beginnings of a people and a faith. The Jews'

---

[1] Professor Ezekiel Kaufman (1889–1964) of Hebrew University, the greatest of modern Jewish Biblical scholars, disagrees with most other scholars on the dating of the Bible and its sources. He claims that other scholars confuse the dates of compilation with the dates of creation of the various narratives. He places P before D, at about 1000 B.C.; he places J and E in the remotest antiquity. Professor Kaufman also disputes the thesis, put forward by several Christian scholars (and Sigmund Freud, who was not a scholar in this field), that Hebrew monotheism is a development of the sun worship of the Egyptian Akhnaton (Amenhotep IV), the Babylonian Marduk, or the Assyrian Asshur. Kaufman offers reasoned arguments that monotheism is an independent and unique development of the ancient Hebrews.

founder-progenitor, Abraham, does not spring full-grown from some God's brow (or other parts) onto a virgin earth. Abraham is placed by the Bible in a verifiable historical context; he travels from one known kingdom to another over a route which can be established geographically and by means in keeping with the historical epoch. His descendants people other known places, meet other historical figures: the Hittites, Amorites, Edomites. And Abraham's ancestors are quite ungodlike except perhaps in the lengths of their lives. They are, if anything, entirely too human. Adam is weak; Cain is a murderer. After the earth is cleansed by the flood, Noah's descendants sink again into evil. In both the prehistorical and historical sections of the Bible, the characters are real, even when the events in which they take part are beyond reality. There are no godlike characters, no Jesus-like or Buddha-like symbols of perfection, nor are their followers ever free of the most human flaws. Even the giving of the Law, perhaps the root event in this history, is marred by human failing: the Jews turn from God to the Golden Calf; Moses' great anger causes him to smash the Tablets.

While archeology and cultural anthropology do not prove the actuality of Biblical history, these disciplines show that some of the recorded events did take place.[2] Archeologists have established the existence of Mesopotamian culture in Sumer and Ur before 3000 B.C., and there probably was a highly developed culture as early as 6000 B.C. The tombs of King Mes-Kalam-dug and Queen Shub-ad establish the use of human sacrifices in the millennium before Abraham, thus providing the context for the Abraham-Isaac story, the Biblical cry against such sacrifices. And there was a flood, although not the world-covering flood of the Bible. A flood covered the valleys of the Tigris and Euphrates Rivers about 3200 B.C., destroying the world of the city dweller, thus the world of civilized man. This flood was great enough to leave a sedimentary layer eight feet thick in places.

Tablets excavated at Nippur in Babylonia, dated about 2000 B.C., tell one flood story. A much more extensive flood story is told in Babylonian tablets from the seventh century B.C. In this later story, the epic of the Babylonian hero Gilgamesh, who combined many of the attributes of Herakles and Odysseus, the gods decide to destroy mankind in a flood. But Ea, god of earth, warns the Babylonian Noah, Utnapishtim, to build a great ship and escape the destruction. He builds the ship, waterproofs it with pitch, stocks it with every variety of living

[2] Since Schliemann's archeological work proved the existence of Troy—until then known only through myth—archeologists and historians have given greater weight to ancient legends. Their more practical uses were further demonstrated in the Israeli war of independence (1948), when Jewish troops used Biblical references to find lost paths through the desert.

thing, and embarks with his family. The Babylonian epic says the flood lasted seven days, after which Utnapishtim sends forth a raven to find dry land.

The comparable Hebrew version is very similar in many details. The Bible says God commanded Noah: "Make thee an ark of gopher wood; with rooms shalt thou make the ark, and pitch it within and without with pitch." The Biblical flood lasted either forty days (the J version) or 150 days (the P version). Noah, too, sent forth a raven, but there was no dry land. Then he sent a dove, who also "found no rest for the sole of her foot." Seven days later a second dove came back "and lo in her mouth an olive-leaf freshly plucked."[3]

The Nippur tablet predates the Biblical story (except by Professor Kaufman's dating) by a millennium. But the much more explicit Gilgamesh tablets were written at least a century after E and several centuries after J wrote his parallel story. Whether the Hebrews embroidered a Babylonian myth or the Babylonians adapted a Hebrew story is not definitively established. But several Eastern religions, notably the Hindu, also tell of world-ending floods. Flood stories are also found in the myths of African and western hemisphere aborigines. Thus the story may be rooted in man's earliest consciousness.

According to the Bible's own reckoning, counting back from a positively dated event, Abraham lived in the twenty-first century B.C. Earlier scholars made him a contemporary of Hammurabi—a conclusion given some weight by evidence that Hammurabi was Amraphel, the Biblical king of Shinar (Genesis 14:1), one of the kings Abraham fought to rescue Lot. More recent scholarship places Abraham in the nineteenth century B.C., Hammurabi at the end of the eighteenth and the beginning of the seventeenth centuries.

There is no direct evidence of Abraham's move to Canaan, but there are collateral proofs. The Biblical stories of Abraham, Isaac, and Jacob include patterns of conduct and customs that were strange to the Biblical writers and redactors. They could not have invented them and did a poor job of explaining them. But these customs were in keeping with those of the Hurrians, the people of Haran. And Abraham, although born in Ur, had been brought by his father to Haran:

And they went forth . . . from Ur of the Chaldees, to go into the land of Canaan; and they came unto Haran, and dwelt there. And the days of Terah [Abraham's father] were two hundred and five years; and Terah died in Haran.[4]

Tablets found at Nuzi, a Hurrian center, show that the non-Hebrew

[3] Genesis 6:14, 8:7–11
[4] Genesis 11:31b–32

customs followed by the patriarchs were quite in keeping with Hurrian customs, with the patterns of family life and protection of family inheritance practiced in Haran. For example, Abraham twice claims his wife as his sister (Isaac does so, too). The explanation given by the Biblical writers of these odd events show how foreign such actions were to the Hebrews; one explanation makes Abraham a coward, a most un-patriarchal quality. But claiming that his wife was also his sister was quite proper for a Hurrian. As explained by Professor E. A. Speiser: "In Hurrian society a wife enjoyed special standing and protection when the law recognized her simultaneously as her husband's sister, regardless of actual blood ties. . . . This dual role conferred on the wife a superior position in society."[5]

Other Hurrian customs followed by Abraham, but strange to the Hebrews, include Sarah's offering her maid to Abraham when she thought she was barren, and Abraham's adoption of Eliezer as his heir. Eliezer's right to inherit ended as soon as Isaac was born.

There is one bit of external evidence of the existence of Abraham. The Bible tells of an invasion from the east led by Chedorlaomer which was beaten back by "Abram the Hebrew."[6] This formulation could have been used only by a non-Hebrew writer. Just as an American historian would not speak of Washington the American, or Lincoln the American, so Hebrew writers would not identify the founder of the nation in such a manner. Scholars suggest that this chapter is an inclusion from a non-Jewish source, providing some independent evidence of the existence of Abraham.

The movements of nomadic herdsmen are hard to establish in any era, particularly when the migrations took place more than three millennia ago. But the drift southward of the Hebrew tribes, then westward into the land of Goshen, is in keeping with the pattern of a nomadic people. Reasonable, too, is the story that the Hebrews were allowed by the Pharaohs to stay in Goshen as a barrier to the incursions of other marauders from the east. Then the Hebrews were taken into Egypt proper as slaves. This is historically evident, since the Hebrews certainly helped build the store cities of Ramses and Pithom. Then, after a sojourn of 430 years according to P, or four generations according to JE (the latter figure makes more sense), the Hebrews left Egypt sometime in the middle of the thirteenth century, B.C.

There is no physical historical evidence of the existence of Moses—or of the miraculous deliverance of the Jews from Egypt. But there are strong cultural and psychological evidences of Moses' leader-

---

[5] E.A. Speiser, "Genesis," *The Anchor Bible*, Doubleday, 1965.
[6] Genesis 14:13

ship of the tribes. The story that Moses lived in Egypt, that he was forced to flee into the desert, and that he returned to lead the Jews out of slavery was so deeply stamped into the national consciousness of the Jews that it must have had substance. No figure out of legend, no creation of mythology could have been so real for so long without historical basis. And the Moses story would be a cultural anomaly if this was the story of the mythological folk hero. A myth adapted from other peoples, a folk tale embroidered over campfires, even the revelation of some later leader would have taken other forms. In such cases, Moses would have been Hero, not man. He would have effected the deliverance of the Hebrews from Egypt by might, by his own superhuman powers, not by a series of God-effected natural phenomena. Moses would not have been a stutterer, would not have sought to escape his duty, would not have been so conciliatory, and would have lived to see the happy ending—the triumph over Canaan—if he had been invented. Only the story of a real man would have been transmitted so realistically; only the reality of a Moses could have made so indelible an impression on a nation.

There is evidence that not all the twelve tribes of the Hebrews went down into Egypt. Some remained in Canaan and carried on a continuing war against the Canaanites. Archeologists have discovered evidence that the Canaanite city of Jericho was destroyed about 1450 B.C.—perhaps by Hebrew tribes. And clay tablets found at Tel el Amarna in Egypt include letters from Ebed-Hopa, vassal king of Jerusalem, to his overlord, the Pharaoh Akhnaton-Amenhotep. In these letters, dated about 1350 B.C., Ebed-Hopa appeals for help against the invading "Habiru" who are "taking the cities of the king." Some scholars suggest that the Habiru were the Hebrew tribes that did not go down to Egypt.

The book of Judges provides some support for the theory that some of the Hebrew tribes remained in Canaan while others were slaves in Egypt. When Deborah called upon the tribes to rally against Sisera, only about half the tribes responded. The division among the tribes between those who answered Deborah's call and those who did not may have been between the resident tribes and those newly arrived from Egypt.

With the death of Moses and the entrance of the tribes of Israel into Canaan, with the book of Joshua, the historical period of the Biblical story begins. According to the Biblical account the conquest of Canaan took six years. It must have taken place much more gradually, but the fact of the destruction of the Canaanite fortresses at about this time has been established archeologically. Jericho, for example, destroyed in 1450 B.C., was again burnt out about 1200.

The magnificent Song of Deborah (in the Book of Judges), dated about 1150 B.C., is the first historical record in the Bible written around the time of the event it describes. It may well be the only contemporary Jewish record predating the period of David.

Then sang Deborah and Barak the son of Abinoam on that day, saying:
    When men let grow their hair in Israel,
    When the people offer themselves willingly,
    Bless ye the Lord.
    Hear, O ye kings; give ear, O ye princes;
    I, unto the Lord will I sing;
    I will sing praise to the Lord, the God of Israel. . . .
    In the days of Shamgar the son of Anath,
    In the days of Jael, the highways ceased,
    And the travellers walked through byways.
    The rulers ceased in Israel, they ceased,
    Until that thou didst arise, Deborah,
    That thou didst arise a mother in Israel.
    They chose new gods;
    Then was war in the gates;
    Was there a shield or spear seen
    Among forty thousand in Israel?
    My heart is toward the governors of Israel,
    That offered themselves willingly among the people. . . .
    Then made He a remnant to have dominion over the nobles
        and the people;
    The Lord made me have dominion over the mighty.
    Out of Ephraim came they whose root is in Amalek;
    After thee, Benjamin, among thy peoples;
    Out of Machir came down governors,
    And out of Zebulun they that handle the marshal's staff.
    And the princes of Issachar were with Deborah;
    As was Issachar, so was Barak;
    Among the divisions of Reuben
    Into the valley they rushed forth at his feet.
    There were great resolves of heart.
    Why sattest thou among the sheepfolds,
    To hear the pipings for the flocks?
    At the divisions of Reuben
    There were great searchings of heart.
    Gilead abode beyond the Jordan;
    And Dan, why doth he sojourn by the ships?
    Asher dwelt at the shore of the sea,
    And abideth by its bays.
    Zebulun is a people that jeoparded their lives unto the death,
    And Naphtali, upon the high places of the field.
    The kings came, they fought;
    Then fought the kings of Canaan,
    In Taanach by the waters of Megiddo;
    They took no gain of money.
    They fought from heaven,
    The stars in their courses fought against Sisera.
    The brook Kishon swept them away,
    That ancient brook, the brook Kishon.

O my soul, tread down with strength.
Then did the horsehoofs stamp
By reason of the prancings, the prancings of their mighty ones. . . .
So perish all Thine enemies, O Lord;
But they that love Him be as the sun when he goeth forth in his
    might.
And the land had rest forty years.[7]

Although the Song of Deborah is the oldest contemporary record in the Bible, it is not the oldest portion of the book. The Song of the Well (Numbers 21:17) is dated before Deborah. Other writers of the Bible also incorporated or used sources predating the monarchy. The Fable of Jotham (Judges 9:7) and the Song of Miriam (Exodus 15:21) are inclusions from ancient sources. The Book of the Wars of the Lord (Numbers 21:14) and the Book of Jashar (Joshua 10:13), which is not quoted, are cited as sources.[8]

The means of transmission of these early sources is unknown, but some of the books must have been written. When Deborah sings, "And out of Zebulun [came] they that handle the marshal's staff," the reference is to scribes. The marshal's staff was an implement of writing, not a sword or spear.

The book of Judges names twelve persons who served in this position, although there probably were many more during the period. (A thirteenth leader, Abimelech, son of Gideon, was "prince over Israel," not a judge.) And of the twelve, six are merely names mentioned in passing; the other six are characters in described events. Nor were the judges cited in the book successive leaders of a more or less united nation. They were charismatic figures who came into prominence when the tribes were in danger and in need of strong leadership. And contrary to popular impression, only one judge led his people in war against the Canaanites; in the wars in which the other judges figured, the tribes and Canaan were allies.

The last judge mentioned in this book is Samson, whose story is completely different from those of the other judges. Samson is a personal rather than a national hero; only his personal feats of strength are celebrated. Nor is there any historical evidence that he existed. However, this section is important historically, because it serves to bring the Philistines into the continuing historical record of the Jewish nation. Non-

---

[7] Judges 5
[8] Later sections of the Bible also cite lost books—the books of Nathan, Gad, Iddo, Shemaiah, and Jehu. Some of these books may have been of the same character as those included in the canon but lost in the centuries of oral transmission. Others may have been inventions of the Chronicler to give credence to this narrative.

Biblical historical sources show that the Philistines did move onto the coast of Palestine about 1200 B.C. and were well established by the time of the judges.

From this point in the Biblical historical narrative, the strongest influence is that of the priestly writers (P). They had a thesis and tried to establish its proofs in their histories. But they were also erudite scholars and would not tamper too much with facts. P embroidered, adapted, and expanded events that were religiously important and slid over events that were not; P added folk tales and incorporated myths of neighboring peoples. But what P wrote was history, quite different from the histories of their contemporaries. P did not write exercises in rhetoric or glorifications of hero kings. The P history is coordinated rather than episodic: generation follows generation, king follows king, prophet follows prophet, and the derelicitions of Judah follow the derelictions of Israel. There are conflicting narratives only because P attempted to tell the entire story.

In essence, this is the P history:

Pressures from the stronger Philistines caused the loosely tied tribes of the period of the judges to come closer together. In the time of Eli, priest of the shrine at Shiloh, the Philistines captured the shrine and carried away the Ark of the Lord. In effect, the Philistines carried away the physical embodiment of a tribal god, thus denying his aid to his people. The Ark was returned, but the Hebrews remained vassals of Philistia.

Early prophets, wild men from the hills, went among the people, stirring them up against their overlords. The prophet Samuel, who judged in Beersheba, brought the tribes together and gave them a hereditary king, Saul. King Saul first turned the tribes against the Ammonites in an attack on Jabesh-gilead. The Philistines, seeing no threat in this attack, remained neutral. But the victory over the Ammonites welded the tribes into a nation and gave Saul the idea of cleansing the land of the more powerful Philistines. He struck at Michmas and chased the Philistines out of the hills of Judah back to the coast. The Philistines eventually counterattacked, defeated Saul at Gilboa, and ruled the land of Canaan once more.

Saul died in the battle at Gilboa, and his son Ish-bosheth established himself on the other side of the Jordan, beyond range of the Philistine armies. David, who had first fought for Saul and then been outlawed, placed himself under the suzerainty of Philistia and became leader of the tribe of Judah. He displaced Ish-bosheth as leader of the nation and conquered Jerusalem as capital of the reunited kingdom. He then turned on Philistia and reduced that nation to vassalage. In a succession of wars with neighboring states, David established an empire.

David's success was due in large part to the reluctance of the two major world powers—Egypt and Mesopotamia—to move into the Palestinian cockpit. Neither of the two great powers wanted to rouse the ire of the other by asserting control over Palestine, the middle ground between them. But David's empire did not know peace; when there were no wars, there were rebellions—one led by David's son, Absalom.

Solomon became the crown prince and ruled after David "slept with his fathers and was buried in the city of David" (I Kings 2:10). Solomon protected and enlarged his empire, not by war, but by marrying foreign princesses. He became rich by levies on the trade between Africa and Asia which had to pass through Palestine, by heavy taxes, by income from his copper mines and the fleets of ships sailing out of Ezion-geber, the modern Elath.

After Solomon's death the Empire fell apart. It had not lasted long enough for the people to have learned to put national patriotism above tribal loyalties. And the cohesive force of the Philistine threat had been removed for good by David's arms and Solomon's successes in diplomacy and economics. The tribes of Judah and Benjamin formed the Southern Kingdom of Judah, with its capital at Jerusalem. The other tribes formed the Northern Kingdom of Israel.

The larger Northern Kingdom had a succession of kings and dynasties in a succession of bloody, brutal internal quarrels. Finally Omri, a general, seized the throne, fortified Samaria, and made that city the northern capital. Omri also made an alliance with Tyre against Damascus—an alliance strengthened when Ahab, Omri's son, married Jezebel, princess of Tyre. But Jezebel brought more to Israel than Tyrian aid; she also brought official recognition of the worship of Baal and Ashtoreth (Astarte). The Israelites succumbed to the bloody worship of these idols, and prophets arose to damn them and call them back to God.

Wars with Assyria almost wiped out Israel, but in the eighth century B.C., Assyria and Damascus were bled white by their warring and had to relax their empire-building. Israel thus had a period of peace and growth. Growth meant enrichment—but mainly for those close to the throne. The obverse side of this coin was growing misery for the landless poor. In this climate, the great social prophets arose and thundered, demanding righteousness instead of ritual, tithes for the poor rather than taxes to uphold the nobles and priests.

The prophets warned that the result of the worship of idols and the social injustices would be the destruction of the kingdom. And destruction came from Assyria in the persons of Tiglath-pileser, Sennacherib, and Sargon. Samaria was destroyed in 722 B.C., and the ten northern tribes were carried away into captivity. Of the original twelve tribes of Hebrews, only Judah and Benjamin remained, in the south.

Judah had avoided being party to the wars between Assyria and Israel and so was not party to the destruction. But now she had a great empire to the north, Assyria, and another great empire to the south, Egypt. There followed two centuries of pulling and hauling between the contending empires. Assyria declined, flamed again, and died before the new power of Babylonia. Alliances between Judah and one or the other great powers generally ended with payment of ransom or conquest. But between, there were periods of grace and of religious growth.

In King Josiah's time, Judah was the vassal of Nebuchadnezzar, king of Babylon. But Josiah, the reformer king, dreamed not only of a kingdom cleansed by God's law; he dreamed also of a nation free of its foreign overlord. His son, Jehoiakim, joined with Egypt in a revolt against Babylon. Nebuchadnezzar marched on Jerusalem to put down the revolt. Jehoiakim died while Nebuchadnezzar was on the march, and punishment was visited on the new king of Judah, Jehoiachin; the king and the nobles were taken into captivity in 591 B.C. Zedekiah, the king's uncle, was left to rule the leaderless nation.

But Zedekiah also plotted with Egypt against Nebuchadnezzar, and the Babylonian returned. This time the Judean threat was eliminated totally. In 586 B.C., Jerusalem was laid waste, the Temple destroyed, and the people taken in chains to Babylon.

Cyrus the Persian gained the throne of Babylon and extended his empire across half the world. He gave the Jews permission to return to Palestine and rebuild their Temple. Some returned; many stayed in Babylon to lay the foundations for what was to become a second Jerusalem in the next millennium. In Jerusalem, Zerubbabel, descendant of the Davidic line, was governor and hoped to rebuild the kingdom, but hope was not enough. In the seventh year of the reign of Artaxerxes, Ezra the Scribe returned from Babylon and began to weld together the nation of the Jews. In Artaxerxes' twentieth year, Nehemiah, the king's favorite, returned and rebuilt the Temple. The nation was viable once more. Nehemiah's diary tells of his success despite the opposition of Sanballat, governor of neighboring Samaria. This story is confirmed by papyri found in Elephantine in Egypt.

The rest of the story of the Jews up to the common era belongs to the books of the Apocrypha. Alexander passed through Jerusalem on his way to conquer the world and was well received by the Jews. In return, he treated the Jews well. On Alexander's death, his empire was divided among his generals. The Ptolemys got Egypt; the Seleucids got the Near East. Palestine swung again between two competing empires.

Palestine was a vassal of Egypt until 198 B.C., then of the Seleucids. The high priest was a creature of the Seleucid kings, and an anti-priestly party grew up and threatened revolt. The revolt, led by the Maccabees, came in 168 and resulted in the establishment of the last Jewish kingdom, under the Hasmonean dynasty. But internecine conflict continued, and Rome asserted its power over the quarrelsome little state in 50 B.C. Nor would the Jews remain quiet under Rome. They revolted again, and Rome destroyed Jerusalem and the Second Temple in the year 70. Rome destroyed the rest of the land during the last revolt, under Bar Kochba, in 135. The Jews entered *Galuth,* the Dispersion, the Diaspora—and the Jewish Bible was closed forever.

The genius of the Biblical historians is best illustrated by the David narrative. In a few pages, relating the history of the later years of David's reign, the writer of Samuel tells of war and rebellion, of a kingly kindness and a royal insult, of the turmoil in a kingly family, of how David's older sons lost the succession and the crown went to Solomon. This is history, but it is the story of the people who make history rather than the story of amorphous powers and the collectivities called states.

And David reigned over all Israel; and David executed justice and righteousness unto all his people. And Joab the son of Zeruiah was over the host; and Jehoshaphat the son of Ahilud was recorder; and Zadok the son of Ahitub, and Ahimelech the son of Abiathar, were priests; and Seraiah was scribe; and Benaiah the son of Jehoiada was over the Cherethites and the Pelethites; and David's sons were chief ministers. . . .

And it came to pass after this, that the king of the children of Ammon died, and Hanun his son reigned in his stead. And David said: "I will show kindness unto Hanun the son of Nahash, as his father showed kindness unto me." So David sent by the hand of his servants to comfort him concerning his father. And David's servants came into the land of the children of Ammon. But the princes of the children of Ammon said unto Hanun their lord: "Thinkest thou that David doth honour thy father, that he hath sent comforters unto thee? hath not David sent his servants unto thee to search the city, and to spy it out, and to overthrow it?" So Hanun took David's servants, and shaved off the one half of their beards, and cut off their garments in the middle, even to their buttocks, and sent them away. When they told it unto David, he sent to meet them; for the men were greatly ashamed. And the king said: "Tarry at Jericho until your beards be grown, and then return."

And when the children of Ammon saw that they were become odious to David, the children of Ammon sent and hired the Arameans of Bethrehob, and the Arameans of Zobah, twenty thousand footmen, and the king of Maacah with a thousand men, and the men of Tob twelve thousand men. And when David heard of it, he sent Joab, and all the host of the mighty men. And the children of Ammon came out, and put the battle in array at the entrance of the gate; and the Arameans of Zobah, and of Rehob, and the men of Tob and Maacah, were by themselves in the field.

Now when Joab saw that the battle was set against him before and behind, he chose of all the choice men of Israel, and put them in array against the Arameans; and the rest of the people he committed into the hand of Abishai his brother, and he put them in array against the children of Ammon. And he said: "If the Arameans be too strong for me, then thou shalt help me, but if the children of Ammon be too strong for thee, then I will come and help thee. Be of good courage, and let us prove strong for our people, and for the cities of our God; and the Lord do that which seemeth Him good." So Joab and the people that were with him drew nigh unto the battle against the Arameans; and they fled before him. And when the children of Ammon saw that the Arameans were fled, they likewise fled before Abishai, and entered into the city. Then Joab returned from the children of Ammon, and came to Jerusalem.

And when the Arameans saw that they were put to the worse before Israel, they gathered themselves together. And Hadadezer sent, and brought out the Arameans that were beyond the River; and they came to Helam, with Shobach the captain of the host of Hadadezer at their head. And it was told David; and he gathered all Israel together, and passed over the Jordan, and came to Helam. And the Arameans set themselves in array against David, and fought with him. And the Arameans fled before Israel; and David slew of the Arameans seven hundred drivers of chariots, and forty thousand horsemen, and smote Shobach the captain of their host, so that he died there. And when all the kings that were servants to Hadadezer saw that they were put to the worse before Israel, they made peace with Israel, and served them. So the Arameans feared to help the children of Ammon any more.

And it came to pass, at the return of the year, at the time when kings go out to battle, that David sent Joab, and his servants with him, and all Israel; and they destroyed the children of Ammon, and besieged Rabbah. But David tarried at Jerusalem.

And it came to pass at eventide, that David arose from off his bed, and walked upon the roof of the king's house; and from the roof he saw a woman bathing; and the woman was very beautiful to look upon. And David sent and inquired after the woman. And one said: "Is not this Bath-sheba, the daughter of Eliam, the wife of Uriah the Hittite?" And David sent messengers, and took her; and she came in unto him, and he lay with her; for she was purified from her uncleanness; and she returned unto her house. And the woman conceived; and she sent and told David, and said: "I am with child."

And David sent to Joab, saying: "Send me Uriah the Hittite." And Joab sent Uriah to David. And when Uriah was come unto him, David asked of him how Joab did, and how the people fared, and how the war prospered. And David said to Uriah: "Go down to thy house, and wash thy feet." And Uriah departed out of the king's house and there followed him a mess of food from the king. But Uriah slept at the door of the king's house with all the servants of his lord, and went not down to his house. And when they had told David, saying: "Uriah went not down unto his house," David said unto Uriah: "Art thou not come from a journey? wherefore didst thou not go down unto thy house?" And Uriah said unto David: "The ark, and Israel, and Judah, abide in booths; and my lord Joab, and the servants of my lord, are encamped in the open field; shall I then go into my house, to eat and to drink, and to lie with my wife? as thou livest, and as thy soul liveth, I will not do this thing." And David said to Uriah: "Tarry here to-day also, and to-morrow I will let thee depart." So Uriah abode in Jerusalem that day, and the morrow. And when David had called him, he did eat and drink before him; and he made him drunk; and at even he went out to lie on his bed with the servants of his lord, but went not down to his house.

And it came to pass in the morning, that David wrote a letter to Joab, and sent it by the hand of Uriah. And he wrote in the letter, saying: "Set ye Uriah in the forefront of the hottest battle, and retire ye from him, that he may be smitten, and die." And it came to pass, when Joab kept watch upon the city, that he assigned Uriah unto the place where he knew that valiant men were. And the men of the city went out, and fought with Joab; and there fell some of the people, even of the servants of David; and Uriah the Hittite died also. Then Joab sent and told David all the things concerning the war; and he charged the messenger, saying: "When thou hast made an end of telling all the things concerning the war unto the king, it shall be that, if the king's wrath arise, and he say unto thee: Wherefore went ye so nigh unto the city to fight? knew ye not that they would shoot from the wall? who smote Abimelech the son of Jerubbesheth? did not a woman cast an upper millstone upon him from the wall, that he died at Thebez? why went ye so nigh the wall? then shalt thou say: Thy servant Uriah the Hittite is dead also."

So the messenger went, and came and told David all that Joab had sent him for. And the messenger said unto David: "The men prevailed against us, and came out unto us into the field, and we were upon them even unto the entrance of the gate. And the shooters shot at thy servants from off the wall; and some of the king's servants are dead, and thy servant Uriah the Hittite is dead also." Then David said unto the messenger: "Thus shalt thou say unto Joab: Let not this thing displease thee, for the sword devoureth in one manner or another; make thy battle more strong against the city, and overthrow it; and encourage thou him."

And when the wife of Uriah heard that Uriah her husband was dead, she made lamentation for her husband. And when the mourning was past, David sent and took her home to his house, and she became his wife, and bore him a son. But the thing that David had done displeased the Lord.

And the Lord sent Nathan unto David. And he came unto him, and said unto him: "There were two men in one city: the one rich, and the other poor. The rich man had exceeding many flocks and herds; but the poor man had nothing, save one little ewe lamb, which he had bought and reared; and it grew up together with him, and with his children; it did eat of his own morsel, and drank of his own cup, and lay in his bosom, and was unto him as a daughter. And there came a traveller unto the rich man, and he spared to take of his own flock and of his own herd, to dress for the wayfaring man that was come unto him, but took the poor man's lamb, and dressed it for the man that was come to him." And David's anger was greatly kindled against the man; and he said to Nathan: "As the Lord liveth, the man that hath done this deserveth to die; and he shall restore the lamb fourfold, because he did this thing, and because he had no pity."

And Nathan said to David: "Thou art the man. Thus saith the Lord, the God of Israel: I anointed thee king over Israel, and I delivered thee out of the hand of Saul; and I gave thee thy master's house, and thy master's wives into thy bosom, and gave thee the house of Israel and of Judah; and if that were too little, then would I add unto thee so much more. Wherefore hast thou despised the word of the Lord, to do that which is evil in My sight? Uriah the Hittite thou hast smitten with the sword, and his wife thou hast taken to be thy wife, and him thou hast slain with the sword of the children of Ammon. Now therefore, the sword shall never depart from thy house; because thou hast despised Me, and hast taken the wife of Uriah the Hittite to be thy wife. Thus saith the Lord: Behold, I will raise up evil against thee out of thine own house, and I will take thy wives before thine eyes, and give them unto thy neighbour, and he shall lie with thy wives in the sight of this sun. For thou didst it secretly; but I will do this thing before all Israel, and before the sun." And David said unto Nathan: "I have sinned against the Lord." And Nathan said unto David: "The Lord also hath put away thy sin; thou shalt not die. Howbeit, because by this deed thou hast greatly blasphemed the enemies of the Lord, the child also that is born unto thee shall surely die." And Nathan departed unto his house.

And the Lord struck the child that Uriah's wife bore unto David, and it was very sick. David therefore besought God for the child; and David fasted, and as often as he went in, he lay all night upon the earth. And the elders of his house arose, and stood beside him, to raise him up from the earth; but he would not, neither did he eat bread with them. And it came to pass on the seventh day, that the child died. And the servants of David feared to tell him that the child was dead; for they said: "Behold, while the child was yet alive, we spoke unto him, and he hearkened not unto our voice; how then shall we tell him that the child is dead, so that he do himself some harm?" But when David saw that his servants whispered together, David perceived that the child was dead; and David said unto his servants: "Is the child dead?" And they said: "He is dead." Then David arose from the earth, and washed, and anointed himself, and changed his apparel; and he came into the house of the Lord, and worshipped; then he came to his own house; and when he required, they set bread before him, and he did eat. Then said his servants unto him: "What thing is this that thou hast done? thou didst fast and weep for the child, while it was alive; but when the child was dead, thou didst rise and eat bread." And he said: "While the child was yet alive, I fasted and wept; for I said: Who knoweth whether the Lord will not be gracious to me, that the child may live? But now he is dead, wherefore should I fast? can I bring him back again? I shall go to him, but he will not return to me."

And David comforted Bath-sheba his wife, and went in unto her, and lay with her; and she bore a son, and called his name Solomon. And the Lord loved him; and He sent by the hand of Nathan the prophet, and he called his name Jedidiah, for the Lord's sake. . . .

And it came to pass, while they were in the way, that the tidings came to

David, saying: "Absalom hath slain all the king's sons, and there is not one of them left." Then the king arose, and rent his garments, and lay on the earth; and all his servants stood by with their clothes rent. And Jonadab, the son of Shimeah David's brother, answered and said: "Let not my lord suppose that they have killed all the young men the king's sons; for Ammon only is dead; for by the appointment of Absalom this hath been determined from the day that he forced his sister Tamar. Now therefore let not my lord the king take the thing to his heart, to think that all the king's sons are dead; for Ammon only is dead."

. . . And Absalom dwelt two full years in Jerusalem; and he saw not the king's face. . . .

And it came to pass after this, that Absalom prepared him a chariot and horses, and fifty men to run before him. And Absalom used to rise up early, and stand beside the way of the gate; and it was so, that when any man had a suit which should come to the king for judgment, then Absalom called unto him, and said: "Of what city art thou?" And he said: "Thy servant is of one of the tribes of Israel." And Absalom said unto him: "See, thy matters are good and right; but there is no man deputed of the king to hear thee." Absalom said moreover: "Oh that I were made judge in the land, that every man who hath any suit or cause might come unto me, and I would do him justice!" And it was so, that when any man came nigh to prostrate himself before him, he put forth his hand, and took hold of him, and kissed him. And on this manner did Absalom to all Israel that came to the king for judgment; so Absalom stole the hearts of the men of Israel.

And it came to pass at the end of forty years, that Absalom said unto the king: "I pray thee, let me go and pay my vow, which I have vowed unto the Lord, in Hebron. For thy servant vowed a vow while I abode at Geshur in Aram, saying: If the Lord shall indeed bring me back to Jerusalem, then I will serve the Lord." And the king said unto him: "Go in peace." So he arose, and went to Hebron. But Absalom sent spies throughout all the tribes of Israel, saying: "As soon as ye hear the sound of the horn, then ye shall say: Absalom is king in Hebron." And with Absalom went two hundred men out of Jerusalem, that were invited, and went in their simplicity; and they knew not any thing. And Absalom sent for Ahithophel the Gilonite, David's counsellor, from his city, even from Giloh, while he offered the sacrifices. And the conspiracy was strong; for the people increased continually with Absalom.

And there came a messenger to David, saying: "The hearts of the men of Israel are after Absalom." And David said unto all his servants that were with him at Jerusalem: "Arise, and let us flee; for else none of us shall escape from Absalom; make speed to depart, lest he overtake us quickly, and bring down evil upon us, and smite the city with the edge of the sword." And the king's servants said unto the king: "Behold they servants are ready to do whatsoever my lord the king shall choose." And the king went forth, and all his household after him. And the king left ten women, that were concubines, to keep the house. And the king went forth, and all the people after him; and they tarried in Beth-merhak. And all his servants passed on beside him; and all the Cherethites, and all the Pelethites, and all the Gittites, six hundred men that came after him from Gath, passed on before the king. . . .

And Absalom, and all the people, the men of Israel, came to Jerusalem, and Ahithophel with him. . . .

When David was come to Mahanaim, Absalom passed over the Jordan, he and all the men of Israel with him. And Absalom had set Amasa over the host instead of Joab. Now Amasa was the son of a man, whose name was Ithra the Jesraelite, that went in to Abigal the daughter of Nahash, sister to Zeruiah Joab's mother. And Israel and Absalom pitched in the land of Gilead.

And it came to pass, when David was come to Mahanaim, that Shobi the son of Nahash of Rabbah of the children of Ammon, and Machir the son of Ammiel of Lo-debar, and Barzillai the Gileadite of Rogelim, brought beds, and basins, and earthen vessels, and wheat, and barley, and meal, and parched corn, and beans, and lentils and parched pulse, and honey, and curd, and sheep, and cheese of kine, for David, and for the people that were with him, to eat; for they said: "The people is hungry, and faint, and thirsty, in the wilderness."

And David numbered the people that were with him, and set captains of thousands and captains of hundreds over them. And David sent forth the people, a third part under the hand of Joab, and a third part under the hand of Abishai the son of Zeruiah, Joab's brother, and a third part under the hand of Ittai the Gittite. And the king said unto the people: "I will surely go forth with you myself also." But the people said: "Thou shalt not go forth; for if we flee away, they will not care for us; neither if half of us die, will they care for us; but thou art worth ten thouasnd of us: therefore now it is better that thou be ready to succour us out of the city." And the king said unto them: "What seemeth you best I will do." And the king stood by the gate-side, and all the people went out by hundreds and by thousands. And the king commanded Joab and Abishai and Ittai, saying: "Deal gently for my sake with the young man, even with Absalom." And all the people heard when the king gave all the captains charge concerning Absalom.

So the people went out into the field against Israel; and the battle was in the forest of Ephraim. And the people of Israel were smitten there before the servants of David, and there was a great slaughter there that day of twenty thousand men. For the battle was there spread over the face of all the country; and the forest devoured more people that day than the sword devoured.

And Absalom chanced to meet the servants of David. And Absalom was riding upon his mule, and the mule went under the thick boughs of a great terebinth, and his head caught hold of the terebinth, and he was taken up between the heaven and the earth; and the mule that was under him went on. And a certain man saw it, and told Joab, and said: "Behold, I saw Absalom hanging in a terebinth." And Joab said unto the man that told him: "And, behold, thou sawest it, and why didst thou not smite him there to the ground? and I would have had to give thee ten pieces of silver, and a girdle." And the man said unto Joab: "Though I should receive a thousand pieces of silver in my hand, yet would I not put forth my hand against the king's son; for in our hearing the king charged thee and Abishai and Ittai, saying:

"Beware that none touch the young man Absalom. Otherwise if I had dealt falsely against mine own life—and there is no matter hid from the king—then thou thyself wouldest have stood aloof." Then said Joab: "I may not tarry thus with thee." And he took three darts in his hand, and thrust them through the heart of Absalom, while he was yet alive in the midst of the terebinth. And ten young men that bore Joab's armour compassed about and smote Absalom, and slew him.

And Joab blew the horn, and the people returned from pursuing after Israel; for Joab held back the people. And they took Absalom, and cast him into the great pit in the forest, and raised over him a very great heap of stones; and all Israel fled everyone to his tent.—Now Absalom in his lifetime had taken and reared up for himself the pillar, which is in the king's dale; for he said: "I have no son to keep my name in remembrance"; and he called the pillar after his own name; and it is called Absalom's monument unto this day.

Then said Ahimaaz the son of Zadok: "Let me now run, and bear the king tidings, how that the Lord hath avenged him of his enemies." And Joab said unto him: "Thou shalt not be the bearer of tidings this day, but thou shalt bear tidings another day; but this day thou shalt bear no tidings; forasmuch as the king's son is dead." Then said Joab to the Cushite: "Go tell the king what thou hast seen." And the Cushite bowed down unto Joab, and ran. Then said Ahimaaz the son of Zadok yet again to Joab: "But come what may, let me, I pray thee, also run after the Cushite." And Joab said: "Wherefore wilt thou run, my son, seeing that thou wilt have no reward for the tidings?" "But come what may, [said he,] I will run." And he said unto him: "Run." Then Ahimaaz ran by the way of the Plain, and overran the Cushite. . . .

And, behold, the Cushite came; and the Cushite said: "Tidings for my lord the king; for the Lord hath avenged thee this day of all them that rose up against thee." And the king said unto the Cushite: "Is it well with the young man Absalom?" And the Cushite answered: "The enemies of my lord the king, and all that rise up against thee to do thee hurt, be as that young man is."

And the king was much moved, and went up to the chamber over the gate, and wept; and as he went, thus he said: "O my son Absalom, my son, my son Absalom! would I had died for thee, O Absalom, my son, my son!"

And it was told Joab: "Behold, the king weepeth and mourneth for Absalom." And the victor that day was turned into mourning unto all the people; for the people heard say that day: "The king grieveth for his son." And the people got them by stealth that day into the city, as people that are ashamed steal away when they flee in battle. And the king covered his face, and the king cried with a loud voice: "O my son Absalom, O Absalom, my son, my son!"[9]

[9] II Samuel 8:15 to 19:5

CHRONOLOGY OF BIBLICAL WRITINGS

	Approximately
The Song of the Well	1200 B.C.
The Song of Deborah	1150 B.C.
The Fable of Jotham	1100 B.C.
The Song of Miriam	1100 B.C.
J document	900 B.C.
E document	800 B.C.
Amos	750 B.C.
Hosea	750 B.C.
Isaiah	750 B.C.
Micah	700 B.C.
JE combined	650 B.C.
Deuteronomy	621 B.C.
Jeremiah	586 B.C.
Ezekiel	580 B.C.
Deutero-Isaiah	550 B.C.
Judges, Samuel, Kings compiled	500 B.C.
Joshua edited	450 B.C.
The Torah canonized	400 B.C.
Job	400 B.C.
Ruth	400 B.C.
Ezra, Nehemiah, Chronicles compiled	300 B.C.
Ecclesiastes	250 B.C.
The Prophets canonized	200 B.C.
Esther	200 B.C.
Daniel	160 B.C.
The Writings canonized	90

THREE

The Bible as Law

IT IS A dangerous oversimplification to say that Judaism is a religion of law, but in the sense that Christianity is essentially a religion of faith, Islam is a religion of action, and Buddhism is a religion of inaction (withdrawal from all human passions and desires), so Judaism is a religion of legal codes. The message of Jesus to His followers was, "Believe in Me." The corollary message of the prophets to the Jews was, "Follow the Law."

The traditional relationship of God to Israel the People, and of God to each individual Jew, was that of Law-giver to Law-follower. The prescriptions, set down mainly in Deuteronomy, Leviticus, and Exodus, are the basis for the civil, religious, and moral laws that governed the total life of the Jews and differentiated them from the Gentiles. Even the much-disputed concept of the election of Israel as the Chosen People is based on the acceptance by the Jews of this body of law. A *midrash*, or illustrative story, offered by the Rabbis to explain the election of Israel says:

Before God gave Israel the Torah, He approached every tribe and nation and offered them the Torah, that they might have no excuse later to say, "Had the Holy One desired to give us the Torah, we would have accepted it."

God went to the children of Esau and said, "Will you accept the Torah?" They answered Him, saying, "What is written therein?" He answered them, "Thou shalt not kill." Then they said, "Our father Esau was blest with the words 'By the sword shalt thou live.' We do not want to accept the Torah."

Thereupon He went to the children of Lot and said to them, "Will you accept the Torah?" They said, "What is written therein?" He answered, "Thou shalt not commit unchastity." They said. "From unchastity do we spring. We will not accept your Torah."

Then He went to the children of Ishmael and said to them, "Do ye want to accept the Torah?" They said to Him, "What is written therein?" He answered, "Thou shalt not steal." They said, "Our father was promised that his hand would be against every man. We do not want to accept the Torah."

Thence God went to all the other nations, who likewise rejected the Torah, saying: "We cannot give up the law of our fathers; we do not want Thy Torah."

Upon hearing this, God came to Israel and spoke to them, "Will ye accept the Torah?" They said to Him, "What is written therein?" He answered, "Six hundred and thirteen commandments." They said, "All that the Lord has spoken will we obey and do."

The 613 commandments which the Jews accepted are explicit rules for the ordering of the life of the nation of Jews. They range from rules governing war and courts to regulation of the manner of killing animals and gleaning fields. The number 613 was not haphazard. Rabbi Simlai, in the third century, explained it thus: "Six hundred and thirteen commandments were revealed to Moses: 365 prohibitions, equal to the number of days of the astronomical year; and 248 commands, equal to the number of [bones and] members of the human body." Another rabbi explained that the prohibitions were related to the days of the year so that each day would remind the Jew not to "transgress the prohibition on me," and that the positive commandments were related to the body so that each member would remind the Jews "to fulfill this commandment through me."

The 613 commandments are not set down in any one place in the Bible. They were not even gathered together into one listing or code of law until about the eighth century. In the next five centuries many great scholars, including Maimonides, offered their own compilations of the 613—and each listing differed from the other. But long before these scholars tried to codify the commandments, the Rabbis of the Talmud had reduced them to their moral essence. They said:

Six hundred and thirteen commandments were given to Moses. . . .
Then came David and reduced them to eleven:
"Lord, who shall sojourn in Thy tabernacle?
Who shall dwell upon Thy holy mountain?
He that walketh uprightly, and worketh righteousness,
And speaketh truth in his heart;
That hath no slander upon his tongue,
Nor doeth evil to his fellow,
Nor taketh up a reproach against his neighbor;
In whose eyes a vile person is despised,
But he honoreth them that fear the Lord;
He that sweareth not to his own hurt, and changeth not;
He that putteth not out his money on interest,
Nor taketh a bribe against the innocent."

Then came Isaiah, and reduced them to six:
"He that walketh righteously, and speaketh uprightly;
He that despiseth the gain of oppressions,
That shaketh his hands from holding of bribes,
That stoppeth his ears from hearing of blood,
And shutteth his eyes from looking upon evil."
Then came Micah , and reduced them to three:
"It hath been told to thee, O man, what is good,
And what the Lord doth require of thee:
Only to do justly, to love mercy, and to walk humbly with thy God."
     Then came Isaiah again, and reduced them to two, as it is said, "Keep ye
judgment and do righteousness." Then came Amos, and reduced them to
one, as it is said, "Seek ye Me and live." Or one may say, then came Habak-
kuk, and reduced them to one, as it is said, "The righteous shall live by his
faith."

By tradition, the entire body of Biblical law was given to Moses on
Mt. Sinai. He received the Ten Commandments directly, engraved on
the tablets of stone; he received the Torah, and he received the Oral
Law. So whenever post-Mosaic writers of the Bible introduced codes,
they ascribed them to Moses. The Deuteronomic code, for example,
contained in the document found in the Temple in 621 B.C., was promulgated as the Law of Moses.

But the systems and compilations of laws in the Bible include codes
that are thought to antedate Moses and many that were developed centuries after Moses; some may have had their sources in the legal systems
of the Babylonians and Canaanites. Whatever their sources, the Jews
added unique moral and ethical values to the codes they wrote into their
Book. Laws requiring justice and regard for one's neighbor are generally
the luxuries of power; only strong nations are assumed able to afford
justice. Yet the Biblical laws governed a weak nation during brutal and
bloody centuries. Unique too for the times and places of the early
Jews—and still unknown in large areas of the modern world—were the
Biblical laws which not only forbade a man to harm his fellow, but
required that he take positive action when his neighbor needed help:
"Neither shalt thou stand idly by the blood of thy neighbor."

Also unknown for millennia, except in the law of the Jews, were laws
against harming or mistreating animals. Until the passage of modern
social legislation, the Biblical code was unique in requiring one day of
rest in every seven not only for freemen but also for servants and slaves
and work animals. And in a law promulgated about twenty-five hundred
years before the Emancipation Proclamation, the Jews ordered the death
penalty for selling a man into slavery: "He that stealeth a man, and selleth him, or if he be found in his hand, he shall surely be put to death."

The Ten Commandments, the basic short formulation of the Law, is not the only decalogue in the Book, nor is it the oldest. The Biblical writers included at least five ten-law codes, one of which was lengthened to twelve to make the number of commandments equal the number of Hebrew tribes.

The oldest decalogue in the Bible, dating from well before 1200 B.C., is tribal legislation. This collection of laws itemizes the ten offenses for which death was the penalty. They were probably composed for group recitation at some tribal ceremony, since most of these laws are stated in five Hebrew words.

1. He that smiteth a man, so that he dieth, shall surely be put to death.
2. He that smiteth his father, or his mother, shall surely be put to death.
3. He that stealeth a man, and selleth him, or if he be found in his hand, he shall surely be put to death.
4. He that curseth his father or his mother, shall surely be put to death.
5. The man that committeth adultery . . . both the adulterer and the adulteress shall surely be put to death.
6. The man that lieth with his father's wife . . . shall surely be put to death.
7. If a man lie with his daughter-in-law, both of them shall surely be put to death.
8. If a man lie with a beast, he shall surely be put to death.
9. A man also or a woman that divineth by a ghost or a familiar spirit, shall surely be put to death.
10. He that blasphemeth the name of the Lord, he shall surely be put to death.[1]

Two things are particularly significant in this earliest of Biblical legal systems: in a patriarchal society in which women had very little place or status, the laws requiring submission to parents (laws 2 and 4) extended equally to father and mother; and in this period before the conquest of Canaan, the tribes had already accepted a stern monotheism (laws 9 and 10).

The J document also included a decalogue establishing the laws of ritual worship. Written toward the end of the tenth or beginning of the ninth century B.C., this system of laws was a reaction against Canaanite and Philistine idol worship, which threatened the monotheism the Hebrews had brought out of the desert. In its edited form, this ritual decalogue orders:

1. Thou shalt bow down to no other God.
2. Thou shalt make thee no molten gods.
3. The feast of unleavened bread [Passover] shalt thou keep.

[1] Exodus 21; Leviticus 20, 24

4. All that openeth the womb [first born] is Mine.
5. Six days thou shalt work, but on the seventh day thou shalt rest.
6. Thou shalt observe feast of weeks [first harvest] . . .
7. and the feast of ingathering at the turn of the year [feast of booths in autumn].
8. Thou shalt not offer [touch] the blood of My sacrifice with leavened bread.
9. Neither shall the sacrifice of the feast of unleavened bread be left unto morning.
10. Thou shalt not seethe a kid in its mother's milk.[2]

In an earlier form, this decalogue was restricted to laws of festivals, sacrifices, and offerings; the first two laws in the J version above, those dealing with idol worship, were left out, and two others were substituted: one required three annual pilgrimages to the Temple, and the second required that the first fruits be brought to the Temple as offerings.[3]

An E version of this decalogue changes the phrase "molten gods" (law 2) to "gods of silver, or gods of gold." The Elohist decalogue also required that altars be built of earth and unhewn stones. These changes reflect the economic differences between J's Southern Kingdom of shepherds and farmers and E's Northern Kingdom of artisans and traders. A citizen of Israel might make a god of gold or silver; a citizen of Judah probably never saw precious metals. And in the Northern Kingdom there was need for a law specifying the materials to be used to raise an altar—earth and unhewn stones. This took care of any Israelite who was tempted to build an altar of hewn stones in competition with the great stone temples to Baal and Ashtoreth.

Still another decalogue is found in the twelve curses which Moses ordered the Levites to utter after they entered the Promised Land.[4] The form of this decalogue indicates that it was used in worship, the Levites uttering the anathemas, the congregation answering "Amen" after each curse. Scholars deduce that this decalogue is a summary of civil and moral law dealing with offenses that are committed in secret—and so beyond reach of mortal punishment. The recitation of this decalogue calls down God's punishment on these lawbreakers. The original anathemas, dating from the ninth century B.C., said:

1. Cursed be the man that maketh a graven or molten image . . . and setteth it up in secret.
2. Cursed be he who dishonoreth this father or his mother.
3. Cursed be he who removeth his neighbor's landmark.
4. Cursed be he who maketh the blind to go astray.

[2] Exodus 34:14–26
[3] Exodus 22–23
[4] Deuteronomy 27:15–26

5. Cursed be he who perverteth the justice due the stranger, the fatherless, and the widow.
6. Cursed be he who lieth with his father's wife.
7. Cursed be he who lieth with his sister.
8. Cursed be he who lieth with his mother-in-law.
9. Cursed be he who smiteth his neighbor in secret.
10. Cursed be he who taketh a bribe to slay an innocent person.

To make the number of these curses correspond to the number of Hebrew tribes, later editors added two more curses: against him who "lieth with any manner of beast"; against him who "confirmeth not the words of this law."

The Ten Commandments grew out of these earlier systems of law, and from these simple one-word[5] shalts and shalt-nots grew the involved, complicated Deuteronomic Code.

The Ten Commandments are given in two versions in the Torah, Deuteronomic[6] and Priestly,[7] although there are few real differences between the two sources. The Decalogue as compiled by D was a compromise between the ritual requirements of the priests and the moral demands of the prophets. Thus the Decalogue (in the Hebrew version, not the Christian) is actually two pentalogues, two codes of five commandments each, one dealing with religious law, the other with oral law. The first five commandments establish the authorship of the Decalogue, monotheism, respect for the Divine Name, proper observance of the sabbath, and respect for parents. The second pentalogue consists of five prohibitions: against murder, adultery, stealing, false witness, and covetousness.

The D and P Decalogues differ mainly in the reasons for observing the sabbath. The Deuteronomist declares the sabbath to be a day of rest for everyone, including laborers, servants, and animals, out of gratitude for the deliverance from Egypt. The Priestly writers say that the sabbath marks the day God rested after the creation.

The differences are shown in the following parallel versions of the Fourth, Fifth, and Tenth Commandments:

The Deuteronomic Commandments	*The Priestly Commandments*
	Fourth Commandment
Observe the sabbath day, to keep it holy, *as the Lord thy God commanded thee.* Six days shalt thou labour, and do all thy work; but the seventh day is a sabbath unto the Lord thy God, in it	*Remember* the sabbath day, to keep it holy. Six days shalt thou labour, and do all thy work; but the seventh day is a sabbath unto the Lord thy God, in it thou shalt

[5] *Lo Tirtzach*—Thou shalt not kill.
Lo Tinaf—Thou shalt not commit adultery.
Lo Tignov—Thou shalt not steal.
[6] Deuteronomy 5:6–18
[7] Exodus 20:2–14

The Deuteronomic Commandments	*The Priestly Commandments*
thou shalt not do any manner of work, thou, nor thy son, nor thy daughter, nor thy man-servant, nor thy maid-servant, nor thine *ox, nor thine ass,* nor any of thy cattle, nor thy stranger that is within thy gates; *that thy man-servant and thy maid-servant may rest as well as thou. And thou shalt remember that thou was a servant in the land of Egypt, and the Lord thy God brought thee out thence by a mighty hand and by an outstretched arm; therefore the Lord thy God commanded thee to keep the sabbath day.*	not do any manner of work, thou, nor thy son, nor thy daughter, nor thy man-servant, nor thy maid-servant, nor thy cattle, nor thy stranger that is within thy gates;
	for in six days the Lord made heaven and earth, the sea, and all that in them is, and rested on the seventh day; wherefore the Lord blessed the sabbath day, and hallowed it.

Fifth Commandment

Honour thy father and thy mother, *as the Lord thy God commanded thee;* that thy days may be long, *and that it may go well with thee,* upon the land which the Lord thy God giveth thee.	Honour thy father and thy mother, that thy days may be long upon the land which the Lord thy God giveth thee.

Tenth Commandment

Neither shalt thou covet thy neighbour's *wife;* neither shalt thou *desire* thy neighbor's *house, his field,* or his man-servant, or his maid-servant, his ox, or his ass, nor anything that is thy neighbour's.	Thou shalt not covet thy neighbour's *house;* thou shalt not *covet* thy neighbor's *wife,* nor his man-servant, nor his maid-servant, nor his ox, nor his ass, nor anything that is thy neighbour's.

The Commandments are not numbered in the Bible, nor are they divided so as to make the divisions between them readily apparent. As a result three systems of numbering the Commandments have developed. In the Jewish version of the Decalogue, the First Commandment is the statement of authorship: "I am the Lord thy God, who brought thee out of the land of Egypt, out of the house of bondage." Christian tradition excludes this statement from the Decalogue. Instead, most Protestant and Orthodox churches divide the Jewish Second Commandment in two: "Thou shalt have no other gods before Me," and "Thou shalt not make unto thee a graven image. . . ." Roman Catholic and Lutheran churches use the entire Jewish Second Commandment as their First Commandment; they divide the Jewish Tenth Commandment in two: thou shalt not covet thy neighbor's wife, and thou shalt not covet thy neighbor's property.

The great code of law contained in the book of Deuteronomy (chapters 12–26) is not a book of statutes or a lawyer's casebook. It is a legal guide for laymen, a manual covering the daily life of the ordinary Jew. It gives directions for keeping the annual feasts and making the principal offerings. It lays down general rules for sacrifices, but where technical knowledge is required, the Deuteronomic Code refers the matter to the priests. It lays down rules for the proper conduct of family life, with examples of the most likely types of disputes. It establishes rules for the proper administration of justice, prescribes the authority of prophets, and indicates how a king may rule over the Jews without invading God's authority over them.

The Deuteronomic Code opens with a long sermon introduced by the Ten Commandments, and the spirit of the Decalogue is evident in the hundreds of laws in the code that follow. Some of the laws in the code are stated simply and without explanation: "One witness shall not rise up against a man for any iniquity, or for any sin . . . at the mouth of two witnesses, or at the mouth of three witnesses, shall a matter be established" (Deuteronomy 19:15). The D lawyers assumed that the justification for this ordinance was self-evident. But more often, the statement of the law incorporates the reason for the law and the reward for following it: "Thou [judges] shalt not wrest judgment; thou shalt not respect persons; neither shalt thou take a gift; for a gift doth blind the eyes of the wise, and pervert the words of the righteous. Justice, justice shalt thou follow, that thou mayest live, and inherit the land which the Lord thy God giveth thee" (Deuteronomy 16:20).

The laws in the D code have no apparent logical arrangement, either by nature of ordinance, type of prohibition, or degree of punishment. In fact, some scholars have suggested, the disarray seems purposeful. The ordinary Jew seeking legal guidance in the code would have to pore over it time and again—or else know it by heart. This may have been the design of the compilers of Deuteronomy. More probably, the Deuteronomic school had already developed a reverential attitude toward the several versions of the laws then extant. When the Deuteronomic redactors combined the differing versions, they did as little cutting and editing as possible. The result had no logical organization.

The Holiness Code, chapters 17–26 of the book of Leviticus, was written about 550 B.C., after the destruction of the First Temple and during the Babylonian exile. This code, too, is presented as a sermon by Moses. It is concerned mainly with ritual and priestly duties and with the preservation of the priesthood, but it is also quite specific about marriage and chastity. This one-sidedness may be explained by the fact that Persian law regulated civil conduct during the period of the compilation of the H code, and so the H writers restricted themselves to religious and family law.

The H code was already an integral part of the Priestly Code when Ezra proclaimed the Pentateuch as canon in the fifth century B.C. Nehemiah, for example, refers to a section of the H code as part of the Law of Moses.

The Priestly Code is not found in any one book or section of the Bible. It was woven into the corpus of the Pentateuch from Genesis to Deuteronomy during the years before the canon was established and while the Mosaic books were receiving their final editing. Although it purports to be an intrinsic part of the early history of the Jews, the P code is the legal structure of the Jewish nation during the early days of the Second Temple; it is the constitution of a religious community in being.

In putting together their code, the P writers made a choice. During the eight hundred years of nationhood preceding the final formulation of the Pentateuch, the Jews had experienced every form of civil organization. They had been a loose federation of independent tribes governed by judges; they had been an independent kingdom; they had been every kind of vassal state to every kind of empire. The realistic P writers, living during the time of the Persian overlordship, worked on the assumption that the Jews would never again achieve true political independence—or that if they did, it would not last. So they framed a legal code which would hold the Jews together as a religious nation, impervious to assimilation. Of course, this required strict prohibitions against intermarriage with non-Jews. But, consistent with their own version of the Noah story, which showed that all nations are members of a single family,[8] the P code opens the congregation of Israel to all individuals and nations accepting the Law. The convert has equal status with the birthright Jew.

The form of the P laws is as varied as their subject matter. Some laws are stated directly, as commands from Moses; other laws are contained in examples; still others are woven into narratives. The law establishing the ceremony for the Day of Atonement during the days of the Temple is an example of the direct statement:

And Aaron [the priest] shall lay both his hands upon the head of the live goat, and confess over him all the iniquities of the children of Israel, and all their transgressions, even all their sins; and he shall put them upon the head of the goat, and shall send him away by the hand of an appointed man into the wilderness.[9]

[8] Genesis 10
[9] Leviticus 16:21

The Noah story includes law-in-narrative. After the Ark has landed and Noah has built an altar, God promises that He will never again "curse the ground." He also blesses Noah and his sons:

Every moving thing that liveth shall be food for you; as the green herb have I given you all. Only flesh with the life thereof, which is the blood thereof, shall ye not eat. And surely your blood of your lives will I require; at the hand of every beast will I require it; and at the hand of every man, even at the hand of every man's brother, will I require the life of man. Whoso sheddeth man's blood, by man shall his blood be shed; for in the image of God made He man. And you, be ye fruitful, and multiply; swarm in the earth, and multiply therein.[10]

These five brief verses of narrative include four laws: a specific prohibition against eating meat taken from animals not yet dead (other nations of the time tore limbs from living animals); a standard for judging whether an animal was dead, and so could be eaten (this is the source of Jewish ritual slaughter in which the neck artery is severed and the blood evacuated); and prohibitions against murder and suicide.

The prohibition against marriage with certain non-Jews is an example of the law stated indirectly. It occurs in the story of Isaac, Jacob, and Esau—but it is repeated three times to make sure the point is understood:

And when Esau was forty years old, he took to wife Judith the daughter of Beeri the Hittite, and Basemath the daughter of Elon the Hittite. And there was a bitterness of spirit unto Isaac and to Rebekah [Esau's parents] ....[11]

And Rebekah said to Isaac: "I am weary of my life because of the daughters of Heth. If Jacob take a wife of the daughters of Heth, such as these, of the daughters of the land, what good shall my life do me?"[12]

And Isaac called Jacob, and blessed him, and charged him, and said unto him: "Thou shalt not take a wife of the daughters of Canaan."[13]

The rules for dividing the booty of war are laid down in a story of a war between Israel and the Midianites. All slaves and animals taken from the enemy were divided into two equal groups; one went to the men of war, the other to the people. From the soldiers' half, one animal and one slave in five hundred were taken for the high priest; from the people's half, one animal and one slave in fifty were taken for the Levites, the servitors of the Temple. But all the gold and silver and precious stones were used for "a memorial for the children of Israel before the Lord."[14]

[10] Genesis 9:3–7
[11] Genesis 26:34
[12] Genesis 27:46
[13] Genesis 28:1
[14] Numbers 31:25–54

And the laws of inheritance were developed out of the story of Zelophehad, who died during the wandering in the wilderness without leaving a son:

> If a man die, and have no son, then ye shall cause his inheritance to pass unto his daughter. And if he have no daughter, then ye shall give his inheritance unto his brethren. And if he have no brethren, then ye shall give his inheritance unto his father's brethren. And if his father have no brethren, then ye shall give his inheritance unto his kinsman that is next to him of his family, and he shall possess it.[15]

Five hundred years after the canonization of the Law, the Rabbis abstracted—out of these scattered decalogues, codes, laws by analogy, and laws by implication—the 613 commandments that governed the Jews for more than two millennia and that established the ethical and moral matrix in which Jews are formed to this day (see pages 57–58).

About one-third of the commandments came from the Deuteronomic Code, the rest from the Priestly and Holiness Codes and early tribal law. But these are not 613 distinct orders and prohibitions; they include many repetitions—many laws are stated twice, once as a commandment and again as a prohibition. For example, one of the 248 positive commandments requires a leper to make himself distinguishable from the healthy members of the community; one of the 365 negative ordinances prohibits a leper from removing the distinguishing marks that identify him as a leper. A positive commandment orders that the ground be allowed to lie fallow every seventh year; a negative commandment prohibits cultivation of the land in the seventh year.

The 613 commandments were the constitution of a religious nation, but a nation whose civic life was also ordered by the laws of whatever secular nation the Jews owed allegiance to at the time whether Persia, Syria, Rome, or Babylonia.[16]

---

[15] Numbers 27:8–11
[16] The social-ethical commandments are listed in Appendix I.

FOUR

The Prophets

DURING A PERIOD of three centuries—from the eighth to the fifth century B.C.—Jewish monotheism gave rise to a unique phenomenon: the literary prophets.[1] All religions have prophets and seers and oracles and men who speak with voices from beyond themselves; generally these are the saints, the fathers of churches, the leader of sects. But the Jewish prophets were neither saints nor fathers of new temples nor founders of new sects. They were driven men, driven by an inescapable inner drive to remind the Jews—and through the Jews, the world—what God demands of man.

These prophets were solitary men acting alone; they did not found schools of disciples or political parties to gain power for their vision of society or community, though some schools of prophecy grew up after them. They took their stand in the market places, in the shrines and temples, or in the courts of rulers; they castigated both the high and the low. In the midst of war, when Israel was beseiged, they demanded capitulation to the enemy. In other religions, saintly men who felt oppressed and defiled by the evils about them would leave the sinful world and lead solitary lives in wasteland or wilderness. The Jewish prophets went into the cities of men to demand adherence to God's Law.

Nor did the prophets—with the single exception of *the* prophet, Moses—come to reveal new truths. They saw themselves as upholders of tradition and ancient pieties rather than as openers of new ways. Rather than enfolders of new visions—except the messianic vision—they were guardians of Israelite tradition against the incursions of foreign gods, foreign customs, and the accretions of new cultures. They

[1] The literary prophets were those whose prophecies were written down at the time they were made, or shortly after. They are quoted directly in the Bible.

were conservatives, although in the context of their times they appeared radical—the old ways they offered had been forgotten long enough to appear new.

For the most part, the words of the prophets recorded in the Bible do not promise victory or conquest or enrichment. They are denunciatory. There are passages of consolation, particularly in the post-exilic prophets, but most of the recorded speeches denounce the religious and moral sins of Israel. Unlike the priests who went before the hosts in pre-prophetic days, and unlike the chaplains of a later period, the prophets did not seek to raise the morale of the hosts or of the beleaguered Jews. Instead they kept repeating Moses' cry: "Justice, justice, shalt thou follow. . . ."[2] Generally, there was little comfort to be gained from that demand.

Preachers of such direful consequences would ordinarily have been driven out of the city—or killed. And in rare instances, notably those of Jeremiah and Elijah, they were thrown into a pit or driven into hiding. But the very people they denounced gave the prophets a terrible respect. Instead of turning against them, the Jews treasured their words and incorporated them in the canon. Thus, alone among Scriptures, the Bible of the Jews catalogues the iniquities of the very people whom the book calls chosen, and holy, and beloved of God.

And the prophets did achieve their purpose. Despite constant warfare with the mighty of the nation, with kings and high priests and nobles, the prophets succeeded eventually in cleansing Israel of idolatry; they succeeded in making an unseeable, incorporeal God the God not only a few great souls, but of a nation of people of all sorts; they succeeded, not in making all Jews follow the Law, but in making all Jews conscious of the Law.

These prophets came from every social and economic group within the community. Samuel, Jeremiah, and Ezekiel were of the priestly caste; Isaiah and Zephaniah were of the nobles and the court; Amos and Micah and Hosea were very common men, workers in the field or forest. But their differing backgrounds did not cause the prophets to favor one group over another, or to examine one group's iniquities more closely than another's. They represented the conscience of the nation—independent of any human power or status.

But the conscience of a nation is the totality of the individual consciences of its people. And the prophets believed that each man had within himself an instinct for good, for right, and for justice. This inner knowledge of the right way—which they equated with God's way—was often buried under equally human desires for power, for riches, or for

[2] Deuteronomy 16:20

sensual pleasures. It was the prophets' purpose to remind man of his true nature, of the right (Godly) way. Thus, in beginning his prophecy, Isaiah compares his mission to that of a teacher of children who know less than some animals:

> Hear, O heavens, and give ear, O earth,
> For the Lord hath spoken:
> Children have I reared, and brought up,
> And they have rebelled against Me.
> The ox knoweth his owner,
> And the ass his master's crib;
> But Israel doth not know,
> My people doth not consider.[3]

Biblical prophecy begins with the supreme prophet, Moses. But by virtue of this very supremacy, Moses was not like the prophets who came after. He was different in degree and in nature. Moses spoke to God; the other prophets heard from God:

And He said: "Hear now My words: if there be a prophet among you, I the Lord do make Myself known unto him in a vision, I do speak to him in a dream. My servant Moses is not so; he is trusted in all My house; with him do I speak mouth to mouth, even manifestly, and not in dark speeches; and the similitude of the Lord doth he behold. . . ."[4]

This thought is repeated in the last verses of the Pentateuch: "And there hath not arisen a prophet since in Israel like unto Moses, whom the Lord knew face to face. . . ."[5]

Moses' special place among the prophets stems also from his position as giver—at one remove—of the Law which the later prophets expounded. And Moses' prophecies provide the philosophical-theological basis for the later prophets' relevance. Before Moses, religion was mainly a system for appeasing or buying favor with the physical world: the world of rain, lightning, fertility, drought, sun, and flood. Moses' prophetic Law made the behavior of man relevant to religion.[6]

Prophecy was quiescent in the two or three centuries between Moses and Samuel. Deborah, a Judge, may have had prophetic visions; she appears at times to speak in the name of God. Trying to stiffen Barak's

---

[3] Isaiah 1:2–3

[4] Numbers 12:6–8

[5] Deuteronomy 34:10

[6] Maimonides, a medieval Aristotelian rationalist, tried to formalize Judaism through a thirteen-point credo. One article of faith in this system was belief in the Mosaic prophecies. But Maimonides was unsuccessful, as were the other attempts to impose a formal creed upon the Jews; one can be a Jew without accepting the Mosaic oracles. However, the one credal statement which all Jews must accept is part of the Mosaic prophecy. It is the *Shema*: "Hear O Israel, the Lord our God, the Lord is One" (Deuteronomy 6:4).

backbone in the war against Sisera, Deborah says: "Is not the Lord gone out before thee?"[7] But Deborah is not considered in the line of true prophets.[8]

Bands of wild men known as seers and prophets ranged the countryside in the years before the monarchy. And they did serve a prophetic function—they cried out against lapses into idolatry—but they also sold magic potions, foretold individual futures, and dealt in amulets. Although in most respects they were akin to the magicians and priests characteristic of primitive religions, they were accepted among the Jews as men of God. Samuel, the first important prophet after Moses, was a member of one of these bands of seers. And Saul, whom Samuel later annointed the first king over Israel, sought the help of Samuel the seer when he could not find his father's lost cattle:

> . . . Saul said to his servant that was with him: "Come and let us return; lest my father leave caring for the asses, and become anxious concerning us." And he [the servant] said unto him [Saul]: "Behold now, there is in this city a man of God, and he is a man that is held in honour; all that he saith cometh surely to pass; now let us go thither; peradventure he can tell us concerning our journey whereon we go." Then said Saul to his servant: "But, behold, if we go what shall we bring the man? for the bread is spent in our vessels, and there is not a present to bring to the man of God; what have we?" And the servant answered Saul again, and said: "Behold, I have in my hand the fourth part of a shekel of silver, that will I give to the man of God, to tell us our way."—Beforetime in Israel, when a man went to inquire of God, thus he said: "Come and let us go to the seer"; for he that is now called a prophet was beforetime called a seer.—Then said Saul to his servant: "Well said; come, let us go." So they went into the city where the man of God was.[9]

This seer was Samuel. But when Samuel assumed his ministry as a true prophet, he outlawed the magicians and diviners. Still the people clung to the seers; even King Saul, after Samuel's death, backslid and went to the "woman that divineth by a ghost at En-dor."[10]

There were other prophets in the great tradition during the first centuries of the monarchy, before the great age of prophecy. The Bible mentions Gad, Shemaiah, and Micaiah by name, and Nathan, Elijah, and Elisha at much greater length. The Rabbis of the Talmud believed there had been many more, but that only those who taught something new were actually mentioned in the canon.

Nathan, in the eleventh century B.C., and Elijah, in the ninth cen-

---

[7] Judges 4:14

[8] Prophets did not have to be male. Huldah was prophetess during the reign of King Josiah.

[9] I Samuel 9:5–10

[10] I Samuel 28:7

tury, indicated the direction of future prophecy. They moved the religion of the Jews from the shrines and the Temple, from the feasts of harvests and the fasts of remembrance, into the homes and counting houses of the people. They insisted that the Law covered personal morality as well as Temple worship. Significantly, both these prophets foretold the doom of kings. Nathan called David to account for stealing Bath-sheba from Uriah; Elijah foretold the death of Ahab for stealing Naboth's vineyards. From these prophets the people learned that if a king could be brought low for trespassing the Law, then certainly ordinary mortals had to obey.

The words and deeds of Samuel, Nathan, Elijah, and Elisha, the early prophets, were transmitted through the writings of others. And the last of these, Elisha, was also the last to deal in miracles and personal prophecy in foretelling the future of individuals. Beginning with Amos, the first of the later prophets and the first of those whose words were recorded at the time they were spoken, prophecy was restricted to what was to befall the nation, to events that would affect the destiny of Israel. Personal prophecy died; national, political, and religious prophecy became the dominant form.

The early literary prophets were men of the desert and the wilderness. The concept of God inherent in their preachings—which became the Jewish concept of God—developed out of the stark, hard world of the open spaces rather than out of the easier world of the cities. These prophets were wanderers rather than farmers, so their God was not tied to fields and trees; they had no need for Baal or Ashtoreth. And since they were nomads, their God had to be everywhere, all-pervading; He could not be resident on a particular hill or "high place."

In keeping with the characterizations of the early writers of the Bible, the prophets were not particularly saintly. Often they were reluctant to accept the burden of prophecy; they didn't rush gladly to be spokesmen for God; sometimes they hid from Him. And they exhibited all the human weaknesses of anger, fear, and desire, all the moods and emotions of man.

The prophets operated in an identifiable historical milieu. Some of the later prophets are hard to date accurately, but this is due to a failure in the physical transmission of scriptural writings rather than to efforts to take them out of the real world. Elijah, for example, prophesied during the reign of (and against) a real historical personage, Ahab. Amos' ministry was during the time of Jeroboam. Isaiah preached during the time of the incursions of Tiglath-pileser and Sennacherib and Sargon. Jeremiah actually saw Nebuchadnezzar.

The great age of prophecy dawned in the middle of the eighth century B.C. during a feast day celebration in the central sanctuary in Bethel, Kingdom of Israel. Amos, a shepherd and gatherer of the fruit of the sycamore tree from the Judean village of Tekoa, had seen a vision which sent him to the Northern Kingdom. Revolted by the social evils he saw about him, he interrupted the celebration of the feast of the harvest to warn the people of the coming judgment of God—not only upon the Jews, but upon all nations. He began with a terrible catalogue of the evils of nations:

> Thus saith the Lord:
>> For three transgressions of Damascus,
>> Yea, for four, I will not reverse it [the judgment]. . . .
>> For three transgressions of Gaza,
>> Yea, for four, I will not reverse it. . . .
>> For three transgressions of Tyre,
>> Yea, for four, I will not reverse it. . . .
>> For three transgressions of Edom . . . . Ammon . . . . Moab. . . .

And then Amos came to Judah, his own nation, and finally to Israel, where he was speaking: "For three transgressions of Israel, yea, for four, I will not reverse it, because they sell the righteous for silver, and the needy for a pair of shoes. . . ." [11]

So terrible were Amos' prophecies that "the land was unable to endure all his words." Amaziah, the priest of Bethel, ordered Amos to leave, to go and prophesy in his own country, Judah. Amos' answer established the prophet's right to preach where he was commanded to preach, without regard to the prophet's lineage or status, and without regard for the comfort of his hearers:

> I was no prophet, neither was I a prophet's son; but I was a herdsman and a dresser of sycamore trees; and the Lord took me from following the flock, and the Lord said unto me: Go, prophesy unto My people Israel. Now therefore hear thou the word of the Lord. [12]

Amos was not only the first literary prophet; he was also the first of the great reformers. Until his time, the religion of the Hebrews was, despite universalist statements, a national religion: God was the God of the Hebrews; His jurisdiction extended over the people of Israel and the land He had given them. Amos proclaimed Him judge over all nations ("Yea, for three transgressions of Damascus. . . . Tyre. . . . Moab. . . ." etc.). He would punish not only Israel for its iniquities, but all nations for the evils they did. Nor was Israel to expect special consideration:

> Are ye not as the children of the Ethiopians unto Me,
> O children of Israel? saith the Lord.

[11] Amos 1–2
[12] Amos 7:10–16

> Have not I brought up Israel out of the land of Egypt,
> And the Philistines from Caphtor,
> And Aram from Kir?[13]

Amos made no distinction between personal social conduct and religion. Allowing the poor to go hungry was a breach not only of social or ethical requirements but of divine command. And if the divine commandments were to be disregarded, then the Covenant itself might be breached—and Israel destroyed. But the destruction of Israel would not end God's reign, for He rules over all nations.

A towering literary figure, Amos used brilliant poetry to rage against dishonesty, venal courts, and ruthless wealth; to demand righteousness instead of empty ritual. Through this poetry Amos gave the Hebrew religion a powerful moral base.

Amos barely mentioned the Hebrews' worship of Baal; Hosea, who preached shortly after Amos, made this worship of idols the major crime of Israel. Hosea did not rail against the exploitation of the poor; instead, he denounced religious and political sins. Israel, Hosea said, had been unfaithful to God in three ways: she had worshiped Baal; she had allowed prostitution—actual prostitution in the temples of Ashtoreth, figurative prostitution through murder, adultery, and robbery; and she had allowed false kings and assassins to usurp the throne of Israel. (Dynastic murders were as prevalent in Israel as in England and Italy two thousand years later.)

In the first three verses of his prophecy, made before 744 B.C. and before Tiglath-pileser revived Assyrian power, Hosea hoped for the reform of his people and their redemption. But in the succeeding verses, written after Assyrian power made the conquest of Israel probable, Hosea described the condition of Israel as beyond help:

> He [Israel] shall not return into the land of Egypt,
> But the Assyrian shall be his king,
> Because they refused to return [to the Law].
> And the sword shall fall upon his cities,
> And shall consume his bars, and devour them,
> Because of their own counsels.[14]

A poet of sentiment and emotion, in contrast to the implacable objectivity of Amos, Hosea changed the concept of religion. The term generally used in the Bible to refer to religion is *irat Adonai,* translated as "fear of the Lord"; Hosea uses the term *da'at Elohim,* translated "knowledge of God." Despite the harsh prophecies he is forced to make, Hosea sees God as a loving Father whose harshest decree has yet a

[13] Amos 9:7–8
[14] Hosea 11:5–6

tender promise, who agonizes over the punishments He gives:

> How shall I give thee up, Ephraim [Israel]?
> How shall I surrender thee, Israel?
> How shall I make thee as Admah?
> How shall I set thee as Zeboim?
> My heart is turned within Me,
> My compassions are kindled together.
> I will not execute the fierceness of Mine anger,
> I will not return to destroy Ephraim;
> For I am God, and not man,
> The Holy One in the midst of thee,
> And I will not come in fury.[15]

Isaiah dates himself in the opening verse of his book: "The vision of Isaiah the son of Amoz, which he saw concerning Judah and Jerusalem, in the days of Uzziah, Jotham, Ahaz, and Hezekiah, kings of Judah." This period was from 744 to 695 B.C., when Assyria was at the height of her power.[16] Challenged only by Egypt, Assyria moved toward the south, a move which put Palestine in her path. Israel joined an alliance against Assyria—and was wiped out. Judah, who kept aloof from the early alliance against Assyria, was pressured by Egypt to join a new revolt against the Assyrian Sennacherib. Threatened with Israel's fate, King Hezekiah paid ransom to Assyria.

This was the world and the time in which Isaiah lived and preached. And, although he was the urbane city dweller, a friend of priest and king, he reacted much as did Hosea, the untutored villager. Revolted by the political double-dealing of the kings of Judah, Isaiah went about Jerusalem barefoot and in rags—the clothing of a captive—and preached:

> And when ye spread forth your hands,
> I will hide Mine eyes from you;
> Yea, when ye make many prayers,
> I will not hear;
> Your hands are full of blood.
> Wash you, make you clean,
> Put away the evil of your doings
> From before Mine eyes,
> Cease to do evil;
> Learn to do well;
> Seek justice, relieve the oppressed,
> Judge the fatherless, plead for the widow.[17]

[15] Hosea 11:8–10
[16] He dates one prophecy exactly: "In the year that King Uzziah died I saw the Lord . . ." (Isaiah 6:1). This was in 737 B.C.
[17] Isaiah 1:15–17

Amos preached the God of absolute justice, and Hosea preached the God of loving-kindness; Isaiah combined the two. To the above denunciation, he immediately added:

> Come now, and let us reason together,
> Saith the Lord;
> Though your sins be as scarlet,
> They shall be as white as snow;
> Though they be red like crimson,
> They shall be as wool.
> If ye be willing and obedient,
> Ye shall eat the good of the land;
> But if ye refuse and rebel,
> Ye shall be devoured with the sword;
> For the mouth of the Lord hath spoken.[18]

Isaiah's God, just and loving, was the God of absolute purity and holiness, perfect in goodness and truth. Thus, where Amos believed that the old, false ideas had to be swept away and the people and their cities with them before the clean Godly world could be rebuilt, Isaiah left a path for personal as well as national salvation: Isaiah offered the concept of the saving, or saved, remnant.

> Your country is desolate;
> Your cities are burned with fire;
> Your land, strangers devour it in your presence,
> And it is desolate, as overthrown by floods.
> And the daughter of Zion is left
> As a booth in a vineyard,
> As a lodge in a garden of cucumbers,
> As a besieged city.
> Except the Lord of hosts
> Had left unto us a very small remnant,
> We should have been as Sodom,
> We should have been like unto Gomorrah.[19]

Isaiah was also the bridge between the pure social prophets and the messianic prophets. He was the first prophet to foresee the time of ultimate peace when the Law of the Lord would be not only proclaimed throughout the earth but followed. Isaiah's Messiah was of the "root of Jesse," that is, of the line of David—a concept adopted by the writers of the Christian gospels in developing the lineage of Jesus. But Isaiah's Messiah, while bringing peace, was not a particularly peaceful person; he smote and he slew:

[18] Isaiah 1:18–20
[19] Isaiah 1:7–9

And there shall come forth a shoot out of the stock of Jesse,
And a twig shall grow forth out of his roots.
And the spirit of the Lord shall rest upon him,
The spirit of wisdom and understanding,
The spirit of counsel and might.
The spirit of knowledge and of the fear of the Lord.
And his delight shall be in the fear of the Lord;
And he shall not judge after the sight of his eyes,
Neither decide after the hearing of his ears;
But with righteousness shall he judge the poor,
And decide with equity for the meek of the land;
And he shall smite the land with the rod of his mouth,
And with the breath of his lips shall he slay the wicked.
And righteousness shall be the girdle of his loins,
And faithfulness the girdle of his reins.
And the wolf shall dwell with the lamb,
And the leopard shall lie down with the kid;
And the calf and the young lion and the fatling together;
And a little child shall lead them. . . .
For the earth shall be full of the knowledge of the Lord,
As the waters cover the sea.[20]

The messianic idea took strong hold among the Jews, as would be inevitable among a persecuted people. Maimonides made this belief, too, a part of his thirteen articles of faith: "I believe, with perfect faith, in the coming of the Messiah. And though he tarry, still I believe and wait his coming every day." Jews recite this statement in their daily services. Religious Jews recited it as they were herded into the Nazi death machines.

Micah also lived during the period of international power-plays, of the quickly forged and quickly broken international alliances that provoked Isaiah's wrath. But Micah, a villager in contrast to the nobly born Isaiah, was far more concerned with social injustice than with kingly quarrels. He warned the people of the final destruction of Israel and Judah because of the evils the rich visited upon the poor:

Hear this, I pray you, ye heads of the house of Jacob,
And rulers of the house of Israel,
That abhor justice, and pervert all equity;
That build up Zion with blood,
And Jerusalem with iniquity.
The heads thereof judge for reward,
And the priests thereof teach for hire,
And the prophets thereof divine for money;
Yet will they lean upon the Lord, and say:

[20] Isaiah 11:1–9

"Is not the Lord in the midst of us?
No evil shall come upon us?"
Therefore shall Zion for your sake be plowed as a field,
And Jerusalem shall become heaps,
And the mountain of the house as the high places of a forest.[21]

The editors of Micah, prior to the canonization of the books of the prophets, were repelled by the unrelieved denunciations of the original manuscript, so they added a messianic vision of the future, a vision not only of peace but of international equality:

But in the end of days it shall come to pass,
That the mountain of the Lord's house shall be established as
        the top of the mountains,
And it shall be exalted above the hills;
And peoples shall flow unto it.
And many nations shall go and say:
"Come ye, and let us go up to the mountain of the Lord,
And to the house of the God of Jacob;
And He will teach us of His ways,
And we will walk in His paths";
For out of Zion shall go forth the law,
And the word of the Lord from Jerusalem.
And He shall judge between many peoples,
And shall decide concerning mighty nations afar off;
And they shall beat their swords into plowshares,
And their spears into pruning-hooks;
Nation shall not lift up sword against nation,
Neither shall they learn war any more.
But they shall sit every man under his vine and under his fig-tree;
And none shall make them afraid;
For the mouth of the Lord of hosts hath spoken.
For let all the peoples walk each one in the name of its god,
But we will walk in the name of the Lord our God for ever and ever.[22]

In the period between Isaiah and Micah (mid-eighth century B.C.) and the last of the pre-exilic prophets, Jeremiah (early sixth century B.C.), there were a number of minor prophets: Zephaniah, Nahum, and Habakkuk. Zephaniah introduced the concept of eschatology—the final judgment—into Hebrew theology. The primitive idea that punishment is almost immediately visited upon the breaker of the law becomes more sophisticated with Zephaniah. He foretells punishment in the distant Day of the Lord. And his vision is dark, very dark:

That day is a day of wrath,
A day of trouble and distress,
A day of wasteness and desolation,

[21] Micah 3:9–12
[22] Micah 4:1–5. See also Isaiah 2:4

> A day of darkness and gloominess,
> A day of clouds and thick darkness,
> A day of the horn and alarm,
> Against the fortified cities, and against the high towers.
> And I will bring distress upon men,
> That they shall walk like the blind,
> Because they have sinned against the Lord;
> And their blood shall be poured out as dust,
> And their flesh as dung.[23]

Nahum is unusual in that his book is largely a hymn of hate against Nineveh. It was written about the time of this great city's fall—and the defeat of Israel's enemy, Assyria—in 612 B.C. Its feeling contrasts sharply with that expressed in the book of Jonah. (The Bible says Jonah prophesied during the reign of Jeroboam II, in the middle of the eighth century B.C. Modern scholars place him much later.) In Jonah, God is as concerned for the non-Jewish people of Nineveh as he ever was for the Israelites; Nahum is venomous against this same people. But although Jonah's religion is on a much higher plane than Nahum's Nahum's writing is much better than Jonah's.

Habakkuk is one of the great books of the Bible, sensitive, profound, and beautifully written. Habakkuk brings out a peculiar relationship between the Jew and God—indicated previously in the Bible but now more fully developed—the Jew's idea that he can challenge, question, even argue with God. This tradition continues from Habakkuk's time into the present. The book of Habakkuk opens with such a challenge:

> How long, O Lord, shall I cry,
> And Thou wilt not hear?
> I cry out unto Thee of violence
> And Thou wilt not save.
> Why dost Thou show me iniquity,
> And beholdest mischief?
> And why are spoiling and violence before me?
> So that there is strife, and contention ariseth.[24]

God answers this argument by saying that the things Habakkuk complains of—the triumphs of the Chaldeans—are by His command. He will, in His own time, chastise the Chaldeans, too. But this answer does not satisfy Habakkuk:

> Thou that art of eyes too pure to behold evil,
> And that canst not look on mischief,

---

[23] Zephaniah 1:15–17. This passage is the basis for the medieval church hymn, the *Dies Irae*.

[24] Habakkuk 1:2–3

> Wherefore lookest Thou, when they deal treacherously,
> And holdest Thy peace, when the wicked swalloweth up
> The man that is more righteous than he. . . .[25]

In this colloquy with God, Habakkuk also begins to introduce the central question in all religion, the question of theodicy: how can an all-powerful and just God permit the existence of evil? This is the problem to which the book of Job is addressed.

Jeremiah came from a priestly family of the tribe of Benjamin. Although the dispersion of the northern tribes had taken place a century before Jeremiah's ministry, his horror at the destruction of Israel still marked Jeremiah's prophecies. In his lifetime, he saw the reformer king Josiah killed and Josiah's son, Jehoahaz, captured by the Egyptians; he saw the Babylonian armies capture Jerusalem (597 B.C.) and take King Jehoiakim and his court into captivity; he saw king Zedekiah betray his word to Nebuchadnezzar and conspire against the Babylonians; he saw the destruction of the kingdom of Judah, of Jerusalem, and of the Temple (586 B.C.). These were imminent, immediate tragedies, and the brooding, sensitive Jeremiah had to proclaim them to his people. He was stoned, imprisoned, sentenced to death, and thrown into a pit—but he persisted in calling Judah to account and to repentance.

Jeremiah was one of the reluctant prophets; when he was called, he answered: "Ah, Lord God! behold, I cannot speak. . . ." [26] But he accepted his terrible burden and went through the villages of Judah and the courts of Jerusalem, stripping illusions from the eyes of the people and compelling them to see their own part in the destruction that was about to overtake them.

Throughout his prophecies, Jeremiah voiced his personal anguish with that of the nation and of the Lord. He was anguished that he had been chosen to foretell so terrible a future for his people:

> O Lord, Thou has enticed me, and I was enticed,
> Thou hast overcome me, and hast prevailed;
> I am become a laughing-stock all the day,
> Every one mocketh me.
> For as often as I speak, I cry out,
> I cry: "Violence and spoil";
> Because the word of the Lord is made
> A reproach unto me, and a derision, all the day.
> And if I say: "I will not make mention of Him,
> Nor speak any more in His name,"
> Then there is in my heart as it were a burning fire

---

[25] Habakkuk 1:13
[26] Jeremiah 1:6

> Shut up in my bones,
> And I weary myself to hold it in,
> But cannot.
> For I have heard the whispering of many,
> Terror on every side:
> "Denounce, and we will denounce him";
> Even of all my familiar friends,
> Them that watch for my halting:
> "Peradventure he will be enticed, and we shall prevail against him,
> And we shall take our revenge on him."[27]

Jeremiah was equally desolated by the fact and the nature of the coming events:

> Though I would take comfort against sorrow,
> My heart is faint within me.
> Behold the voice of the cry of the daughter of my people
> From a land far off:
> "Is not the Lord in Zion?
> Is not her King in her?"—
> "Why have they provoked Me with their graven images,
> And with strange vanities?"—
> "The harvest is past, the summer is ended,
> And we are not saved."
> For the hurt of the daughter of my people am I seized with anguish;
> I am black, appalment hath taken hold on me.
> Is there no balm in Gilead?
> Is there no physician there?
> Why then is not the health
> Of the daughter of my people recovered?
> Oh that my head were waters,
> And mine eyes a fountain of tears,
> That I might weep day and night
> For the slain of the daughter of my people![28]

The book of Jeremiah (large parts of it were dictated by Jeremiah to his secretary Baruch) includes several dialogues between the prophet and God in which he bemoans the task he has been given and in which he entreats God to allay the judgment against Judah. This is a further and fuller development of the God-challenge noted earlier in Habakkuk.

Although he was wellborn, Jeremiah was a man of the countryside rather than of the city. He lived in Anathoth, a village outside Jerusalem, and was always reluctant to leave his home. To him, as to many present-day sociologists, the city was the natural breeding place of evil. The complexities of urban life offered greatly increased opportunities to

[27] Jeremiah 20:7–10
[28] Jeremiah 8:18–23

break the Law, and the people of the city took easier advantage of the offer.

Jeremiah's major contribution to the prophetic stream—in addition to great literature—was to move the center of religious gravity away from the nation and closer to the individual. Despite his messages of destruction, he offered a God who loved Israel with "an everlasting love," who would make a new covenant with the Jews to replace the covenant they had broken. This new covenant would not be written on stone, a contract between God and the people Israel, but would be "written in their hearts," a contract between God and each individual.

Ezekiel, whose ministry dates from about 593 to 571 B.C., was a younger contemporary of Jeremiah and like him came from a priestly family. But Ezekiel, who must have been taken to Babylon from Jerusalem in the first captivity (596 B.C.) is the first of the line of exilic and post-exilic prophets; prophets who preached to a different need and in a different tone. The difference is evident in the book of Ezekiel; the prophecies are sharply divided by that cataclysmic event, the destruction of the Temple in 586.

During the first part of his prophetic career, Ezekiel, like Jeremiah, told of the coming destruction of Judah. But his bill of indictment was not so much for current crimes; he reached back into the centuries, citing every violation of the Law since Egypt. And although Ezekiel's denunciations leaned more heavily on religious and ritual crimes than upon social and ethical evils, they were even stronger than Jeremiah's.

And He said unto me: "Son of man, I send thee to the children of Israel, to rebellious nations, that have rebelled against Me; they and their fathers have transgressed against Me, even unto this very day; and the children are brazen-faced and stiff-hearted, I do send thee unto them. . . .[29]

Behold, I, even I, will bring a sword upon you, and I will destroy your high places. And your altars shall become desolate, and your sun-images shall be broken; and I will cast down your slain men before your idols. And I will lay the carcasses of the children of Israel before their idols. . . .[30]

A third part of thee shall die with the pestilence, and with famine shall they be consumed in the midst of thee; and a third part shall fall by the sword round about thee; and a third part will I scatter unto all the winds. . . .[31]

Yet even after this prophecy of total destruction, Ezekiel recalls Isaiah's saving remnant:

Yet will I leave a remnant, in that ye shall have some that escape the sword among the nations, when ye shall be scattered through the countries.

[29] Ezekiel 2:3–4
[30] Ezekiel 6:3–5
[31] Ezekiel 5:12

And they that escape of you shall remember Me among the nations whither they shall be carried captives, how that I have been anguished with their straying heart, which hath departed from Me, and with their eyes, which are gone astray after their idols. . . .[32]

But with the actual occurrence of the destruction he had warned against, with the end of the Temple and the transport of the people to Babylon, Ezekiel's concern turned away from the evils of the past to the problems of the present and the future. His task now was to convince the exiled Jews that God had acted justly in desolating Judah, but that He had not forsaken them—nor should they forsake Him. Ezekiel's message now became that of survival, return, and the eternal covenant between the stricken people and God.

For thus saith the Lord God: Behold, here am I, and I will search for My sheep, and seek them out. As a shepherd seeketh out his flock in the day that he is among his sheep that are separated, so will I seek out My sheep; and I will deliver them out of all places whither they have been scattered in the day of clouds and thick darkness. And I will bring them out from the peoples, and gather them from the countries, and will bring them into their own land; and I will feed them upon the mountains of Israel, by the streams, and in all the habitable places of the country.[33]

To make the promise of the future real to the often hopeless captives, Ezekiel offered them a vision so explicit that it had to be accepted. He described in great detail, so that it would seem inevitable, the nature of the new community, its religious structure, even the exact dimensions of the new temple:

And behold a wall on the outside of the house round about, and in the man's hand a measuring reed of six cubits long, of a cubit and a handbreadth each; so he measured the breadth of the building, one reed, and the height, one reed.
Then came he unto the gate which looketh toward the east, and went up the steps thereof; and he measured the jamb of the gate, one reed broad, and the other jamb, one reed broad.[34]

Ezekiel's prophecies reflect the revolutionary changes through which he lived. Before the fall of Judah, when there was a nation and a land and a king, he was a prophet of priestly concerns. After 586 B.C. when the usual ties which bind a nation together had disappeared, Ezekiel was the prophet of a Holy Congregation, telling of its apocalyptic future. He preached a concept of God beyond nation; he preached a religion that would enable the Jews to persist without king or country or Temple.

[32] Ezekiel 6:8–9
[33] Ezekiel 34:11–13
[34] Ezekiel 40:5–6

When the prophetic books were canonized about 200 B.C., they consisted of four volumes: Isaiah, Jeremiah, Ezekiel, and The Twelve (minor prophets). But Isaiah, which consisted of only thirty-nine chapters, did not fill its scroll. So the book was completed with the oracles of an unknown prophet. These chapters, 40 through 66, were ascribed by early scholars (Abraham ibn Ezra, eleventh century, for example) to a prophet since called Deutero-Isaiah. Later scholars have found evidences that chapters 56 through 66 were the work of still a third author, or several third authors.

The second Isaiah wrote immediately before and after Cyrus of Persia took Babylon in 538 B.C. He spoke to the Jews in the Babylonian exile a generation or two after Ezekiel, and his prophecy was that of the forthcoming deliverance and the return to Jerusalem.

Deutero-Isaiah was a rhapsodic poet and theologian rather than a prophet in the traditional mode. The earlier prophets, preaching in times of power and riches, foretold destruction and exile. Deutero-Isaiah, preaching in a time of exile, foretold the coming great days. Purified by suffering, Israel would return to Zion across a desert made Eden:

> Comfort ye, comfort ye My people,
> Saith your God.
> Bid Jerusalem take heart,
> And proclaim unto her,
> That her time of service is accomplished,
> That her guilt is paid off;
> That she hath received of the Lord's hand
> Double for all her sins.
> Hark! one calleth:
> "Clear ye in the wilderness the way of the Lord,
> Make plain in the desert
> A highway for our God.
> Every valley shall be lifted up,
> And every mountain and hill shall be made low. . . ."[35]

The third part of Isaiah, chapters 56 through 66, was probably written about 400 B.C. These chapters interpret Deutero-Isaiah for a new generation and a new condition. Some Jews have returned from the captivity, and the Temple has been rebuilt; but foreign kings still rule Judah, and religion is the only force holding the nation to its ancient birthright. Thus this writer is concerned mainly with the Law, with nationalistic fervor, with the trappings of religion that will bind the people together. Still, he was a prophet in the great tradition, and so he repeated the great social messages. The third Isaiah's version is among the most magnificent:

[35] Isaiah 40:1–4

Is such the fast that I have chosen?
The day for a man to afflict his soul?
Is it to bow down his head as a bulrush,
And to spread sackcloth and ashes under him?
Wilt thou call this a fast,
And an acceptable day to the Lord?
Is not this the fast that I have chosen?
To loose the fetters of wickedness,
To undo the bands of the yoke,
And to let the oppressed go free,
And that ye break every yoke?
Is it not to deal thy bread to the hungry,
And that thou bring the poor that are cast out to thy house?
When thou seest the naked, that thou cover him,
And that thou hide not thyself from thine own flesh? . . .
Then shalt thou call, and the Lord will answer. . . .[36]

The post-exilic prophets—Haggai, Zechariah, Malachi, Obadiah, Joel, Daniel—although mainly prophets of the apocalypse, also had a specific contemporary function. Where the pre-exilic prophets were mainly anti-priest and anti-Temple, the post-exilic prophets were mainstays of the evolving religious organization. In this time of adaptation, of change from a nation like other nations, with a land and a king, to a nation that was a congregation of the Lord, the prophets provided the visions on which the adaptation could be effected.

From the days of the monarchy, particularly from the time of king Josiah and the promulgation of the Deuteronomic Code, Jews accepted the concept that the Law was of divine origin. Still, there was a king and his army and his bailiffs to give the divine law a mortal reality. Without a king, ruled by foreign emperors under foreign law, the Jewish law had to become *the* Law—the Torah—if it was to be followed, particularly when it conflicted with the civil law of their foreign rulers.

The post-exilic prophets were particularly important in this changing concept of the Law. They taught and retaught the lesson that all aspects of living were under God's watchful eye and covered by God's universal law. Keeping the sabbath was the Law, and bringing the first fruits to the Temple; but equally so were the lines of inheritance and the requirement for two witnesses in a criminal trial.

Amos, for example, was uninterested in legislation; he demanded ethical conduct regardless of what was written on the royal rescripts. The post-exilic prophets insisted that the Law be followed in every word and comma, for only the Law guaranteed ethical conduct in a dispersed people.

[36] Isaiah 58:5–9

Witch doctors and shamans of primitive, animistic tribes could hold their people with terror, although they did promise food, water, and women if the gods were appeased. But among more highly developed cultures, prophets of doom were rejected. In Egypt, even the messenger who brought bad tidings was strangled. Unusual, then, is the peculiar regard in which the prophets were held by the Jews, even by their kings:

Now it came to pass, when Jeremiah had made an end of speaking all that the Lord had commanded him to speak unto all the people, that the priests and the prophets and all the people laid hold on him, saying: "Thou shalt surely die."

But after Jeremiah explained his mission:

Then said the princes and all the people unto the priests and to the prophets: "This man is not worthy of death; for he hath spoken to us in the name of the Lord our God."[37]

At first, all the people, including priests and prophets (probably seers), demanded Jeremiah's death. But when the decree was averted, it was the princes and the people against the priests and prophets. This was another version of the quarrel found throughout the Biblical books of prophecy between the moral and physical service of God. The pre-exilic prophets in particular were vehement against ritual:

To what purpose is the multitude of your sacrifices unto Me?
Saith the Lord;
I am full of the burnt-offerings of rams,
And the fat of fed beasts;
And I delight not in the blood
of bullocks, or of lambs, or of he-goats.
When ye come to appear before Me,
Who hath refused this at your hand,
To trample My courts?
Bring no more vain oblations;
It is an offering of abomination unto Me;
New moon and Sabbath, the holding of convocations—
I cannot endure iniquity along with the solemn assembly.
Your new moons and your appointed seasons
My soul hateth;
They are a burden unto Me;
I am weary to bear them.
And when ye spread forth your hands,
I will hide mine eyes from you;
Yea, when ye make many prayers,
I will not hear;
Your hands are full of blood.
Wash you, make you clean,

[37] Jeremiah 26:8,16

> Put away the evil of your doings
> From before Mine eyes,
> Cease to do evil;
> Learn to do well;
> Seek justice, relieve the oppressed,
> Judge the fatherless, plead for the widow.[38]

The post-exilic prophets were defensive of ritual, and modern scholars echo that defensiveness. They say that a careful reading of the pre-exilic prophets indicates that most were not opposed to ritual as such; they were opposed to ritual only when it was used as a substitute for moral service. The post-exilic prophets, living in a time when the practice of religion, including highly formalized ritual, was indispensable to the preservation of Israel, stressed the forms and patterns of religious service.

The prophets were not merely voices crying doom. They were human beings aware of the destruction they proclaimed, and they felt its pain even as they warned of it. Their stern monotheism came out of their love of God; and the more they loved Him, the more they accepted the burden He put upon His people.

Nor did any prophet turn away from that concept of Israel as the Chosen People that makes modern religionists uneasy: God is the Father of all peoples, but Israel is His first-born son; Israel therefore carries a greater burden of obedience to His law than the other children of God. Nor can the Lord be bribed or cozened to be more indulgent to His chosen people than to others; indeed, He must be harsher to them. And the prophets, the most God-loving of the chosen, are horrified at the doom they must proclaim. The prophet saw most clearly the terrible justice; he also felt most keenly the terrible sentence.

Involved constantly with this idea of chosenness, the prophets did not equate it with superiority—except in the sense that one who has greater knowledge (of God) is superior to one who has less knowledge. Even when He was a tribal God, He was the God of all nations. He requires love and justice because His nature is love and justice; and in a world of love and justice, the divisions among nations are unimportant. Chosenness is a temporary condition, until the Day of the Lord, when "a shoot out of the stock of Jesse" shall declare the end of strife. In that time of the Messiah, nations will still be separate, but there will be universal peace and justice.

> And it shall come to pass in the end of days,
> That the mountain of the Lord's house shall be established
>   as the top of the mountains,

[38] Isaiah 1:11–17

And shall be exalted above the hills;
And all nations shall flow unto it.
And many peoples shall go and say:
"Come ye, and let us go up to the mountain of the Lord,
To the house of the God of Jacob;
And He will teach us of His ways,
And we will walk in His paths."
For out of Zion shall go forth the law,
And the word of the Lord from Jerusalem.
And He shall judge between the nations,
And shall decide for many peoples;
And they shall beat their swords into plowshares,
And their spears into pruning-hooks;
Nation shall not lift up sword against nation,
Neither shall they learn war any more.[39]

---

[39] Isaiah 2:2–4

Wisdom Literature in the Bible

THE CENTRAL AUTHORITIES IN THE BIBLE and the protagonists of the Biblical narratives are prophets, priests, and kings. They differ, very widely at times, about the relative importance of moral and institutional religion, but they agree on essentials: Israel's election and Israel's special obligations because of that election. The overwhelming concern of prophet, priest, and king is Israel.

But there was always another source of power, another source of authority: wisdom and its possessors, wise men. This force is represented in the Bible by the wisdom books, Proverbs, Ecclesiastes, and Job. The apocryphal books of Ben Sirach and The Wisdom of Solomon are also part of the wisdom literature; so, too, are certain didactic psalms, for example, Psalms 37, 49, and 73.

In its most ancient Biblical sense, wisdom meant skill, skill in working and fashioning things. A musician was considered a wise man, a midwife a wise woman; even an accomplished mourner was considered wise. Jeremiah says, "And send for the wise women, that they may come; And let them make haste, and take up a wailing for us. . . ."[1] The Bible describes most fully the wisdom of the artist, perhaps because he was considered by the Jews the wisest of men in earliest days.

See, I have called my name Bezalel . . . And I have filled him with the spirit of God, in wisdom, and in understanding, and in knowledge, and in all manner of workmanship, to devise skilful works, to work in gold, and in silver, and in brass, and in cutting of stones for setting, and in carving of wood, to work in all manner of workmanship . . . and in the hearts of all that are wise-hearted I have put wisdom, that they may make all that I have commanded thee: the tent of meeting, and the ark of the testimony, and the

[1] Jeremiah 9:16–17

ark-cover that is thereupon, and all the furniture of the Tent; and the table and its vessels, and the pure candlestick with all its vessels, and the altar of incense; and the altar of burnt-offering with all its vessels, and the laver and its base; and the plaited garments, and the holy garments for Aaron the priest, and the garments of his sons. . . ."[2]

This primitive conception of wisdom (which is also the most modern idea of wisdom) developed through the centuries to include the fashioning of all things necessary for the good life. It was extended in time to include not only skills in making things for the good life, but skills in living well. And having, or not having, this wisdom to live well assumed moral implications. Wisdom came to mean that knowledge required to decide between the beneficient and the harmful, between the good and the evil. And knowledge of the difference between good and evil had to be of divine origin; it became "knowledge of His ways," because only by following "His ways" could man know truly which action was good and which was evil, which application of skills was harmful and which was helpful.[3]

Thus wisdom became a religious concept: "The fear of the Lord [religion] is the beginning of wisdom."[4] And in the Eighteen Benedictions, a prayer repeated in the synagogue service every day, the Fourth Benediction is a prayer for wisdom.

The Torah legislated right (that is, ethical, or wise) conduct for the community and the congregation of Israel. The prophets broadened the application of the Law to require this right conduct of each individual. The wisdom books gave practical rules and advice by which the individual could attain the norm of right conduct—and its rewards. The wisdom books became the basis for the *Pirke Aboth,* the Sayings of the Fathers, of the homiletic stories in the Talmud and the Midrash, and of sermons and homilies delivered from pulpits by generations of priests, ministers, and rabbis ever since the wisdom books were compiled.

In developing their standards of right living for the average man, the wisdom books, particularly Proverbs and Ecclesiastes, broke with the mood and the content of the other books of the Bible. There is no talk in these books of the Temple, of Israel, of Zion, of Jerusalem, of kings and battles and history. They emphasize conduct rather than belief; their goal is happiness rather than righteousness.

---

[2] Exodus 31:2–10

[3] The idea of work went through the same metamorphosis in Western industrial society more than two thousand years later. Work was economically necessary; therefore it was good; therefore it became a "value" in the Protestant ethic, and no-work became morally bad. The non-worker not only committed an economic crime; he was guilty of a moral religious lapse in eighteenth- and nineteenth-century Great Britain and America.

[4] Psalms 111:10

The development of the concept of wisdom from skill with the hands to skill in living, to sound judgment in daily affairs, to moral understanding—eventually to the consideration of the most profound problems of human destiny—took place over centuries. The Bible says that wisdom existede even before the creation of the world.[5] By the end of the fifth century B.C., when it became evident that the organization of Jewish life would be that of a theocracy in which the priests would control religious and secular life, the line between secular and religious, including secular and religious wisdom, had to disappear. Wisdom, which had referred to secular knowledge in the previous centuries, came to be regarded as another form of divine revelation. *Hochmah,* the Hebrew word for wisdom, became an essential part of the Torah. The wisdom books formalized this transformation.

Wisdom literature was not unique to the Jews. Almost every highly developed culture had a tradition of this kind of literature. In Egypt, wisdom books took the form of instructions given by a king or other important person to his son. The Egyptian books of wisdom cover a period of more than two thousand years. One of the earliest of these books, *Instruction of Ptah-hotep,* was written in the third millennium B.C. One book, *Instruction for King Meri-ka-re,* was written about 2100 B.C.; it gives such advice as this: "The tongue is a sword . . . and speech is more valorous than any fighting."[6] The most widely known of the Egyptian wisdom books, *Instructions of Onchshesheqy* (fifth century B.C.), says: "Do not go to your brother if you are in trouble; go to your friend."[7]

The Jews had known the Greeks casually from the time of Greek beginnings during the period of the Northern and Southern Kingdoms. After the death of Alexander the Great toward the end of the fourth century B.C., Greek and Hebrew cultures met head on—mainly in conflict with each other. But it was inevitable that they should also complement each other, learn from each other. The second largest Jewish community in the centuries immediately befeore the birth of Christ was in Alexandria, and it was as Greek as it was Jewish. In this confrontation of Hebrew and Greek thought, their concepts of wisdom became inter-

---

[5] The Lord made me [wisdom] as the beginning of His way.
   The first of His works of old.
   I was set up from everlasting, from the beginning,
   Or ever the earth was.
   When there were no depths, I was brought forth. . . .
   Before the hills was I brought forth. . . .
   When he appointed the foundations of the earth;
   Then I was by Him, as a nursling. . . . (Proverbs 8:22–30)
[6] J. B. Pritchard, *Ancient Near Eastern Texts,* Princton University Press, 1955.
[7] Catalogue of Demotic Papyri in the British Museum, S.R.K. Glanville, ed.

twined. The Greek Stoics conceived of a universal mind or wisdom they called *sophia,* which Greek Jews equated with the Hebrew *hochmah.* Greek philosophers spoke of a quality of reason, and the power to reason, so perfect as to be divine. This concept was identified by the word *logos,* which also became part of, and confused with, the idea of *hochmah.*[8] It was in this period that the book of Proverbs was compiled.

The proverb is the most usual form of folk wisdom—a short, pithy statement generally in the form of an epigram. But the Hebrew name for the book of Proverbs is *Mishle,* which means much more than proverb. *Mishle* can also mean sayings of truth, sayings with hidden meanings, oracles, parables, even fables and riddles. The book of Proverbs includes most of these types in seven forms. The first form is direct association: "A faithful witness will not lie. . . ." (Prov. 14:5). The second is the opposite of the first, contrast or paradox: ". . . a soft tongue breaketh the bone" (Prov. 25:15). The third idiom is analogy: "A word fitly spoken is like apples of gold in settings of silver" (Prov. 25:11). Fourth is the mocking taunt: "As a dog that returneth to his vomit, so is a fool that repeateth his folly" (Prov. 26:11). The fifth idiom categorizes or characterizes:

> There are three things which are too wonderful for me,
> Yea, four which I know not:
> The way of an eagle in the air;
> The way of a serpent upon a rock;
> The way of a ship in the midst of the sea;
> And the way of a man with a young woman (Prov. 30:18–19).

The sixth idiom deals with values and priorities: "Houses and riches are the inheritance of fathers; but a prudent wife is from the Lord" (Prov. 19:14). The last idiom is a statement of consequences: "Whose diggeth a pit shall fall therein" (Prov. 26:27).

These flat, unquestioning statements exude a kind of confidence that is in marked contrast to the other major wisdom books, to the all-embracing scepticism of Ecclesiastes and the deep philosophical questioning of Job.

The book of Proverbs deals with earthly happiness rather than with inward peace, or emotion, or the practice of formal religion. The book's thesis is this: earthly happiness is the direct result of righteousness;

---

[8] The Gospel according to St. John opens with the verse: "In the beginning was the Word, and the Word was with God, and the Word was God." The Greek original uses *logos* where the English translation uses Word. This is a version of the Hebrew concept of wisdom existing prior to the creation (Proverbs 8:22)—taken several steps beyond Jewish theology.

follow the precepts recorded in this book and you will become rich, successful, and happy; disregard these proverbs and you will be poor, miserable, and a failure. It defines happiness as long life, good health, wealth, and a contented family life.

Nor does Proverbs have any of the doubts that are evident in every chapter of the other two wisdom books. There are no theoretical discussions of the nature of happiness and unhappiness or of good and evil. Everything in Proverbs is practical; there is unquestioning faith that wisdom in practical matters not only leads to happiness, but is also the equivalent of following God's Law.

The advice given in Proverbs reflects urban, middle-class morality. But the theology of Proverbs is the same as that of Ecclesiastes and Job. God is real and just. He is the Creator of the earth and everything on it; He is responsible for everything that occurs on the earth. Though man can do nothing against God's will, he must achieve his goals through his own efforts. Wealth, that most important measure of a man's success, is achieved through wisdom—which is demonstrated by the intelligent handling of practical affairs.

Like so many books of the Bible, Proverbs includes sections going back to the second millennium B.C. But internal evidence indicates that it could not have been compiled before 400 B.C.: it uses certain Aramaic and Hebrew forms unknown before that time, and it refers to the Law and the Prophets as completed works. External evidence from references in the apocryphal book of Ben Sirach shows that Proverbs already existed by about 200 B.C. It was probably completed about 250 B.C.

A major section of Proverbs (see Appendix III for the seven sections of Proverbs) is ascribed to Solomon, because he was assumed to have been the wisest of kings. (The compilers of Proverbs may also have been swayed by the fact that the Hebrew name for Solomon has the numerical value of 375, which is the number of proverbs linked to his name—Proverbs 10:1 to 22:16.)

The book of Ecclesiastes is called Koheleth in Hebrew, a word whose literal meaning is "one who addresses an assembly," therefore a teacher or preacher. The opening verse identifies this teacher, perhaps someone named Teacher, as "the son of David, king in Jerusalem." Taken literally, this would mean Solomon, which is most unlikely; Koheleth is very unlike that king. The ascription was probably added, just as in Proverbs, because of Solomon's reputation for wisdom.

Ecclesiastes is, in tone, temper, and philosophy, the most unlikely book in the Bible. It has nothing in it of Israel or of the God of the Hebrews; it is far closer in spirit and in time to the Greek sceptics and stoics and cynics than to the God-intoxicated earlier writers of the Book.

Its writer was the most original author in the Bible, and a most radical thinker. He could not have composed this book before the death of Alexander (323 B.C.); he needed the close knowledge of Greek philosophy. Nor could he have written it after the Jews established the Hasmonean kingdom (141 B.C.); he is too free of the zealous nationalism that was fashionable then. A likely date is early in the second century B.C.—less than three hundred years before the book became part of the canon of the third section of the Bible, the Writings.

In view of the pessimism and open agnosticism, why did the Rabbis allow this book in the canon? Its teachings are too specific to be interpreted as allegory, the excuse used in permitting the Song of Songs into the Bible. It may be that the Rabbis recognized the great wisdom and beauty to be found in Ecclesiastes and thus bravely accepted a book that appeared to deny their most deeply held belief.

The Talmud records some of the debate on this issue. Some rabbis were opposed to the inclusion of Ecclesiastes because "its words contradicted each other."[9] But the winning argument was that the book's "beginning is religious teaching and its end is religious teaching."[10] Some scholars have suggested that the "religious" ending, Chapter 12, was added by a later hand. A modern Jewish scholar holds: "This may be the case, but the theory [of another author] is quite unnecessary, for the same author might easily have lost the courage of his lack of convictions."[11]

The decision of the Rabbis to include Ecclesiastes in the canon has been applauded and disputed since the canon was set. The first Christian commentator on Ecclesiastes, Thaumaturgus (third century), held that the book was designed "to show that all affairs and pursuits of men are vain and useless, in order to lead us to the contemplation of heavenly things." But this concept is foreign to Judaism; in fact, a Jewish scholar is more likely to view the book as a sophisticated analysis of reality than as an abnegation of life—thus as the essence of Judaism.

Ecclesiastes is a work of philosophy and opens with a philosophical statement, the kind that incurs immediate acceptance or immediate—and strong—argument. "Vanity of vanities, saith Koheleth; Vanity of vanities, all is vanity."[12]

---

[9] "Who knoweth the spirit of man whether it goeth upward, and the spirit of the beast whether it goeth downward to the earth?" (Eccl. 3:21) appears to contradict "And the dust returneth to the earth as is was, And the spirit returneth unto God who gave it" (Eccl. 12:7). "That which is crooked cannot be made straight; And that which is wanting cannot be numbered" (Eccl. 1:15) seems opposed to "He hath made every thing beautiful in its time" (Eccl. 3:11).

[10] Tractate Shabbat 30b

[11] Samuel Sandmel, *The Hebrew Scriptures*, Alfred A. Knopf, 1963.

[12] Ecclesiastes 1:2

A modern Jewish commentator says a better translation would be: "Futility of futilities, all is futility."[13]

And the most recent scholarly translation puts it: "A vapor of vapor (says Koheleth). Thinnest of vapors. All is vapor."[14]

But the meaning is the same in all translations: nothing is substantial, nothing is lasting, nothing matters.

> All things toil to weariness;
> Man cannot utter it,
> The eye is not satisfied with seeing,
> Nor the ear filled with hearing.
> That which hath been is that which shall be,
> And that which hath been done is that which shall be done;
> And there is nothing new under the sun.[15]

The succeeding verses expand on this thesis, basing the agrument on Koheleth's own experience.

> I Koheleth have been king over Israel in Jerusalem. And I applied my heart to seek and to search out by wisdom concerning all things that are done under heaven; it is a sore task that God hath given to the sons of men to be exercised therewith. I have seen all the works that are done under the sun; and, behold, all is vanity and a striving after wind.[16]

Having found little difference between wisdom and folly, Koheleth turns to pleasure. But he finds no lasting value in mirth and enjoyment. All are canceled by death—which itself has no meaning.

> And whatsoever mine eyes desired I kept not from them; I withheld not my heart from any joy, for my heart had joy of all my labour; and this was my portion from all my labour. Then I looked on all the works that my hands had wrought, and on the labour that I had laboured to do; and, behold, all was vanity and a striving after wind, and there was no profit under the sun. . . . For of the wise man, even as of the fool, there is no remembrance for ever; seeing that in the days to come all will long ago have been forgotten. And how must the wise man die even as the fool! So I hated life; because the work that is wrought under the sun was grievous unto me; for all is vanity and a striving after wind.[17]

The beautiful and terrible third chapter—"To everything there is a season, and a time to every purpose under the heaven"—accepts God's plan for the universe. But in accepting, Koheleth denies that man can ever penetrate the mystery of why these things are; man cannot understand his purpose on earth or the purpose of existence itself. (More than two thousand years ago, Koheleth stated the central philosophical and

---

[13] Sandmel, *op. cit.*
[14] R.B.Y. Scott, "Proverbs and Ecclesiastes," *The Anchor Bible,* Doubleday.
[15] Ecclesiastes 1:8–9
[16] Ecclesiastes 1:12–14
[17] Ecclesiastes 2:10–11, 2:16–17

psychological problem of the twentieth century: Who am I; what am I? In effect, he was searching for identity.) It is even useless to fight against personal and social evils, Koheleth finds, for they, too, are part of the immutable, unknowable laws of the universe. Therefore, death is probably preferable to life.

But I returned and considered all the oppressions that are done under the sun; and behold the tears of such as were oppressed, and they had no comforter; and on the side of their oppressors there was power, but they had no comforter. Wherefore I praised the dead that are already dead more than the living that are yet alive; but better than they both is he that hath not yet been, who hath not seen the evil work that is done under the sun.[18]

Experience, says Koheleth, contradicts the religious idea that goodness brings prosperity and that wickedness brings poverty and despair—the central thesis in Proverbs and the central question in Job. It doesn't matter whether man is good or evil; the end is the same: death negates all that a man was and did. This idea is expressed in a series of proverbs that directly contradict those in the book of Proverbs.

All things have I seen in the days of my vanity; there is a righteous man that perisheth in his righteousness, and there is a wicked man that prolongeth his life in his evil-doing. Be not righteous overmuch; neither make thyself overwise; why shouldest thou destroy thyself? Be not overmuch wicked, neither be thou foolish; why shouldest thou die before thy time?[19]

What then is man to do? Enjoy that which gives you joy, says Koheleth, but don't overdo either pleasure or pain. The most you can have out of this life is a moderately good time.

> Go thy way, eat thy bread with joy,
> And drink thy wine with a merry heart;
> For God hath already accepted thy works.
> Let thy garments be always white;
> And let thy head lack no oil.

Enjoy life with the wife whom thou lovest all the days of the life of thy vanity, which He hath given thee under the sun, all the days of thy vanity; for that is thy portion in life, and in thy labour wherein thou labourest under the sun. Whatsoever thy hand attaineth to do by thy strength, that do; for there is no work, nor device, nor knowledge, nor wisdom, in the grave, whither thou goest.[20]

In sum, says the teacher, God is not known through revelation, nor can He be discovered through reason. In fact, wisdom is a disappointment; it cannot bring happiness and may have no value at all.

[18] Ecclesiastes 4:1–3
[19] Ecclesiastes 7:15–17
[20] Ecclesiastes 9:7–10

But after this doctrine of despair, which if followed to its logical conclusion might lead to suicide, Koheleth asks himself why men fight to live. Why do the satisfactions men find in life, however temporary, appear to have value to man? Perhaps because life itself has value, because there is a kind of wisdom in the act of living.

Koheleth makes three major points. First, man must face reality; he must disregard the teachings of the past if they cannot be substantiated by experience and logic, even if they are presented as the word of God. Second, man must learn to live with reality; he cannot divine, let alone change, the order of the universe; he cannot even change the orders of evil kings, so let him accept his role in life. Third, man should enjoy whenever enjoyment is available to him; he must particularly learn to enjoy work, wisdom, and the fact of living; but he must enjoy these things for their own sake, not for what they might bring in the hereafter or for what can be left to heirs.

Wisdom, then, according to the wisdom book of Koheleth, lies not in the facts man accumulates, but in his knowledge and acceptance of his limits. Happiness lies in the personal satisfaction gained from work and good living; but these must be accepted as a sort of windfall, not as the obligation of a higher power.

According to Scott,[21] Koheleth teaches that "Man is not the measure of all things. He is the master neither of life nor of death. He can find serenity only in coming to terms with the unalterable conditions of his existence and in enjoying real but limited satisfactions." Koheleth's own summing up (which may have been the contribution of a later editor) says:

The end of the matter, all having been heard: fear God, and keep His commandments; for this is the whole man. For God shall bring every work into the judgment concerning every hidden thing; whether it be good or whether it be evil.[22]

The book of Job is the literary masterpiece of the Bible. Tennyson called this book the "greatest poem of ancient or modern times." Other scholarly critics have placed it on a level with Lucretius' *On Nature,* Dante's *Divine Comedy*, and Goethe's *Faust*. Its tremendous profundity, its poetic beauty, and its theological daring are the product of an unknown author who was a writer of genius and a gifted scholar, with the awesome vocabulary that generally marks the pattern-setting, ground-breaking writer.[23]

---

[21] R.B.Y. Scott, "Proverbs and Ecclesiastes," *The Anchor Bible,* Doubleday.
[22] Ecclesiastes 12:13–14

The Rabbis placed the book of Job in the period of the patriarchs, and there are many internal evidences that link Job to that time: he lived a pastoral life in which wealth was measured by flocks and slaves, he lived as long as the patriarchs, and he made his own sacrifices without priests and shrines. But that is the time in which the Job story takes place; it is not the time in which it was written. Modern scholars tend to place the writing between the sixth and fourth centuries B.C. (Similar Sumerian, Akkadian, and early Canaanite stories date from as early as 2000 B.C.) One clue to the time of composition is the appearance in the narrative of Satan. The idea of a devil, particularly an embodied devil, is foreign to the Jewish concept of the cosmos. Satan came to the Jews from the Persians, so Job must have been written after the Persian-Babylonian culture had made its impress upon the Jews, that is, after about 530 B.C.

The greatness of this wisdom book lies not only in its beauty, but in its content. It is a masterly exposition of the central ethical problem of religion, the problem of theodicy: since God is just, merciful, and all-powerful, why do the righteous who follow God's ordinances suffer, while the wicked flourish? Or stated as a thesis: the existence of evil and injustice in the world is incompatible with the existence of a just and omnipotent God.

Job also answers the simplistic, even childlike idea of the more primitive writers of the Bible, including the early prophets, that man's suffering is punishment for breaking the Law. They pictured God as a father figure who gives sweets when man is good and a whipping when man misbehaves. Jeremiah, for example, asks God why he suffers when he has done no evil. Five centuries after Job was written, the writers of the New Testament were still trying to counter this idea.[24] Nor is Job the patient sufferer of the cliché; he is instead outraged, angry, demanding that God give reasons if He cannot give justice.

The book of Job is made up of a prose prologue and epilogue which tell the story; a series of dialogues in poetic form among Job and his three friends, Eliphaz, Bildad, and Zophar; four speeches by a young man, Elihu; God's answer to Job; and Job's answer to God. Both the content of the book and its form, dramatic dialogue, bring it close to Greek tragedy, particularly since what happens to Job is determined by

---

[23] The author of a recent translation of the book of Job notes that "there are more *hapax legomena* (words which occur only once in a manuscript) and rare words in Job than in any other biblical book." Marvin H. Pope, "Job," *The Anchor Bible,* Doubleday.

[24] And his disciples asked him, saying, "Master, who did sin, this man, or his parents, that he was born blind?" (John 9:2).

fate (by the gods, to the Greeks) rather than by anything Job does or can do.

The narrative tells of Job, a man of Uz, who was "whole-hearted and upright, and one that feared God, and shunned evil." This formulation indicates that Job was not a Hebrew but a Gentile, probably an Edomite; however, he did believe in the One God. He was the greatest man in his country, for he had seven sons, three daughters, seven thousand sheep, three thousand camels, five hundred yoke of oxen, five hundred she-asses, "and a very great household."

"Now it fell upon a day" that God pointed out Job to Satan as the example of a godly man. Satan questions whether Job would be so good if he were not so blessed with possessions. God accepts Satan's challenge and gives Satan permission to test Job, but without causing him any personal harm. Satan destroys Job's children and beggars him. But Job does not waver in his faith.

Then Job arose, and rent his mantle, and shaved his head, and fell down upon the ground, and worshipped; and he said:
Naked came I out of my mother's womb,
And naked shall I return thither;
The Lord gave, and the Lord hath taken away;
Blessed be the name of the Lord.
For all this Job sinned not, nor ascribed aught unseemly to God.[25]

Satan again challenges God and is permitted to test Job even further. Job is afflicted with "sore boils from the sole of his feet unto his crown." Job's wife rages at him and demands that he curse God and die. But Job remains steadfast.

But he said unto her: "Thou speakest as one of the impious women speaketh. What? shall we receive good at the hand of God, and shall we not receive evil?" For all this did not Job sin with his lips.[26]

Job's three friends come to comfort him. They weep, tear their clothes, and put dirt on their heads. Since words cannot help, they remain silent. After seven days and seven nights, Job breaks the silence by cursing the day he was born; he longs for death and questions the reason for living if life brings such suffering.

Eliphaz answers Job in the first of the cycle of dialogues. Eliphaz affirms the idea that God visits misery on the sinner, that he rewards the righteous man, although He may chasten him. Job will be restored to his former luxury, says Eliphaz.

But Job answers that his friends are false; let them prove that he

---

[25] Job 1:20–22
[26] Job 2:10

was ever unrighteous, that he ever did evil. Better death than this punishment for crimes he did not commit.

Bildad compares Job's answer to a big wind and points to the lesson of history, which proves that righteousness is rewarded and wickedness is punished. How can Job accuse God of injustice? If Job is innocent, he will be raised up again.

Job answers Bildad that if God is all-powerful, how can man contest with Him? The contest is too unequal, particularly since God does not appear to distinguish between the innocent and the guilty. How can He, when He cannot understand man's lot?

> My soul is weary of my life;
> I will give free course to my complaint;
> I will speak in the bitterness of my soul.
> I will say to God: Do not condemn me;
> Make me know wherefore Thou contendest with me.
> Is it good unto Thee that Thou shouldest oppress,
> That Thou shouldest despise the work of Thy hands,
> And shine upon the counsel of the wicked?
> Hast Thou eyes of flesh,
> Or seest Thou as man seeth?
> Are Thy days as the days of man,
> Or Thy years as a man's days,
> That Thou inquirest after mine iniquity,
> And searchest after my sin,
> Although Thou knowest that I should not be condemned;
> And there is none that can deliver out of Thy hand?[27]

Zophar doesn't answer Job; instead he accuses Job of pleading innocence when he knows that he is guilty. If God so wished, He could reveal Job's sin.

In Job's last answer in the first round of dialogues, he reminds his friends that he is just as wise as they. All nature—beasts, birds, and fishes—know that God is omnipotent. Therefore God is as responsible for Job's condition as He is responsible for everything. Job asks for a fair trial, with a specific indictment and without terror. But this God does not deign to give him. This earth, says Job, is nothing, and the hereafter is nothing, too.

Eliphaz begins the second round of dialogues with a more severe charge: that Job is guilty of the sin of impiety for challenging God. Job isn't the first man to try to divine God's secrets, but he, too, will fail. No one is innocent of evil, not even the angels. Why should Job assume that he is pure? Job is being punished by God; therefore, there must be just cause for punishment.

[27] Job 10:1–7

Job scorns Eliphaz' "windy words." He demands a fair counsel in heaven to plead his case with God against the vicious and unfair assaults made upon him. But all he gets is mockery, from God and from his friends.

This argument continues until each friend has spoken three times and Job has answered each speech. The thread of the friends' arguments is much the same: God is not indifferent to man, but knows his innermost thoughts and most secret actions. When man is punished, there must be wickedness. Human virtue is of value to man, but it is not "profitable to God." God's actions may not always appear just, but they are. Job's answers repeat his insistence that he is innocent, that he is unjustly punished; as evidence, see how many wicked men are untroubled. God is so powerful in comparison to that worm, man; why should He terrorize Job? Job closes the dialogue with a terrible catalogue of sins—sins of which he is innocent. He rests his case and demands an answer of God.

> If I have walked with vanity,
> And my foot hath hasted to deceit. . . .
> If my heart have been enticed unto a woman,
> And I have lain in wait at my neighbour's door. . . .
> If I did despise the cause of my man-servant,
> Or of my maid-servant, when they contended with me. . . .
> If I have withheld aught that the poor desired,
> Or have caused the eyes of the widow to fail. . . .
> If I have seen any wanderer in want of clothing,
> Or that the needy had no covering . . .
> If I have lifted up my hand against the fatherless,
> Because I saw my help in the gate . . .
> If I have made gold my hope,
> And have said to the fine gold: "Thou art my confidence". . . .
> If I rejoiced at the destruction of him that hated me,
> Or exulted when evil found him. . . .
> Oh that I had one to hear me!—
> Lo, here is my signature, let the Almighty answer me—
> And that I had the indictment which mine adversary hath written! . . .
> The words of Job are ended.[28]

The three friends are silenced by Job's continued rejection of their arguments and his insistence upon his innocence. But Elihu, a young man who has been listening, takes up the argument. He summarizes all the answers given by Job and refutes them: God may afflict a man to chasten him, or to warn him, but admission of guilt, and repentance, may avert the punishment. Job's very denial of guilt may in itself be part of Job's crime. In the end, God's justice is proved.

[28] Job 31:5–40

With the close of Elihu's speech, the arguments of men are finished. Now God answers Job in the great theophany, the most powerful poem in the Bible. God describes the physical world He created, the earth, the skies, the winds, the beasts. Where were you, He asks, when I created these things that you should attempt to understand the nature of man and God, of evil and good, of justice and retribution?

> Then the Lord answered Job out of the whirlwind, and said:
> Who is this that darkeneth counsel
> By words without knowledge?
> Gird up now thy loins like a man;
> For I will demand of thee, and declare thou unto Me.
> Where wast thou when I laid the foundations of the earth? . . .
> Hast thou commanded the morning since thy days began,
> And caused the dayspring to know its place;
> That it might take hold of the ends of the earth,
> And the wicked be shaken out of it? . . .
> Hast thou entered into the springs of the sea?
> Or hast thou walked in the recesses of the deep?
> Have the gates of death been revealed unto thee?
> Or hast thou seen the gates of the shadow of death?
> Hast thou surveyed unto the breadths of the earth?
> Declare, if thou knowest it all. . . .
> By what way is the light parted,
> Or the east wind scattered upon the earth?
> Who hath cleft a channel for the waterflood,
> Or a way for the lightning of the thunder;
> To cause it to rain on a land where no man is,
> On the wilderness, wherein there is no man;
> To satisfy the desolate and waste ground,
> And to cause the bud of the tender herb to spring forth?
> Hath the rain a father? . . .
> Canst thou bind the chains of the Pleiades,
> Or loose the bands of Orion?
> Canst thou lead forth the Mazzaroth in their season?
> Or canst thou guide the Bear with her sons?
> Knowest thou the ordinances of the heavens?
> Canst thou establish the dominion thereof in the earth?
> Canst thou lift up thy voice to the clouds,
> That abundance of waters may cover thee?
> Canst thou send forth lightnings, that they may go,
> And say unto thee: "Here we are"?
> Who hath put wisdom in the inward parts?
> Or who hath given understanding to the mind? . . .
> Wilt thou hunt the prey for the lioness?
> Or satisfy the appetite of the young lions,
> When they couch in their dens,
> And abide in the covert to lie in wait?

> Who provideth for the raven his prey,
> When his young ones cry unto God,
> And wander for lack of food?
> Knowest thou the time when the wild goats of the rock bring forth?
> Or canst thou mark when the hinds do calve?
> Canst thou number the months that they fulfil? . . .
> Who hath sent out the wild ass free?
> Or who hath loosed the bands of the wild ass?
> Whose house I have made the wilderness,
> And the salt land his dwelling-place. . . .
> Doth the hawk soar by thy wisdom,
> And stretch her wings toward the south?
> Doth the vulture mount up at thy command,
> And make her nest on high? . . .
> Moreover the Lord answered Job, and said:
> Shall he that reproveth contend with the Almighty?
> He that argueth with God, let him answer it.[29]

God has invited Job to answer, but Job cannot: "Once have I spoken, but I will not answer again; yea, twice, but I will proceed no further."[30] God then continues His description of His wonders. When God concludes His second answer, Job capitulates; he repents his challenge to God. Though he cannot understand, he will accept.

> Then Job answered the Lord, and said:
> I know that Thou canst do everything,
> And that no purpose can be withholden from Thee.
> Who is this that hideth counsel without knowledge?
> Therefore have I uttered that which I understood not,
> Things too wonderful for me, which I knew not.
> Hear, I beseech Thee, and I will speak;
> I will demand of Thee, and declare Thou unto me.
> I had heard of Thee by the hearing of the ear;
> But now mine eye seeth Thee;
> Wherefore I abhor my words and repent,
> Seeing I am dust and ashes.[31]

The epilogue tells of the end of the test of Job's faith.

So the Lord blessed the latter end of Job more than his beginning; and he had fourteen thousand sheep, and six thousand camels, and a thousand yoke of oxen, and a thousand she-asses. He had also seven sons and three daughters. And he called the name of the first, Jemimah; and the name of the second, Keziah; and the name of the third, Kerenhappuch. And in all the land were no women found so fair as the daughters of Job; and their father gave them inheritance among their brethren. And after this Job lived a hun-

[29] Job 38:1 to 40:2
[30] Job 40:5
[31] Job 42:1–6

dred and forty years, and saw his sons, and his sons' sons, even four generations. So Job died, being old and full of days.[32]

The book of Job has troubled theologians and laymen for two thousand years. It seems to refute the basic pessimism of Ecclesiastes, but it
also denies very strongly the Pollyanna-ism of Proverbs. It raises questions about the very foundations of faith (in the central poem, not in the
prose epilogue, which puts a happy ending on a tragic dramatic dialogue), and so might serve as a threat to established religion. But the
rejection in the book of Job of the Deuteronomic concept—if man follows the divine commandments, he will be rewarded with health, wealth,
children, and long life—allows for a much more sophisticated and intellectually acceptable view of the God-man relationship.

Job says that suffering is not necessarily a sign of punishment for
evil; in fact, suffering may be a trial of faith and may serve to strengthen
faith. Nor can God be viewed primitively as a mere dispenser of rewards
and punishments. Neither is the view of man so simple; he is not a child
or an animal who responds only to rewards and punishments. Man is
capable of goodness without reward, of love for its own sake. And the
moral problems of man cannot be viewed egocentrically; they require a
conception of man and God and the universe that is vastly larger and
more complex than any individual. In effect, there are no answers within
man's comprehension.

[32] Job 42:12–17

The Talmud:
History and Authors

IF THE BIBLE is the heart of Judaism, of the continuing, persistent Congregation of Israel, the Talmud is the moving, changing bloodstream nourishing every organ and extremity of that corpus. These books, as much as any physical property or intellectual concept, kept the Jews alive as a community, however dispersed, through fifteen hundred years in which all logic dictated their disappearance.

The Talmud is two very distinct books (and book is used here in its very broadest sense): the Mishnah; and the commentary on the Mishnah, the Gemarah. The Mishnah, from the Hebrew *shonah,* to repeat, therefore to study by repetition, is the recorded Oral Law of the Jews in use about the year 200, the period when the Mishnah was finally compiled and edited by Judah haNasi (Judah the Prince). There are two Gemarahs, the Palestinian and the Babylonian, each a record of the comments and discussions of the Mishnah by different schools of rabbis, sages, and scholars. The Mishnah of Judah haNasi and the Gemarah of the Palestinian scholars make up the *Talmud Yerushalmi,* the Jerusalem (or Palestinian) Talmud. The Mishnah of Judah haNasi and the Gemarah of the Babylonian academies make up the *Talmud Babli,* the Babylonian Talmud.

The deliberations of scholars in Palestine were interrupted many times by persecutions and the unsettled conditions of that country in the centuries after the end of the Second Roman War in 135. Toward the end of the fourth century, times were so desperate that the work was rushed to completion. It was in its final form by 400. The Babylonian scholars lived in a relatively more peaceful and free environment. They could therefore be much more deliberate. The Babylonian Talmud was completed a century after the Palestinian Talmud, about 500. During the period of the compilation of the Talmud and for five hundred years afterward, Babylon was the new Jerusalem, the center of world Jewry. Thus the fuller Babylonian Talmud became the dominant work: when reference is made to *the* Talmud, the Babylonian Talmud is meant; reference to the Palestinian Talmud requires the place-name adjective.

Jewish tradition says that Moses received two Laws on Mt. Sinai: the Torah or written law, and the Oral Law. The genealogy of the written Bible as recorded in the Talmud is given in Chapter 1 (page 16). The Oral Law, according to the Talmud, was handed down as follows:

Moses received the [Oral] Law from Sinai and delivered it to Joshua, and Joshua to the elders, and the elders to the Prophets, and the Prophets committeed it to the men of the Great Synagogue. . . . Simeon the Just was of the survivors of the Great Synagogue. . . . Antigonus of Socho received it from Simeon the Just. . . . Jose ben Joezer of Zeredah and Jose ben Jochanon of Jerusalem received from them. . . . Joshua ben Perahyah and Nittai the Arbelite received from them. . . . Judah ben Tabbai and Simeon ben Shetah received from them. . . . Shemaiah and Abtalion received from them. . . . Hillel and Shammai received from them. . . . Jochanon ben Zakkai received [the Law] from Hillel and from Shammai.[1]

This genealogy passes quickly over the almost one thousand years between Moses and the men of the Great Synagogue (circa 450–325 B.C.), but it details the later transmission almost generation by generation. This is realistic, because the Oral Law was relatively unimportant during the years of the Judges, the monarchy, the divided kingdoms, and the Babylonian exile—the years of the development of the Torah. As a more or less self-governing nation, the Jews had little need for the collection of adapted customs, interpretations of various decalogues, and common usages that was the Oral Law before 450 B.C. But with their return from Babylon as vassals of a foreign king, and the acceptance by the priestly schools of the realistic probability that the Jews would henceforth always be subject to foreign law, the need for defined religious-secular Judaic law became intense. The need became desperate when the Torah was canonized (400 B.C.) and the Written Law became fixed and unalterable. For despite the Jews' insistence on its divine origin, the Torah, like man-made laws, did not answer all legal questions. It lagged behind the need and the practice in both religious and secular areas.

For example, as soon as the Palestinian Jewish community was well organized, there was need for specific interpretations of the Biblical prohibition of work on the sabbath: "Six days shalt thou labor and do all

[1] Tractate Aboth 1:1–12, 2:8

thy work; but the seventh day is a sabbath unto the Lord thy God. . . ."[2] "Ye shall keep the sabbath therefore, for it is holy unto you; everyone that profaneth it shall surely be put to death. . . ."[3] But the Mosaic Law identified only three kinds of work prohibited on the sabbath: "Ye shall kindle no fire throughout your habitations upon the sabbath day"[4]; ". . . abide ye every man in his place, let no man go out of his place on the seventh day"[5] ; ". . . they found a man gathering sticks on the sabbath day . . . . and [they] stoned him with stones . . . ."[6] Obviously, the work prohibited on the sabbath was not limited to making fire, gathering kindling, and walking outside your "place." And what constitutes "place"?

The Oral Law had begun a redefinition of prohibited work long before the Written Law was closed. Jeremiah reproved people for carrying packages on the sabbath,[7] although this was not specifically barred by the Bible; and Nehemiah drove the traders out of Jerusalem on the sabbath,[8] also without Biblical authority. Thus, over centuries the Oral Law widened the meaning of "labor" that "profaneth" the sabbath—always referring to some Biblical authority for the new meanings. The scribes ("men of the book" is a better translation) developed a list of thirty-nine types of prohibited work which they took from the list of jobs itemized in the Bible as necessary to build the Temple.

The Bible refers several times to the transfer of real property: "And if a man sell a dwelling-house in a walled city, then he may redeem it within a year after it is sold. . . ."[9] But how is a sale effected? When is a sale valid and when invalid? What are the instruments for the transfer of property? Jeremiah describes one process for the sale of land which requires weighing the money and subscribing and sealing the deed before witnesses,[10], but even this detailed description was not sufficient as a model for transactions in an increasingly commercial society.

On a more personal level, the Bible admonishes everyone to marry. It also says they can get divorced: "When a man taketh a wife, and marrieth her, then it cometh to pass, if she find no favor in his eyes, because he hath found some unseemly thing in her, that he writeth her a bill of divorcement, and giveth in her hand. . . ."[11] An orderly society certainly needed a description of the size and nature of the "unseemly

[2] Exodus 20:9–10
[3] Exodus 31:14
[4] Exodus 35:3
[5] Exodus 16:29
[6] Numbers 15:32–36
[7] Jeremiah 17:21
[8] Nehemiah 13:15–23
[9] Leviticus 25:29
[10] Jeremiah 32:9–11
[11] Deuteronomy 24:1

thing," plus some regulation of the content and manner of giving the bill of divorcement.

The men of the Great Synagogue (more properly, Great Assembly) were the first body to assume authority for interpreting the sparse Biblical commandments and developing a law capable of regulating the affairs of an increasingly sophisticated community. Little is known about this body, despite rather frequent mention in the Talmud, but it must have functioned as a combined religious and secular court in post-exilic Palestine. The authority of the Great Assembly was transferred to the Sanhedrin during the Hellenistic period, beginning with the death of Alexander the Great. But the Sanhedrin had more than a single voice. It is assumed by some scholars that the Sanhedrin was a bicameral body, much like the British Parliament before the power of the House of Lords was wiped out. These scholars believe that the upper house of the Sanhedrin (like the Lords) was representative of the priests of the Temple and the ruling class; the lower house (like the Commons) represented the people. Each house became the stronghold of a religious-political party, the upper house of the Sadducees (from Zadok, high priest in the first Temple), the lower house of the Pharisees (separatists). The Sadducees were strict interpreters of the Torah and refused to give any authority to the Oral Law; the Pharisees insisted upon the validity of a developing Oral Law. The historian Josephus, writing of the period of King John Hyrcanus (135–104 B.C.), described the differences between the two parties:

The Pharisees have delivered to the people a great many observances [laws] by succession from their fathers [oral transmission] which are not written in the Law of Moses [the Torah]; and for that reason it is that the Sadducees reject them, and say that we are to esteem observances to be obligatory which are in the Written Word [the Torah], but are not to observe what are derived from the tradition of our forefathers [the Oral Law].[12]

The Sadducees, the royalist nationalistic party, the party of the Temple in Jerusalem, were eliminated as a force in Jewish life when the Romans destroyed their power centers in the Temple and the court and the commonwealth in the year 70. The Pharisees' power, on the other hand, was based on the synagogues; scattered throughout the land, they could withstand the destruction of the religious and governmental centers. Thus the Pharisaic tradition continued, while the Sadducees disappeared. Jochanon ben Zakkai, disciple and successor to the great Hillel and leader of the Pharisees, gathered the surviving scholars of Judah and established an academy in the village of Jabneh. This body assumed the religious and legal authority of the Sanhedrin. (This was the body

---

[12] Josephus, *Antiquities of the Jews,* Book XIII, Chapter 6.

that canonized the last section of the Bible in the year 90). During the
sixty years of peace—comparative peace—from 70 to 130, the Academy at Jabneh adapted Jewish law to the new conditions of Jewish life,
the life of a dispersed nation without king or title to any land. At Jabneh
the sages began compiling and ordering the great body of civil and religious and ethical legislation that existed outside the Bible, existed only
in the trained memories of the scholars.

Early in the second century, the leading scholar among the compilers
of the Oral Law [13] was Rabbi Akiba ben Joseph, one of the great
romantic figures of Jewish history and the architect of the Mishnah.
According to Jewish tradition, Akiba was an unlettered workman until
he was forty years old; then he turned to a life of scholarship and
became the greatest scholar and teacher of his generation. He was martyred by the Romans during the Bar Kochba rebellion, the Second
Roman War, for refusing to heed their order prohibiting the teaching of
the Torah.

Rabbi Akiba had two scholarly passions: to find a Biblical source
for every law and judgment and opinion in the developing Oral Law,
and to organize the Oral Law so that it would be readily available and
readily applicable to every condition. The first pursuit led Rabbi Akiba
into some rather tenuous interpretations; the second led to the
Mishnah[14] of Rabbi Akiba, whose structure and organization was the
basis of the Talmud.

With the complete destruction of the Palestinian community after
the defeat of Bar Kochba and the persecutions under Emperor Hadrian,
the Jewish academies were closed, and the disciples and sages were dispersed. But the need for maintaining and transmitting the Oral Law was
intensified. This task was carried forward by Akiba's greatest disciple,
Rabbi Meir. Building on Rabbi Akiba's framework, his student erected
the Mishnah of Rabbi Meir.

The real authorities among the Jews, even during the last years of
the Hasmonean kings, were the chief scholars of the community, the
heads of the Sanhedrin before the year 70, and the hereditary patriarchs
after the destruction of the Temple. The two groups of rulers were really
one, since the patriarchs were the descendants of Hillel, head of the
Sanhedrin from 30 B.C. to the year 10. (The only nonmember of the
House of Hillel to head the ruling council—from 70 to 90—was Jochanon ben Zakkai.)

Judah haNasi, called simply Rabbi, held the patriarchate from 165

[13] The Rabbis who compiled the Oral Law were called *tannaim* (singular,
tanna), from the Aramaic word *tneh*, to tell or teach.

[14] Mishnah, initial capital, refers to the entire Oral Law compiled by Judah
haNasi, or to sum of the teachings of a single *tanna* (the Mishnah of Rabbi
Akiba); *mishnah,* lower case (plural, *mishnayot*), refers to the statement of a
single law.

to 219. He was born, according to tradition, on the day that Rabbi Akiba was martyred. Legend endows Rabbi with every positive attribute: he was very wise, very rich, and personally beautiful; he had the friendship of Roman emperors, very deserving children, and a long life. Although the Mishnah doesn't actually say that Rabbi was the final editor and redactor of the Mishnah, the Talmud (both Jerusalem and Babylonian) accepts the fact without question.

Rabbi, himself a great scholar, gathered a remarkable school of sages and with them put together the final Mishnah. Through the authority of his scholarship and of his status in the world Jewish community, Rabbi's Mishnah became the accepted standard of Jewish law.

According to one source, Rabbi made use of some thirteen compilations of the Oral Law in making his Mishnah, but there is internal evidence that the principal sources were the Mishnayot of Rabbis Akiba and Meir: "Anonymous rulings in the Mishnah are those of Rabbi Meir, and all are according to the teaching of Rabbi Akiba."[15] There are also frequent references to other and older Mishnayot: "Such was the Mishnah of R. Akiba; but the First Mishnah. . . ." [16] Still earlier sections of Oral Law are identified by the introductory phrase, "Beforetimes they used to say . . . ."

Cyrus of Babylon had released the Captivity and permitted the exiled Jews to return to Palestine toward the end of the sixth century B.C. But, much like the case of twentieth-century Israel, only a minority of Jews returned to the Holy Land. The majority remained in Babylonia; considering the later histories of the two communities, particularly during the three centuries ending with the Second Roman (or Jewish) War in 135, the choice was reasonable. The Persian kings were, in the main, far more tolerant of their Jewish subjects than the successive overlords and rulers of Palestine. And unlike the dispersed congregations of Jews to the West, the Babylonian Jews held tightly to the ties with Palestine. They accepted the authority of the Temple, of the Palestinian academies, and of the Palestinian patriarchs. Although the Babylonian Jews had active scholarly academies of their own, they sent their brightest pupils to be trained in the Jerusalem centers of learning.

Among the students in Jerusalem during the final redaction of the Mishnah was Abba Areka, son of a distinguished Babylonian family and foremost student-disciple of Judah haNasi. Abba Areka, called Rab,[17]

[15] Tractate Sanhedrin 86a
[16] Tractate Sanhedrin 3:4
[17] Ordained scholars were given titles, much like graduates of modern universities. The *tannaim* were called Rabbi, the individual Babylonian scholars cited in the Gemarah (the *amoraim*) were called Rab, and certain patriarchs and heads of the Jerusalem academy were titled Rabban. All these titles were versions of "master" or "teacher."

returned to his native country and established an academy at Sura, on the Euphrates River. This academy became one of the great centers of Jewish learning—and remained so for more than seven hundred years.

Another Babylonian student at the Jerusalem academy was Samuel, called Mar, who returned to Babylonia to become head of the academy at Nehardea. Like so many Jewish scholars before the modern period, Mar Samuel was renowned not only for his scholarship in Judaic studies but also for other scholarly pursuits; he was a great astronomer and a much sought-after physician. At their respective academies, Abba Areka and Mar Samuel began the process that was to result in the Gemarah.

In 259, the city of Nehardea was destroyed during a Roman-Persian war. The Nehardea Academy was re-established in the city of Pumbeditha—and it, too, lasted more than seven hundred years. In those centuries, beginning with Mar Samuel and Abba Areka, generation after generation of scholars—the *amoraim*—participated in the study of the Mishnah and in the accumulation of comment, explanatory material, and illustrative stories that was to form the Gemarah.

Using the Mishnah as a text, the scholars at the academies analyzed the Oral Law and its basis in the Written Law—line by line. The analysis—in fact, the dissection—was aimed at uncovering the meaning behind the meaning, the source behind the source. Most of the material offered to make or support an argument was relevant, but as with most discussions of points of law in any country and period, some of the comments and explanations wandered far afield. And in wandering so far afield, the commentaries encompassed the entire body of Jewish knowledge of the time. Thus, in the Gemarah, on the Mishnaic section dealing with the division of property, there is discussion of the line: "Sacred writings, however, may not be divided. . . ." (See pages 114–15.) In the course of this discussion, there is an analysis of the meaning and relevance of Scripture. This seeming side issue takes twenty pages of the Talmud.

Although the Mishnah was the text on which the studies were based (some *mishnayot* are self-explanatory and were not given a *gemarah*), the scholars did not limit themselves to this one collection of law. Judah haNasi had not exhausted the statements of Oral Law when he closed the Mishnah in 200. Many opinions were excluded from that compilation. This excluded matter termed *Baraitah,* "that which is excluded," was often used by the Rabbis of the Talmud in their investigations.

The scholars of the academies were not students in the modern school sense. That is, with the exception of those seeking ordination as rabbis, they were not young men studying to attain some mark of qualification, a degree, or admission into a professional society. There were many young men among the scholars at the academies—there were at one time twelve hundred scholars at Sura—but by their side were scholars of all ages whose vocation or avocation or passion was to seek knowledge, without thought of career or reward. The completed Talmud includes citations from more than a thousand of such *amoraim*.

Even these thousands did not constitute the total body of students involved in the creation of the Gemarah. The Jews of Babylon were highly literate; they belonged to a nation in which literacy was a religious commandment, a social requirement, and a cultural necessity. In this environment, scholarship was a form of holiness—and even the average citizen had to be given an opportunity to partake of the scholarly process. So on sabbath afternoons throughout the year and during two entire months (the Kallah months: Adar, preceding Passover, when the seed is in the ground but not yet ready for harvest, and Elul, preceding the High Holy Days, when the first harvest is in and the second not yet ready), the people came to the academies. Artisans, farmers, traders, and laborers came to the academies to hear about the discussions that had taken place during the preceding half year and the decisions that had been made by the scholars. They discussed the work of the *amoraim* and listened to stories illustrating the results of the work.

As with the Mishnah before Rabbi Akiba gave it a structure, the Gemarah grew without limit or form for two centuries. In 375, Rab Ashi became head of the academy at Sura and began the process of compilation and order. During more than a half-century of leadership of the academy (375–427), Rab Ashi assembled the great commentary on the Mishnah. He not only performed for the Gemarah the counterpart of Rabbi Judah haNasi's work on the Mishnah; he was also very much like Rabbi, as rich in worldly goods and in spiritual and scholarly attainments. Unlike Judah haNasi, Rab Ashi did not close his book; that took another seventy years or so, but the form of the Talmud was fixed by Ashi.

Throughout this period, from the closing of the Mishnah until about 400, the Palestinian Talmud and the Babylonian Talmud developed independently—but cooperatively. Scholars moved regularly back and forth between the Babylonian academies and the Palestinian academies at Caesarea, Sepphoris, and Tiberias, transmitting the discussions and opinions. Rab Ashi's Gemarah, therefore, includes much material that had been developed in Palestine.

For a time after Ashi's death, the Persians were infected with missionary zeal and tried to suppress the Jews, hoping to convert them to Zoroastrianism. The students were scattered and teaching was forbidden. It was time to close the Babylonian Talmud. When the persecutions abated, the discussions were rounded out, legal points were sharpened, and additional homiletic material was added. The final touches were

BEROCHOT CHAPTER 1

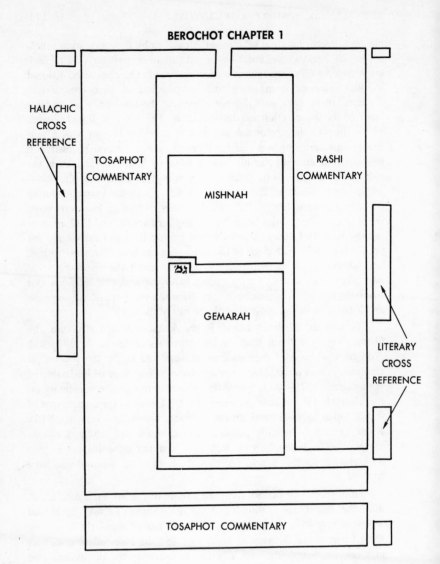

HALACHIC CROSS REFERENCE

TOSAPHOT COMMENTARY

MISHNAH

גמ׳

GEMARAH

RASHI COMMENTARY

LITERARY CROSS REFERENCE

TOSAPHOT COMMENTARY

מסורת הש"ס

מאימתי קורין את שמע בערבית. משעה שהכהנים נכנסים
לאכול בתרומתן. כהנים שנטמאו וטבלו והעריב
שמשן והגיע עתם לאכול בתרומתן: עד סוף האשמורה הראשונה.
שליש הלילה כדאמרינן בגמרא (דף ג.) ומתם וליצן עבר זמן
דלא מקרי תו זמן שכבה ולא
קרינן ביה בשכבך. ומקמי הכי
נמי לאו זמן שכבה הוא לפיכך
הקורא קודם לכן לא יצא ידי חובתו. אם
כן למה קורין אותה בבית הכנסת
כדי לעמוד בתפלה מתוך דברי
תורה. והכי תניא בברייתא בברכות
בירושלמי. ולפיכך חובה עלינו
לקרותה משתחשך. ובקריאת
פרשה ראשונה שאדם קורא על
מטתו יצא: עד שיעלה עמוד השחר.
שכל הלילה קרוי זמן שכבה.
הקוטר חלבים ואברים. של קרבנות
שנזרק דמן ביום: מצותן. להעלות
כל הלילה ואינן נפסלים בלינה
עד שיעלה עמוד השחר. וכן למטה
וכן ההכנה דכתיב (שמות לז) ולא
ילין לבקר: חלבים. של כל הקרבנות
אברים. של עולה: כל הנאכלים
ליום אחד. כגון חטאת ואשם וכבשי
עצרת ומנחות ותודה: מצותן. זמן
אכילתן: עד שיעלה עמוד השחר.
והוא מביאן לידי נותר דכתיב
בתודה (ויקרא ז) לא יניח ממנו
עד בקר אם כן למה אמרו חכמים
עד חצות: כדי להרחיק אדם מן העבירה.
ואסרום באכילה קודם זמנן כדי
שלא יבא לאכלן לאחר עמוד השחר
ויתחייב כרת. וכן בקריאת שמע
לזרז את האדם שלא יאמר יש
לי עוד שהות ובתוך כך יעלה
עמוד השחר ועבר לו הזמן. והקטר
חלבים דקתני הכא לא קתני
לה גבי קריאת שמע דלא מפסלי
בלינה מיד אלא משיעלה עמוד
השחר כדאמר לקמן (דף ב:) דאמר
הקריבהו נא לפחתך וגו:

גמ' הכא קאי. מהיכא קא פסיק
ותני דתנא קורא שמע
שחרית שלא שנאה היכן שנויה
אקרא קאי: ואי בעית אימא. יליף
דתנא גבי גבול בתחיה:

מאימתי

קורין את שמע בערבית **משעה שהכהנים**
נכנסים לאכול בתרומתן עד סוף האשמורה
הראשונה דברי ר' אליעזר וחכמים אומרים
עד חצות רבן גמליאל אומר עד שיעלה עמוד
השחר מעשה ובאו בניו מבית המשתה אמרו
לו לא קרינו את שמע אמר להם אם לא עלה
עמוד השחר חייבין אתם לקרות ולא זו בלבד
אמרו אלא **כל** מה שאמרו חכמים עד חצות
מצותן עד שיעלה עמוד השחר **הקטר** חלבים
ואברים מצותן עד שיעלה עמוד השחר **וכל**
הנאכלים ליום אחד מצותן עד שיעלה עמוד
השחר אם כן למה אמרו חכמים עד חצות
כדי להרחיק אדם מן העבירה: **גמ'** תנא
היכא קאי דקתני מאימתי ותו מאי שנא דתני
בערבית ברישא לתני דשחרית ברישא תנא
אקרא קאי דכתיב בשכבך ובקומך והכי
קתני זמן קריאת שמע דשכיבה אימת משעה
שהכהנים נכנסים לאכול בתרומתן ואי בעית
אימא יליף מברייתו של עולם. וקקרני
ערב ויהי בקר יום אחד אי הכי סיפא דקתני
בשחר מברך שתים לפניה ואחת לאחריה
בערב מברך שתים לפניה ושתים לאחריה
לתני דערבית ברישא תנא פתח בערבית והדר
תני בשחרית עד דקאי בשחרית פריש מילי
דשחרית והדר פריש מילי דערבית: אמר מר
משעה שהכהנים נכנסים לאכול בתרומתן מכדי
כהנים אימת קא אכלי תרומה משעת צאת
הכוכבים לתני משעת צאת הכוכבים מלתא
אגב אורחיה קמשמע לן כהנים אימת קא
אכלי בתרומה משעת צאת הכוכבים והא מלתא
דכפרה לא מעכבא כדתניא **ובא השמש**
וטהר ביאת שמשו מעכבתו מלאכול בתרומה
ואין כפרתו מעכבתו מלאכול בתרומה וממאי
דהאי ובא השמש ביאת השמש והאי וטהר
טהר

רש"י קורין וכו'. פ"ה רש"י ואם הכי קרין ונגמר יום משהס
ואין אנו מחזירין ללאת הכוכבים כדמוכח בגמרא. גר מצוה
על כן פי' רש"י שקריאת שמע שעל
המטה היא עיקר. והכי איתא בירושלמי. אם קרא קודם לכן
לא יצא הכוכבים. וא"ת למה אנו מתפללין ק"ש בבית
הכנסת כדי לעמוד בתפלה מתוך
דברי תורה. היימו לפירוש והלא
העולם רגילין לקרות קודם
שכיבה אלא פרשה ראשונה היה
נו לקרות. ואם כן שלא שנה פרשה ראשונה היה
נו לקרות. ואם כן שלא פרשיות
בקריאת שמע קודם שתחשך לפני
שהיא שעת שכיבה ועוד דאותה
קריאה שמן כמין ל' מנוס היכא
אלא בשביל להתחיל על ידי כן בתפלה
אינו נו ליד. ועוד תניא חכם הוא

תוספות

made by the master of the Sura Academy known as Rabbina II. On his death in 499, the Babylonian Talmud was closed.

The Talmud is unique not only in content but also in form and pagination. A page of the Talmud beginning a section has in the center the *mishnah* under discussion; around it is written the *gemarah* interpreting and discussing the *mishnah*; in the margins are comments by noted sages (see photo and diagram).

The Mishnah was first printed in 1492 in Naples by the Soncino Press. The first printed Talmud was produced by Daniel Bomberg in Venice, 1520. Every printed version of the Talmud since that day has exactly the same paging. Whether a Talmud was printed in Amsterdam, Vilna, Berlin, or New York, in the seventeenth or eighteenth or twentieth centuries, each page begins with the same word and ends with the same word. Thus, a reference to page 60b of the tractate Gittin is the same in any edition printed by any press at any time.

Beginning about the eleventh century, the Talmud—rather than the Bible—became the major study source of European Jews. The Pentateuch was read through every year or every three years, appropriate passages of the Prophets, called *Haftorah*, were read after each Torah reading, and the Five Scrolls—Ruth, Esther, the Song of Songs, Lamentations, Ecclesiastes—were read on the appropriate holidays; but the Bible as such was studied very little in the *Beth haMidrash,* the house of study. Young boys were taught to read in the *Chumash*, the Pentateuch, but they were graduated to the Talmud as soon as their scholarship allowed. And every man who considered himself a pious Jew tried to read *"a blat Gemarah,"* a page of Gemarah, every day.

To Christians, the Talmud became the symbol of all that was alien, all that was exotic, all that was stubbornly Jewish in the Jews. Since the Bible was canon for the Christians also, it could not be attacked. But the Talmud was believed by the Church to contain mysteries, devilish powers, even orders to kill Christians—and so was the focus of the legal attack upon the Jews from the thirteenth century on.

In 1240, an apostate Jew, Nicholas Donin of La Rochelle, France, formally accused the Talmud before Pope Gregory IX of blasphemy against Jesus and the Church, and of other crimes. The Pope gave orders for the confiscation and destruction of all the Talmuds in the lands of Christian kings. Most sovereigns disregarded the papal order, but pious King Louis IX of France (St. Louis) ordered all Talmuds seized and put on trial. The conclusion was foregone; all the Talmuds found in Louis' realm were burned.

In 1264, Pope Clement IV ordered the death penalty for anyone found with a copy of the Talmud in his house. And in 1286 Pope Honorius IV ordered the Archbishop of Canterbury "vehemently to see that it [the Talmud] be not read by anybody, since all other evils flow from it." The Talmud was burned publicly in Rome in 1322 on order of Pope John XXII. A century later Pope Martin V reissued a bull forbidding Jews to study or teach it. The Christian scholar Johann Reuchlin got the Emperor Maximilian in 1510 to rescind his order to burn all copies of the Talmud, but thirty-four years later Martin Luther branded the Talmud "nothing but godlessness lies, cursing, and swearing [*Von den Juden* and *Ihren Luegen.*]" The Talmud was placed on the Index Expurgatorius in 1599; and ten years later the Jewish library at Cremona, Italy, was plundered, and twelve thousand Talmudical books were burned. Still, Pope Clement VIII had to renew the interdiction against reading or owning the Talmud in 1593. The Talmud was also publicly burned in Barcelona, 1263; Paris, 1299 and 1309; Toulouse, 1315; throughout Spain, 1490; Germany, 1509; Rome, 1553 and 1558; Poland, 1757.

Modern anti-Semitism got its theoretical basis in a book supposedly based on the Talmud, *Judaism Unmasked*, written in 1700 by Johann Eisenmenger. A supporting work was written in 1871 by August Rohling, *The Talmud Jew*. Russians got their anti-Semitic text in 1892 from Justin Pranaitis, *The Christian in the Jewish Talmud*. Among twentieth-century attacks on the Talmud are Walter Forstat's *Basic Principles of the Talmud*, Breslau, 1935, and Dr. Alfred Rosenberg's *Immorality in the Talmud*, Berlin, 1935.

SEVEN

The Talmud: Mishnah, Transcription of the Oral Law

THE TALMUD, including the Mishnah, is not a literary work. The earlier part, the Mishnah, certainly was not written down before the year 200, and scholars disagree whether it was actually put on parchment then. Whatever the date, it was not composed by writers with a sense of literary form. The Talmud is recorded discussion; sometimes the discussions are abstracted or digested, but they remain talk rather than literary composition. The work both suffers and gains from this peculiarity: "in a literary work, you see things; in the Talmud you hear voices."[1] Nor are these recorded voices making set speeches; instead, they are the interacting, discussing voices of great sages met in an academy or in a vineyard or in study groups.

Neither is the Mishnah a code of law in the sense in which this phrase would describe a modern book of statutes. Legal rules are given in the *mishnayot,* but as opinion, not as legislated ordinances. Sometimes the opinion given in a *mishnah* is unanimous, therefore authoritative—but a later unanimous, equally authoritative *mishnah* may offer a differing opinion; sometimes the opinions are divided, and the differing opinions are recorded with as much space and prominence as the unanimous ones. In either case, there is room left for later scholars and judges to amend or adapt or reverse the Mishnaic opinion. According to Rabbi's system, opinions recorded without attribution to a sage are assumed to be unanimous; opinions are ascribed to individual sages when they differ with the majority or with each other. For example:

A courtyard may not be divided unless it will allow four [square] cubits

---

[1] Judah Goldin, *Wisdom of the Fathers,* University of Chicago Press.

[one cubit equals six handbreadths, about twenty inches] for each occupant; nor may a field be divided unless there are nine *kabbim* [one *kab* equals 416 square cubits] space of ground to each jointholder—R. Judah says: unless there are nine half-*kab* of space to each—nor may a garden be divided unless there is a half-*kab* space of ground for each—R. Akiba says: a squarter-*kab* space—nor [can] an eating hall, a watchtower, a dovecote, a cloak, a bathhouse, or an olive-press [be divided] unless there is a portion sufficient for each jointholder. This is a general rule: whatsoever when divided can still be called by the same name may be divided; otherwise it may not be divided. This applies if either of the jointholders is not willing to divide their joint property; but if both are willing, they may divide it even if it is yet smaller. But the Sacred Books may not be divided even if both are willing.[2]

In the earlier centuries of the development of Oral Law, *mishnayot* were developed by the method of *midrash,* or interpretation (from the verb *darosh,* to investigate or search). The process began when a specific case for which no specific rule could be found in the Torah was brought to the scribes or courts. The scholars would find an applicable general rule in the Torah; this would be discussed and commented on by the other scribes and scholars and priests, and an interpretation covering the specific case would be drawn. In order to explain the relationship of the *mishnah* to the Torah passage, and to make the rule easily understood by simpler folk, the explanations sometimes included analogies, homilies, and parables, which became integral parts of the particular *mishnah.*

As society became more complex and the Oral Law more refined, the method of *midrash* became too cumbersome; nor could every individual situation be related to a Biblical text. Rabbi Akiba tried to find a Torah text for every *mishnah* and was forced into rationalizations that were dismissed by his peers. The often long-winded midrashic explanations also made the problem of memorizing—the only means of transmitting the Oral Law then—too difficult even for scholars who were mnemonic geniuses. A new method of abstraction was developed by which comparatively simple legal statements were gathered from the mass of references and interpretations and examples. This method, and the statements of law derived by it, was termed *halachah,* from the Hebrew root *halach,* to go, thus the proper way to go, the proper rule of conduct.

The rule of *prosbol,*[3] developed by Hillel, illustrates the operation of the mishnaic methods. The Torah rule of *shemitah* required forgiveness

---

[2] Tractate Baba Bathra 1:6
[3] *Prosbol,* from the Greek *pros bouleh,* in the presence of the council or court.

in the seventh year of all loans between Jews.[4] This ordinance of the sabbatical year could not operate in a commercial culture, particularly one in which trade was both internal, among Jews, and external, among Jews and non-Jews. A Jewish bank or moneylender, for example, would hesitate to give a long-term loan to a Jewish borrower in the sixth year, because the debt would have to be forgiven at the end of the year. Hillel reasoned that a debt presented to the court was as good as collected and so could not be forgiven. He ruled that a lender could present to the court a document, attested by witnesses, enumerating the debts owed him, and declaring that he intended to collect the debts at any time he saw fit. Since these debts were accepted by the court, in effect already collected, they were not subject to *shemitah*.

A legal code may reflect the community's prevailing religious concepts or those of the makers of the code, but codes are seldom religious documents in themselves. The Mishnah, however, is a religious book. According to Herbert Danby, it is, "after Sinai, the greatest landmark in the history of Judaism."[5] But despite its religious standing, the Mishnah is not religious authority; the laws contained in the work are not creed. Judaism, by its very nature, does not permit creed or dogma, or any absolute authority except God. The Torah itself, accepted as the revealed word of God, contains processes for continual adaptation, change, and elaboration. The Mishnah was the result of that process applied to law, specifically to the law as it affected Jewish life in the second century. And like all legal codes, major parts of the Mishnah were obsolescent the day they were compiled.

There undoubtedly were among the sages of the Mishnah some who saw it merely as the Jewish Revised Statutes of the year 200, an attempt to order the conduct of the Jewish community in peace and legality. But most of the sages had higher motives. They were attempting through the compilation of the Oral Law to make Jewish life conform to the ethical and religious commandments of the Bible.

Thus the question of what is permitted to be carried on the Sabbath, a question that on the surface appears to be purely ritual and legalistic, is answered in such a way as to provide an ethical imperative: war is evil.

A man may not go out with a sword or a bow or a shield or a club or a spear; and if he went out with the like of these he is liable to a sin-offering. R. Eliezar says: They are his adornments. [The wearing of adornments on the Sabbath is sinful.] But the Sages say, they [the weapons] are naught but a reproach, for it is written, and they shall beat their swords into plough-

[4] Deuteronomy 15:1–2
[5] Herbert Danby, *The Mishnah*, Oxford University Press, 1933.

shares, and their spears into pruning hooks: nation shall not lift up sword against nation, neither shall they learn war any more [Isaiah 2:4].[6]

To the *tannaim* and to the succeeding generations of Jews, the Mishnah was a religious book relating daily life to the traditional doctrines of Judaism, with special emphasis on the particular problems of the second Christian century. In this view, the nature of the opening *mishnah* becomes inevitable: it deals with the Shema, the statement of the unity and universality of God which every Jew is enjoined to make every day.

In its religious philosophy, the Mishnah says that there is reward and punishment both in this world and the hereafter, that man has free will to choose between good and evil, that the Torah was given from God and therefore has final authority, and that the Messiah *will* come [has not yet come]. The last two doctrines—the Torah as revelation and the eventual coming of the Messiah—were of special relevance in the Mishnaic period when Christianity was ascendant and the fathers of the Church were proclaiming that the Messiah had come and the Torah was no longer relevant. The last *mishnah* in the first tractate sums it up:

Man is bound to bless God for the evil even as he blesses God for the good . . . . At the close of every benediction in the Temple they used to say, For everlasting; but after the heretics had taught corruptly and said there is but one world, it was ordained that they say, From everlasting to everlasting. . . .[7]

This *mishnah* closes with an opinion from Rabbi Nathan that in times of emergency it may be right to set aside or amend the Law, that the Law may sometimes best be served by breaking it.

The last tractate in the Mishnah deals pragmatically with ritual uncleanness in plants and animals. It records, for example, Shammai's opinion that fish become susceptible to uncleanness as soon as they are caught; Hillel says they are susceptible only after they are dead; R. Akiba says at some point in between, i.e., when, if put back in the water, the fish would recover. But the last *mishnah* in this prosaic collection is totally different from the preceding *mishnayot* in the chapter. The last *mishnah* in the Mishnah deals with rewards in heaven and the ultimate reward on earth: The saints (meaning "those that love Me") will be rewarded in the hereafter, but the "Holy One, blessed is he, found no vessel that could hold Israel's blessing except Peace."

The language of the Jews at the time of the final compilation of the Mishnah was Aramaic, but the Mishnah was written in Hebrew. Tradi-

---

tion says Judah haNasi was such a confirmed Hebraist that in his house even the servant girls spoke Hebrew, a most unusual state of affairs. However, the purity of Rabbi's Hebrew did not keep out of the Mishnah a number of Aramaic, Greek, and Latin words and constructions.

The Mishnah, following Rabbi Akiba's structure, is divided into six orders, somewhat similar to volumes; each order is divided into tractates, or books, the tractates into chapters, and the chapters into sections. A section is a *mishnah*. In all there are 524 chapters in the Mishnah. The orders and tractates are identified by names, but references are made only to the tractate, without indicating to which order it belongs. Thus the reference Sanhedrin 3:4 is to the fourth section (or *mishnah*) in the third chapter of the tractate Sanhedrin—without indicating that the tractate Sanhedrin is in the fourth volume or order, Nezikin.

The complete order of the tractates is given in Appendix II. Here are representative *mishnayot* from several of them.

From the tractate Peah of the first order, Zeraim (Seeds):

1:1. These are things for which no measure is prescribed [have no limit]: corners, first fruits, the festal offering, deeds of loving-kindness, and the study of the Law. These are things whose fruits a man not only enjoys in this world but which accrue to him in the world to come: honoring father and mother, deeds of loving-kindness, making peace between a man and his fellow; and the study of Torah is equal to them all.

1:2. Corners [of the fields, which cannot be harvested] should be not less than one-sixtieth part [of the harvest]. And although they have said that no measure is prescribed for *Peah*, it should ever accord with the size of the field and the number of the poor and the yield [of the harvest].

1:4. A general rule have they enjoined concerning *Peah*: whatsoever is used for food and is kept watch over and grows from the soil and is reaped all together and is brought in for storage is liable to the law of *Peah*. Grain and pulse come within this general rule.

1:5. Among trees, sumach, carob, walnut trees, almond trees, vines, pomegranate trees, olive trees, and palm trees are subject to the law of *Peah*.

From the tractate Betzah of the second order, Moed (Set Feasts):

1:1. If an egg was laid on a Festival day, the School of Shammai say: It may be eaten. And the School of Hillel say: It may not be eaten. The School of Shammai say: An olive's bulk of leaven and a date's bulk of what is leavened [may not remain at Passover]. And the School of Hillel say: An olive's bulk of either.

1:2. The School of Shammai say: They may not remove a ladder from one dovecot to another but only incline it from one opening to another [of the same dovecot.] And the School of Hillel permit it. The School of Shammai say: A man may not take pigeons for slaughtering on a Festival day unless he stirred them up the day before. And the School of Hillel say: He need only go up and say, "This one and this one shall I take."

1:5. The School of Shammai say: They may not take off cupboard doors on a Festival day. But the School of Hillel even permit them to be put back. The School of Shammai say: They may not lift up a pestle to hack meat on it. And the School of Hillel permit it. The School of Shammai say: They may not put a hide before the treading-place and they may lift one up only if there is an olive's bulk of flesh on it. And the School of Hillel permit it. The School of Shammai say: They may not carry out a child or a *Lulab*[8] or a scroll of the Law into the public domain. And the School of Hillel permit it.

From the tractate Ketubah, of the third order, Nashim (Women):

5:1. Although they have said: "The *Ketubah* [marriage contract] of a virgin is two hundred denars [one denar equals one-half shekel] and of a widow one mina [one hundred denars]," but a man may add thereto if he wishes, even a hundred minas. If she was left a widow or was divorced, whether after betrothal or after wedlock, she may lay claim to the whole. R. Eleazar b. Azariah says: If after wedlock, she may lay claim to the whole; but if after betrothal only, a virgin may lay claim but to two hundred denars and a widow to one mina, since he assigned her the whole only on the condition that he married her. R. Judah says: If he was so minded, a man may write out a bond for two hundred denars for a virgin while she writes, "I have already received from thee one mina"; and he may write out a bond for one mina for a widow, while she writes, "I have already received from thee fifty zuz [denars]." R. Meir says: If they assign less than two hundred zuz for a virgin or less than one mina for a widow, such is accounted fornication.

5:5. These are works which the wife must perform for her husband: grinding flour and baking bread and washing clothes and cooking food and giving suck to her child and making ready his bed and working in wool. If she brought him in one bondwoman, she need not grind or bake or wash; if two, she need not cook or give her child suck; if three, she need not make ready his bed or work in wool; if four, she may sit all the day in a chair. R. Eliezer says: Even if she brought him in a hundred bondwomen, he should compel her to work in wool, for idleness leads to unchastity. Rabban Simeon b. Gamaliel says: Moreover if a man put his wife under a vow to do no work, he should put her away and give her her *Ketubah,* for idleness leads to lowness of spirit.

5:6. Disciples [of the Sages] may continue absent for thirty days against the will of their wives while they occupy themselves in the study of the Law; and laborers for one week. The duty of marriage enjoined in the Law is: every day for them that are unoccupied; twice a week for laborers; once a week for ass-drivers; once every thirty days for camel-drivers; and once every six months for sailors. So R. Eliezer.

---

[8] A *Lulab* is a wand used in celebrating the festival of Succot. It is formed from the interwoven branches of palm, myrtle, and brook willow trees.

5:8 If a husband maintained his wife at the hands of a third person, he may not give her less than two kabs [the equivalent of the contents of twenty-four eggs] of wheat or four kabs of barley every week. R. Jose said: Only R. Ishmael provided her with barley because he lived near Edom. The husband must also give his wife half a kab of pulse and half a log [one-fourth kab] of oil and a kab of dried figs or a mina of fig cake; and if he has none of these he must provide her with other produce in their stead. He must also give her a bed and a bedcover and if he has no bedcover he must give her a rush mat. He must also give her a cap for her head and a girdle for her loins, and shoes at each of the [three] Feasts, and clothing to the value of fifty zuz every year. He may not give her new clothes for summer or worn-out clothes for winter; but he should give her clothes to the value of fifty zuz for winter, and she may clothe herself with the rags thereof in the summer time; and the discarded garments belong to her.

From the tractate Baba Bathra of the fourth order, Nezikim (Damages):

10:1. An unfolded document has the signatures within the single page; a folded document has the signatures behind each fold. If in an unfolded document its witnesses signed behind, or if in a folded document its witnesses signed within, they are invalid. R. Hanina b. Gamaliel says: If its witnesses signed within a folded document, it is valid, since it can be made into an unfolded document. Rabban Simeon b. Gamaliel says: Everything should follow local custom.

10:2. An unfolded document requires two witnesses; a folded one three. If an unfolded document has but one witness or a folded one but two, both are invalid. . . .

10:3. They may write a bill of divorce for the husband even if his wife is not with him, or a quittance for the wife even if her husband is not with her, provided that he knows them; and the husband must pay the fee. They may write a bond for the debtor even if the creditor is not with him, but they may not write a bond for the creditor unless the debtor is with him; and the debtor must pay the fee. They may write a deed of sale for the seller although the buyer is not with him; but they may not write it for the buyer unless the seller is with him; and the buyer must pay the fee.

10:4. They may not write deeds of betrothal or marriage save with the consent of both the parties, and the bridegroom must pay the fee. They may not write deeds of tenancy save with the consent of both the parties, and he that assumes the tenure must pay the fee. They may not write a deed of arbitration or any document drawn up before the court save with the consent of both the parties, and both must pay the fee. Rabban Simeon b. Gamaliel says: Two documents are written for the two parties, a separate one for each.

10:5. If a man had paid part of his debt and the bond was placed with a third party, and the debtor said to him, "If I have not paid thee by such a day, then give him his bond," and the time came and he had not paid, R. Jose says: He should give it to him. R. Judah says: He should not give it to him.

From the tractate Kerithot of the fifth order, Kodashim (Holy Things):

1:1. For thirty-six transgressions is extirpation prescribed in the Law: if a man has connection with his mother, his father's wife, his daughter-in-law, or with a male or with a beast; if a woman has connection with a beast; or if a man has connection with a woman and her daughter, with a married woman, with his sister, his father's sister, his mother's sister, his wife's sister, his brother's wife, or his father's brother's wife, or with a menstruous woman; if a man blasphemes, commits idolatry, offers of his seed to Molech, has a familiar spirit, or profanes the Sabbath, or eats what is consecrated while unclean, or enters the Temple while unclean, or eats the fat, or the blood, or remnant or refuse, or slaughters or offers up an offering outside the Temple Court, or eats leavened bread during Passover, or eats or does any work on the Day of Atonement, or compounds anointing oil, or compounds incense like that compounded in the Temple, or anoints himself with the oil of unction; or if he transgresses the laws of the Passover and circumcision.

EIGHT

The Talmud: Gemarah,
Commentary on the Oral Law

SINCE THE TORAH is the Law revealed by God, it must contain answers to every legal question that can arise, reasoned the Rabbis. And for them, legal meant also ethical and moral; thus legal questions encompassed every activity of man. So if situations arose which did not appear to be covered in the Torah, the fault must lie with the scholars, not, of course, with the Torah itself. "Search in it and search yet again, for everything is contained in it," they said.

The Mishnah was the first post-Biblical codification of these "searchings." But even as the Mishnah was set down, conditions changed; new problems arose that were not covered in the Mishnah. The process of elaboration, of interpretation, had to continue. The records of this second series of searchings is the second strand of the Talmud, the Gemarah, from the Aramaic word for study or instruction. As the Mishnah is, in effect, a commentary on an elaboration of the Torah, so the Gemarah is a commentary on an elaboration of the Mishnah. The two strands are not separate; the Talmudic form interweaves Mishnah sections with Gemarah comment.

The more than a thousand rabbis who contributed to the Talmud used every philosophical method from Aristotelian logic to mystical intuition, but for the most part they were dialecticians, using the method of critical investigation of the truth of any statement. The method that came to be most associated with the Talmud was the dialectical method called *pilpul*.[1]

---

[1] *Pilpul,* meaning pepper, therefore sharp, came to define the sharp arguer. One of the greatest pilpulists said, "I prefer a single pungent pepper to a basketful of melons," to show his disdain toward the slower-moving traditional analyzers.

The method of *pilpul* involved the detailed analysis of a detailed examination of a detailed dissection of the Mishnah text. Used properly, it gave free range to ingenuity and cleverness in argument; taken to extremes, it became meaningless hairsplitting. The traditional scholar went in a straight line from case to case, seeking to find the most significant cases that had relevance to the situation before him. The pilpulist sought to break down a *mishnah* into its smallest component parts, then to recombine the parts into a new concept. He reasoned that if the whole is true, then the component parts are valid; therefore any rearrangement of the valid components should create a true statement. The fifth century pilpulists did to logic, philosophy, and law what twentieth century chemists were to do in breaking down compounds and synthesizing new ones. Admiring students called the great pilpulists "uprooters of mountains" because of their skill in reducing monumental opinions to their basic elements.

The Palestinian and Babylonian versions of the Talmud are quite different in size, in spirit, and according to some scholars, in purpose. The Palestinian Talmud is about one-sixth the size of the Babylonian record. It is more direct and simpler in language, but its Babylonian counterpart is more intellectually stimulating and has greater scope. It is said that the Palestinian Talmud was written as a reference for rabbis and judges, the Babylonian Talmud as a text for scholars. The two versions also use different dialects, the Palestinian being written in a mixture of Hebrew and west-Aramaic, the Babylonian in a mixture of Hebrew and east-Aramaic.

The thousands upon thousands of words in the Talmud are not—in fact, could not be—concerned only with law in a lawyer's sense. But they all refer to law in the sense of the Torah: ethical conduct, which encompasses law of commerce and law of social relations, law of court, law of the family, law of the exact moment at which evening begins, and law of birth and death ceremonies. Thus the Talmud deals with the totality of the conduct of the Jew from long before birth to long after death—which is a paradox, since the totality of man cannot be encompassed or ruled by law.

Life is ruled by spontaneous outbursts of feeling, of emotions, of hope and despair, of thoughts and reflection. Hence the Talmud deals not only with law but with medicine as far as it affects conduct, with astronomy and meteorology in their relations to human life and occupations, with the rules and methods of agriculture as it was practiced by the people in their daily tasks, and a host of other matters which in life are linked together directly and indirectly, with the wisdom of the everyday man culled from hard experience and expressed for brevity's sake in adages, proverbs, saws, and epigrams, and finally with the suffering of the people in the present, as well as with their hopes for a better and brighter future. This is only a partial description of the world embodied in the Talmud.[2]

The Talmud is also the means of expressing and the result of expressing the relationship of the Jew to the Torah. The Torah, to the Jew, is not a book or a code or even only the Word. The lines of division between God and Torah, between Torah and Israel, blur in the Talmud. The Torah becomes, in a sense, the reason for man's existence. It follows, then, that study of the Torah is a fulfillment of the reason for man's existence: it cannot lead to anything; it is an end in itself. There is no time at which the study is completed; in fact, no man's lifetime is sufficiently long for the study. And the Talmud is the record of the greatest concentrated study of the Torah by the greatest sages over a period of five hundred years.

As a commentary on the Mishnah, the Gemarah follows the order of the Mishnah. Section by section, the Mishnah was put before the scholars and analyzed, discussed, compared, and illustrated. If *baraitah*, material excluded from the Mishnah, was pertinent, it was brought into the discussion—which might then turn to an analysis of the *baraitah* itself. If a great scholar commented on the same *mishnah*, his comments were entered and analyzed in turn. Often a word, an idea, or a name triggered a new train of thought. And to confuse logical order still further, the introduction of the opinion of some sage—an opinion pertinent to the *mishnah* under examination—might be followed by a recitation of all the important opinions of that sage, relevant or irrelevant. This occurred because the students used the names of authorities as mnemonic devices. Once the name was brought up, it triggered recall of all the legal opinions connected with the name.

As a result, the Gemarah has no logical order. Even the comparative order of the Mishnah is lost as the Gemarah wanders from subject to subject, from sage to sage, from legal opinion to illustrative story. It is, as the Jews termed it, the ocean of Talmud. Appendix IV, p. 247, shows the Talmudic form and nature.

The Gemarah, as transmitted from Babylon to the medieval Jews in Europe, and from them to modern Jews, does not include commentary on each of the sixty-three tractates in the six orders of the Mishnah. The existent Babylonian Talmud includes Gemarah on thirty-seven tractates; the Palestinian Talmud covers thirty-nine tractates. When the Talmud was closed in the year 500, it may have included commentary on all the tractates, but if so, much was lost in the years of handwritten transmission. And what evidence exists appears to indicate that not all the trac-

---

[2] Meyer Waxman, *History of Jewish Literature,* Vol. 1, Bloch, 1938.

tates of the Mishnah were covered. With some exceptions, the existing Babylonian Gemarah covers the tractates that have most meaning to post-Temple, Diaspora Jews, passing over those tractates that are not particularly relevant to Jewish life outside a Temple-centered Palestine.

The Palestinian Talmud, for example, includes Gemarah on all the tractates in the first order, Seeds. However, since this order deals mainly with the land and tithing of the products of the land, rules not pertinent to life outside Palestine, the Babylonian Talmud includes Gemarah on only the first tractate, Berachot, Blessings. On the other hand, the Babylonian Talmud includes Gemarah on most of the tractates of the fifth order, Kodashim, dealing mainly with the Temple cult, while the Palestinian Talmud includes none of the tractates of this order.

The Gemarah, like the Mishnah on which it is based, is not a book of laws; it is not a book of statutes in which each statement is validly binding. Diverging opinions appear next to each other in the Mishnah; the Gemarah often has the character of minutes of a meeting of *amoraim* called to resolve the divergencies of the *tannaim*—not always successfully. The inference is that what is religiously valid at any time is what the rabbis declare to be valid, after an examination of the scholarly works going back to the Gemarah, the Mishnah, and the elemental source itself, the Torah.

Despite its quicksilver nature, definite currents of consensus can be found within the ocean of Talmud. These define the Rabbis' concepts of God, man, and the universe, of the proper forms of family, social, and community life, of the moral and ethical standards that measure man and men. These concepts are authoritative, but not authority; they have great weight, but they can be questioned and reexamined. The Rabbis said: "Akiba's opinion is always authoritative in conflict with a single scholar, but not when he is opposed by more than one scholar." And the scholars did not die out with the *amoraim*.

Following are some of the significant ideas of the Rabbis of the Talmud grouped, as they are not grouped in the Talmud, by pertinence to four broad concepts: God, heaven and hell, moral man, and social man.

The God of the Rabbis is not the Greek Prime Mover or First Cause. He is a personal God in the sense that he is both real and available to those who accept Him. His existence is axiomatic—no proofs have to be offered. Man accepts or does not accept, and that is that; in fact, theorizing about His existence, His beginning and His end, is not only pointless but dangerous. Most people *learn* about God; that is, they gain knowledge of Him from others, but it is quite possible to gain knowledge of Him through spiritual consciousness. The Rabbis said: "Abraham perceived the Holy One, blessed be He, by himself, and no one taught him this knowledge." Equally axiomatic is the idea of total monotheism; the existence of other gods is unthinkable.

Although both the Bible and the Talmud make anthropomorphic references to God—He cries, He sits upon a throne, He has arms, etc.—the Talmud strongly reinforces the Biblical concept of the incorporeal God. He has no form, no physical properties of any kind. The Rabbis explain the anthropomorphic terms: "We borrow terms from His creatures to apply to Him in order to assist understanding."

God is omnipresent: He encompasses space; space does not encompass Him. The Torah source offered by the Rabbis for this concept is Jeremiah 23:24: "Do I not fill heaven and earth?"

God is omnipotent—except for one small but very important area: "Everything is in the power of heaven except the fear of heaven." God can do anything except cause man to love (fear) Him. However, the Rabbis discouraged the idea that God might use his omnipotence to change the orderly process of the universe. Miracles which appear to change this order—the opening of the Sea of Reeds for Moses, the halting of the sun for Joshua—were said by the Rabbis to have been put into the plan of creation when God formed the heavens and the earth. In effect, they had already been programmed.

His omniscience is also unlimited; He has knowledge of everything that has happened, is happening, will happen. The Rabbis said: "From the creation, the Holy One, blessed be He, foresaw the deeds of the righteous and the wicked." And to the Rabbis, God was transcendent, immanent, and eternal. He was immeasurably removed from finite limits and immeasurably close to everyone who called upon Him. And "everything decays, but Thou dost not decay."

Justice and mercy are God's most obvious attributes. The Rabbis used the Jahvist term, Adonai, to refer to God in His aspect as the Merciful One; they used the Elohist term, Elohim, to refer to Him as the Judge. But most references to God include both attributes: Merciful Judge, or Judge full of compassion.

The Rabbis also frequently use the term "Father in heaven" to denote His paternal attribute. This fatherhood extends to all men, and man is adjured to respond to God as a child to a father: "All miracles and mighty acts which I performed for you were not with the object that you should give Me a reward, but that you should honor Me like a dutiful child and call Me your father."

The love/fear relationship between man and God was not viewed as a paradox by the Rabbis. (In Hebrew, the word used for love, as in the Decalogue, is *ahavah;* fear is *yirah.*) Just as both love and fear are (or were until very recent years) intrinsic to the relationship between parent and child, so are they essential to the father/child relationship of God and man. And contrary to contemporary Christian theology, which is heavily love-centered, love and fear have almost equal importance in Judaism. If there were no fear, said the Rabbis, man might wrong his fellow man.

God's love for Israel is seen as the fulfillment of the covenant. "And it shall come to pass, because ye hearken to these ordinances, and keep, and do them, that the Lord thy God shall keep with thee the covenant and the mercy which He swore unto thy fathers, and He will love thee. . . ." [3] Commenting on the commandment, "And thou shalt love the Lord thy God with all thy heart, and with all thy soul, and with all thy might," [4] Rashi asserts that man should obey God's commands out of love rather than out of fear. And anticipating the twentieth-century view of love as multi-faceted, this eleventh-century scholar says that a special grammatical construction is used in the commandment: the Hebrew word for heart is *lev* but here the word *levav* is used, to indicate that God is to be loved with "both hearts" that are in every man, the good heart and the evil one.

Yet fear is necessary, for "The fear of the Lord is the beginning of wisdom." [5] In this context, fear is understood to be the feeling of awe necessary as the starting point of a life which must be lived on a higher plane than that of the animals who do not know love. However, this fear can have only one object—God; a God-fearer does not have to be a man-fearer. "The Lord of Hosts, Him shall ye sanctify; and let Him be your fear, and let Him be your dread" [6] is explained to mean that only the King, not mortal kings, are to be feared.

The relationship is summed up in the next to last verse in Ecclesiastes, "The end of the matter, all having been heard: fear God, and keep His commandments; for this is the whole of man." [7] The Rabbis interpret this: rejoice in God's statutes; love God by serving Him without thought of reward, but be wary of His anger when you transgress.

The Rabbis were not metaphysicians. Although they were acquainted with Greek philosophy, their ideas of nature were far from those of Aristotle and Plato. They did not, for example, accept the Aristotelian concept of the eternity of matter. To the Rabbis, God pre-existed all things. And while they did not give much thought to natural science, the Rabbis developed a picture of a three-layered cosmos: heaven, earth, and hell.

[3] Deuteronomy 7:12–13
[4] Deuteronomy 6:5
[5] Psalms 111:10
[6] Isaiah 8:13
[7] Ecclesiastes 12:13

Since the Bible has seven designations for heaven, the Rabbis reasoned that heaven has seven stories or levels. These range from the lowest level, Vilon, where the process of creation is renewed daily; to the highest level, Arabot, where dwell righteousness, charity, and judgment and where the Throne of Glory stands. The ministering angels and the souls of the yet unborn are also kept in the top level. On the middle level, Zebul, is the heavenly Jerusalem and the celestial Temple where the archangel Michael offers sacrifices.

Earth, too, has seven layers or strata, and is, of course, flat. [Discoveries, circa 400, confirmed this.] This flat earth rests upon pillars. This was unanimously accepted by the Rabbis, although they differed sharply as to the number of pillars. R. Eleazar ben Shammua said one pillar; others said seven; the consensus was twelve. The pillars rest on water, which is on a mountain, which stands on the wind, which rests on the storm, which is suspended from the arm of God.

Gehinnom, from which the term Gehenna derives, also has seven levels.[8] The Rabbis speak of descending into Gehenna, but they were not sure that it lies under the earth. There was strong argument that hell is beyond the mountains to the west, as evidence the color of the descending sun which reflects the fires of hell. Fire is the principal feature of hell, but there is also mire. The Rabbis did not accept weird beasts or devils with pitchforks.

Heaven is inhabited by seraphim and cherubim—that is, angels. The angels are not intermediaries between God and man; the major purpose of the heavenly host is to glorify the Lord—to sing His praises. The heavenly choir is headed by four archangels: Michael, guardian of Israel and instructor of Moses; Gabriel, messenger of God; Raphael, healer; and Uriel, transmitter of knowledge.[9] The Rabbis rejected the idea of fallen angels. The evil angels, the destroying angels (Sammael, for example), are merely the expressions of God's wrath. The Rabbis said: "Satan, the *yetzer harah* (the evil inclination in man), and the angel of death are all one."

On death, man is judged by the Great Tribunal to determine whether he will spend the years until the World-to-Come in heaven or hell. He is judged again at the last judgment:

They that are born will die; and the dead will be brought to life again; and they that live again will be judged, will know, will make known, and will be made aware that He is God, He the Maker, He the Creator, He the Discerner, He the Judge, He the Witness, He the Complainant, He it is that will

---

[8] Dante got his idea of the seven circles of hell from the Talmud.

[9] Angels were not given names until the book of Daniel. The Rabbis said: "Names of angels came into the possession of Israel from Babylon (the Captivity)."

judge, blessed be He, with whom there is no unrighteousness, nor forgetfulness, nor respect for persons, nor taking of bribes. Know also that everything is in the reckoning. And let not your imagination persuade you that the grave will be a place of refuge for you; for perforce you were formed, and perforce you were born, and perforce you live, and perforce you die, and perforce you will in the hereafter have to give account and reckoning before the supreme King of kings, the Holy One, blessed be He.[10]

The Sadduccees had rejected any idea of life after death; the Pharisees held as strongly to the idea of the resurrection of the dead. The Rabbis of the Talmud were in the Pharisaic tradition, but there was no agreement as to who would be resurrected. The Rabbis were divided into those who believed that only the good would be resurrected, those who believed only Israel would be resurrected, and those who believed that every soul would be resurrected. They also differed sharply as to the length of punishment of those souls who were sent to Gehenna. A minority argued that punishment was eternal. But the majority could not reconcile eternal punishment with a merciful God. Some Rabbis said the maximum term of punishment in Gehenna was four thousand years; some said seven weeks; others set the limit between these extremes. Rabbi Akiba's dictum is considered authoritative:

The judgment on the generation of the Flood [which was so evil it had to be destroyed] was twelve months, on Job twelve months, on the Egyptians twelve months, on Gog and Magog in the hereafter twelve months, and on the wicked in Gehenna twelve months.

Most cultures place their golden age in the past, generally a time when gods or men-more-than-men walked the earth. The Jews place their golden age in some distant future when the *Moshiach* or Messiah will have come. *Moshiach* means the annointed one. The Rabbis believed that the coming of the Messiah was part of the plan of creation. But they insisted that the Messiah would be a human and would not have superhuman attributes.

Some venturesome Rabbis played numerological games to try to determine when the Messiah would come. Generally they came up with dates somewhere toward the end of the fifth century or the beginning of the sixth. Two favorites were the year 4291 of the Hebrew calendar and the period beginning 4250, or eighty-five jubilees after the Creation.[11] But this practice of numerological prediction was frowned upon by the more serious scholars, who felt that the Messiah would come only in a

---

[10] Tractate Aboth 4:29

[11] The Hebrew calendar counts years from the Creation, believed to have been in 3760 B.C.; these two dates are 531 and 490 in the modern calendar. The year of jubilee comes after the seventh sabbath—that is, after the forty-ninth—year, thus every fiftieth year.

period of universal peace and goodness and righteousness—probably after a period of tremendous man-made cataclysms (Armageddon). "If Israel observed a single sabbath properly, the son of David would come," they said.

The coming of the son of David will usher in the world-to-come. The Rabbis described it thus: "While in this world one man builds and another uses, one man plants and another eats the fruit, what is written about the hereafter? They shall not build and another inherit, they shall not plant and another eat . . . they shall not labor in vain, nor bring forth calamity."

Man was created in the image of God. The Rabbis reasoned from this that man was supremely important to God, to the universe, and to himself; he is central to the economy of creation. They said: "Man was first created a single individual to teach the lesson that whoever destroys one life, it is as though he had destroyed the whole world; and whoever saves one life, it is as though he had saved the world."

Man's purpose on earth is to glorify God, his Creator and Father, a purpose best served by faithful adherence to His law. But man is so important to himself and to God that if he is faced with a choice between breaking the law and death, he is to "choose life." Only three laws cannot be broken to save life: the laws against idolatry, bloodshed, and unchastity, that is, adultery and incest. (Some rabbis add a fourth to this list of most grievous sins: slander.) It follows then that suicide is against God's Law except to avoid idolatry, killing, and unchastity. In the time of the Crusades, Jews accepted the choice of murder and suicide, rather than life, when parents killed their children and then themselves to avoid forced conversion. These Jews are considered to have died *Kiddush haShem,* for the glorification of the Holy Name.

Just as there are certain laws which cannot be broken to save life, there are laws which bar life if broken. The Rabbis said, "The evil eye [meaning envy in this context], the evil inclination [meaning hedonism here], and hatred of his fellow creature put a man out of the world."

The soul is the most Godlike feature of man, who is created in His image. The Rabbis saw the soul as the spiritual force in man that raises him above the animals, which must always follow their nature, gives man his ideals, and enables him to choose between good and evil. The soul can get help in its spiritual purpose from prayer, as an act of fellowship with God. Prayer is also the truest expression of faith, since if man did not believe, he would not pray. There are two forms of prayer: that which blesses God and sings His praises, and a lesser form which petitions Him. But even the petitionary prayer is not couched in terms of I; it asks in the name of "we," in the name of men rather than of one man.

The Rabbis rejected totally the idea of original sin. Being sinless, the soul is perfect at birth, and the Rabbis cautioned: "Give it back to Him as He gave it to you, in a state of purity." Still, sin is inevitable, since without it there would be no death. If nothing else, there is always some sin of idolatry: "There is no generation in which there is not at least an ounce of the sin of the Golden Calf." But there can be no inheritance of sin, no punishment for another's sin. The Rabbis insisted that man cannot be guilty of a sin for which he is not personally responsible.

The foundation of Rabbinic ethics at the heart of the Rabbis' concept of man is free will. Man's life is basically in his own hands. He may do evil, he may become a slave to his senses, but the Rabbis believed, contrary to the Greek conception of fated tragedy and the Christian concept of original sin, that man is never compelled to sin by forces outside himself. He may be tempted by the evil inclination, but he chooses whether to follow the evil impulse or to reject it. The choice is his—and the greatest sin is to lead another into sin.

The ability to commit a sinful act appears at birth, for that is when the evil inclination—the *yetzer harah*—enters man's being. But the child is not morally responsible until he reaches age thirteen, for that is when the *yetzer tov*, the good impulse, appears within him. This concept expresses the Rabbinic idea that moral consciousness is learned from family and society and implies the necessity of studying the Law. It also explains the Jewish ritual of *bar mitzvah*, at which point a boy becomes responsible for the moral consequences of his acts.

Aware of the ease with which the evil inclination can dominate a man ("The evil impulse is first like a passer-by, then like a lodger, then like the master of the house"), the Rabbis suggested: "If a man sees that his evil impulse is gaining mastery over him, let him go to a place where he is not known, put on black clothes [as a sign of mourning, which might sober him], and do what his heart desires; but let him not profane the Name publicly [where he is known]."

If wickedness is a disease to which all men are susceptible, reasoned the Rabbis, then a merciful God would provide a readily available antidote. This antidote is repentance. But repentance must be more than verbal: "Who says I will sin and repent and again sin and repent will be denied the power of repentance." Repentance through prayer and confession is valid only when it is accompanied by a change in conduct and by making recompense.

By the time of the Rabbis, the Day of Atonement had become the symbolic equivalent of the atonement sacrifices at the Temple. But the Rabbis set harsher terms for atonement than the priests of the Temple. A sin against God only, such as a violation of ritual law, could be atoned by confession and prayers of repentance; but a sin against man, such as slander or theft, first had to be put right by admitting the slander or repaying the theft before repentance was possible.

Theoretically, even in the time of the Rabbis, there was no punishment without sin and no sin without punishment. They even had a list of specific punishments for specific sins: drought for not tithing; pestilence for not punishing criminals; war for perverting justice; poisonous snakes and insects for false swearing; slavery for idolatry. But reality—and the Rabbis were realists—proved that the innocent often suffered and the guilty grew rich. The Rabbis made valiant efforts to explain this gap between religious theory and reality. Some offered the idea that the merit of the fathers, or lack of merit, saved some sinful and punished some good. But this explanation ran counter to the axiom that sin cannot be inherited. Other rabbis said: "When there are righteous in a generation, the righteous are punished for the sins of that generation. If there are no righteous, then the schoolchildren [the innocent] suffer for the evil of the time." But this appeared to invalidate the rule that the innocent shall not suffer for the guilty. Some tried to reject the problem by saying that the service of God had to be without thought of earthly or heavenly reward: "Blessed is the man who delighteth greatly in His commandments—in His commandments, not in the reward of His commandments." In sum, the Rabbis of the Talmud had no better answer to the problem of theodicy than Job had.

The commandment in Leviticus 19:18 to "love thy neighbor as thyself" was hailed by Rabbi Akiba as the fundamental principle of the Torah. The Rabbis strongly associated themselves with this dictum. Some Rabbis, particularly those active during periods of persecution, refused to accept Gentiles—the persecutors—within the meaning of "neighbor." But the Rabbinic consensus is for the universality of love. The most usual formulations carefully used the word *berriot*, creatures or human beings, rather than neighbor or brother, which might be misconstrued as referring only to Jews. The Talmud says: "Our Rabbis taught: we must support the poor of the Gentiles with the poor of Israel, visit the sick of the Gentiles with the sick of Israel, give honorable burial to the dead of the Gentiles as to the dead of Israel, because of the ways of peace."

In general, the Rabbis saw an equal share for Gentiles in the world-to-come: "A Gentile who obeys the Torah is equal to the High Priest." However, the Talmud includes many statements—usually made during times of persecution—damning Gentiles out of hand: "A Gentile who occupies himself with the study of Torah is deserving of death." Since the Talmud is a recording of opinions, such opinions are recorded, too. The consensus was that even a Gentile who could not accept the

Torah entirely was eligible for a share in the world-to-come if he followed the seven laws enjoined upon all of Noah's descendants (the Noahide commandments): against inequity, idolatry, immorality, bloodshed, robbery, blasphemy, and eating meat torn from a living animal.

The Rabbis said the world was divided into seventy nations with seventy languages, traced from the genealogy in Genesis. And whenever God addressed man, he addressed all seventy nations: "Every phrase which issued from the mouth of the All-Powerful divided itself into seventy languages." However, this did not invade the special intimate relationship between God and Israel: "I am God over all who come into the world; but I have associated My Name with you. I am not called the God of the idolators, but the God of Israel."

This special relationship was not due to any inherent superiority of the Jews, according to the Rabbis. The unique God-Israel relationship stemmed from Israel's acceptance of the burden of the Torah—which they said, had first been offered to, and rejected by, the other nations of the world. But this relationship was open to all persons of any lineage who associated themselves with the covenant, so the Rabbis welcomed proselytes.

Since everything stemmed from God, everything belonged to God, and a man's possessions were merely on loan from Him, reasoned the Rabbis. Therefore, the practice of charity was necessary to create a more equitable distribution of God's gifts to man, which tend to accumulate in comparatively few pockets. (Tsedakah, translated "charity" in English, is more properly translated "acts of righteousness.") So strongly did the Rabbis feel about the requirement of tsedakah that they said: "Even a begger who is maintained by charity must himself practice charity."

Nor could charity be measured only by the ability of the giver to give; it must be consistent with the needs of the receiver. If a needy man's former style of life required it, charity might have to extend to the giving of clothes better than those worn by the giver.

The highest type of charity is that in which the giver does not know the receiver and the receiver does not know the giver. The Rabbis reported that in the Temple there had been a Room of Secret Charity: no one knew who deposited how much in the room; no one knew who took how much from it.

Far more important than almsgiving was the practice of gemilut chasadim, acts of loving-kindness. These acts of benevolence were superior to the usual acts of charity because, said the Rabbis, charity can be given only to the poor, but benevolence can be extended to rich and poor; charity can be given only in money, but benevolence can be either money or personal service; charity can be extended only to the living, but benevolence to either the living or the dead. Essential acts of benevolence were visiting the sick, giving hospitality to strangers, caring for orphans, and honoring the dead by sitting up with the corpse and attending the funeral.

The Rabbis differed as to whether saintliness or humility was the greater virtue, with the majority choosing humility, at least for scholars. Scholarship and learning were so highly regarded in the Jewish community that the learned man was constantly being tempted to pride. They said: "If a man makes himself like a wilderness in which all may walk, his learning will endure in him; otherwise it will not."

Honesty, particularly in trade, was also a superior virtue. In fact, the Rabbis thought it so important that they said the first question put to the dead by the Heavenly Tribunal was, "Have you been honest in your dealings?" They said: "Jerusalem was destroyed because honest men ceased. therein."

God created both the means of pleasure and the ability in man to take pleasure. To refuse to accept these gifts is in a sense to reject Him. The Rabbis rejected both extremes of conduct: abstinence, celibacy, and strict austerity on the one hand; a life of sensuality and pleasure on the other. They did not believe there was any virtue intrinsic in poverty, nor was there in luxury. Abstinence from wine concerned them in particular: "Where wine is lacking, drugs are necessary"—but, "Do not become intoxicated and you will not sin." They summed it up: "Sufficient for you is what the Torah forbids, and do not seek to add further restrictions."

Among the other virtues important to the Rabbis were kindness to anmials and personal cleanliness. They believed that inconsiderateness to animals provoked God's wrath: "A man must not eat his meals until he has fed his cattle." The rabbis went a little further than the Romans in the *mens sana* philosophy; they said: "Physical cleanliness leads to spiritual purity."

The first command in the Bible (Genesis 1:28) is to marry and rear children, and the Rabbis warned that "the unmarried person lives without joy, without blessing, and without good." The prime reason for marriage is to have children, preferably sons, but the wife was more than a child-bearer; she was also a partner in life. R. Jose said: "Never have I called my wife by that word, but always 'my home.' "

The Rabbis' view of women was somewhat paradoxical. They insisted on the absolute authority of the husband, but they also insisted that he honor his wife; "Honor your wife, for thereby you enrich yourself," and, "A man should spend less than his means on food and drink, according to his means on clothing, and more than his means in honoring his wife and children."

Theoretically, divorce is possible only at the request of the husband. However, the Rabbis recognized the inherent injustice in this rule and provided means whereby a husband could be forced to give his wife a divorce if she had cause: "The court may bring strong pressure to bear upon a husband until he says, I am willing to divorce my wife."

Polygamy, although quite legal, also troubled the Rabbis. One Rabbi said: "A man may marry as many wives as he pleases"; another said, "He may not exceed four"; still a third said a man must offer his first wife a divorce if he takes a second, but if he does take a second wife and divorces the first, "even the altar sheds tears on her behalf."[12]

Having children was the prime purpose of marriage and "a childless person is accounted as dead," since the childless person's name died with him and there was no one to say prayers for him. Having had children, parents' first responsibility was for their education. A child was taught the Torah so that he could follow God's Law, but he had also to be taught that learning was for the love of learning—there could be no monetary rewards. A scholar could be a smith or a porter as easily as a merchant or a judge. "If you have acquired knowledge, what do you lack? And if you lack knowledge, what have you acquired?" There was one avenue of reward for learning: to become a scholar-teacher. This was the position with the highest status in the community. In some areas, the teacher even took precedence over the parent, "for a parent only brings the child to the life of this world, while a teacher brings him to the life of the world to come."

And to safeguard the quality of teaching, the Rabbis placed strict limits on the size of classes. "The maximum number of elementary pupils that should be placed under one teacher is twenty-five. . . ."

Elementary schools taught Hebrew and the Pentateuch; higher schools had broader curricula. But the Rabbis were troubled about teaching languages other than Hebrew, particularly Greek. Many agreed that Greek might be taught, but the consensus was that Greek philosophy, which had seduced so many young men during the Hellenic period, could not be taught.

Views as to the education of girls diverged widely. The Rabbis agreed that girls should receive elementary education, that is, become literate. But their opinions on education beyond literacy ranged from "A man is obliged to have his daughter taught Torah" to "Whoever teaches his daughter Torah, it is as if he had taught her obscenity."

The Rabbis anticipated modern psychology in understanding the subtle difference in relationship between boy and mother and boy and

---

[12] Polygamy was formally ended in the West by the ban of Rabbi Gershom, c. 1000.

father. Noting that the Decalogue puts the father first in the commandment to "Honor thy father and thy mother," they pointed to Leviticus
19:3, which says, "Ye shall fear every man his mother, and his father."
They explained: "It was revealed and known before Him who spoke
and the universe came into being that a son has a tendency to honor his
mother more than his father because she wins him over with kindly
words; for that reason the Holy One, blessed be He, gave the father precedence in the commandment concerning honoring the parents. It was
also revealed and known before Him that a son has a tendency to fear
his father more than his mother because he instructs him in Torah; for
that reason the Holy One, blessed be He, gave the mother precedence in
the commandment concerning fear of parents."

Despite the great importance the Rabbis placed on children, they
did not bar contraception; they even urged it in particular cases: in a
young girl, when pregnancy might prove fatal; in a pregnant woman,
since abortion might result; and in a nursing mother, since a new pregnancy might cause her to lose her milk, thus endangering the nursing
child.

The Talmud describes man as a social creature with strong social
responsibilities. His actions are measured against the standard of social
good as well as his own welfare—in this world and the next. To illustrate this idea, the Talmud includes the parable of the man aboard ship
who began to drill a hole in the side. When his fellow passengers remonstrated with him, he said that he was drilling a hole only under his seat,
which was not his neighbor's concern. But, they answered, the water
that will come in the hole under your seat will drown us all.

Key to the Rabbis' concept of the relationship between individual
and society is Hillel's aphorism: "If I am not for myself, who will be for
me? And if I am for myself [alone], what am I? And if not now,
when?" They even put man's responsibility toward his fellow man on a
higher plane than his responsibility to God: "He who is wicked toward
God and wicked toward his fellow man is a wicked man who is evil; but
he who is wicked toward God but not wicked towards his fellow man is
a wicked man who is not evil." They also said that God would rather
have man forget Him than forget His commandments.

Social responsibility also means loyalty to the constituted government, because were it not for government, "men would swallow each
other alive." Therefore, the Rabbis cautioned that a man should not
speak against the king: the law of the country is the law. But neither
should he curry favor with the same king: "Love work, hate lordship,
and do not get too close to the ruling power."

The advice to "love work" points up the Talmudic idea that work,
even the most menial, is ennobling. "Great is work, for it honors the

workman." Nor should a man work only for the immediate rewards it will give him. The Talmud tells of the Emperor Hadrian, who saw an old man breaking the ground preparatory to planting a tree. Hadrian asked the workman how old he was and was told that he was one hundred years old. "You are one hundred years old and you break the earth to plant trees? Do you expect to live long enough to eat the fruit?" asked the Emperor. The man replied: "If I am worthy, I shall eat the fruit. If not, as my fathers labored for me, so I labor for my children."

Second only to the duty to educate a son was the duty to teach him a trade: "A man is obliged to teach his son a trade, and he who does not teach his son a trade teaches him to be a thief." But not all trades were equally worthy to the Rabbis. Some cautioned against teaching a son the trades of camel-driver, ass-driver, sailor, barber, or shopkeeper, because these were thieving occupations. The one occupation that the Rabbis unanimously rejected was moneylending, or usury.

Employers were strictly enjoined to treat their workmen fairly. The master was specifically barred from oppressing his workers and from withholding their pay. A master who did less than he had promised his workmen was equated with a merchant who gives his customers short weight.

The Talmud speaks of three grades of courts: a court of seventy-one for the most serious crimes and disputes, a criminal court of twenty-three, and a civil court of three judges. Two witnesses were necessary to establish a point, and circumstantial evidence was not admitted. The Rabbis offered this case to show the strictness of this rule: "We saw the accused run after a man with a sword in his hand. The man he pursued ran into a shop and the accused ran after him. Then we saw the man dead and the accused with a bloody sword in his hand." But the accusation did not stand, since the witnesses could not say of their own direct knowledge that the accused actually killed the man. On the other hand, circumstantial evidence was admissible for the defense if it would tend to free the accused. Because of these very strict rules of evidence, giving evidence was mandatory. The Rabbis said that God hated a man "who knows evidence in connection with his fellow man and does not testify for him."

Methods of punishment were limited, and there were many capital crimes. But a prisoner did not go to his execution in cold blood. He was given a grain of frankincense in a cup of wine to numb his senses. Even so, capital punishment was so abhorrent to the Jews that a court that sentenced a man to death was known as a murderers' court.

The Rabbis rejected totally the literal interpretation of the Biblical law of an eye for an eye. "Eye for eye—that means a payment of money. . . . Supposing that the eye of the one is larger and the eye of the other small, how can I in that case apply the Scriptural order of eye for eye? . . . Or suppose a blind man knocked out the eye of another, or a lame man made another lame, or a man with one hand cut off the arm of another, how can I fulfill in this case eye for eye? And the Torah declared, Ye shall have one manner of law—that means a law which shall be the same for all. . . ."

Spotted through the Talmud are all manner of medical recipes and cures for all manner of ailments. For example: "If blood flows from the mouth, we examine with a piece of wheat straw. If the straw adheres to the blood, it flows from the lungs and there is a remedy; if it does not adhere, the blood is from the liver and there is no cure. What is the remedy if the blood flows from the lungs? Take three handfuls of sliced beets, seven handfuls of sliced leeks, five handfuls of juice berries, three handfuls of lentils, one handful of cumin, one handful of spices, an equal quantity of the intestines of a first-born animal, and boil them together. The bleeding one should eat this and then drink strong beer brewed in Tebet [a winter month]."

NINE

Midrash: The Aggadic Tales

POST-BIBLICAL JEWISH LITERATURE was a natural development of the strongly held belief that the Bible must contain far more than could be grasped from a surface reading. In modern literary terms, the Bible had to be read on several levels; the means of reaching the more meaningful levels below the obvious was the method of *midrash*, of searching investigation. Out of the early searchings came the legal codes, the moral and practical rules of conduct that governed the Jews—the *midrash halachah*. But even during the development of the Bible, and particularly after the destruction of the first Temple and the kingdom, midrashic searchings were also expressed in illustrative stories and homilies. These were the *midrash aggadah,* from the Hebrew *haged,* to impart instruction. And, as always, these stories, parables, allegories, and pithy sayings had great popular appeal. The statement of an ordinance is never as welcome as the recitation of a fable, though both may make the same point.

Midrash halachah, generally referred to as *halachah,* came to define the laws that governed the Jews' secular and religious life. *Midrash aggadah,* referred to either as *midrash* (plural *midrashim*) or *aggadah* (plural *aggadot*), came to define the entire mass of Jewish literature which supplements history, illustrates ethics, inspires hope, and comforts the bereaved.[1]

After the great religious revival under Ezra during the mid-fifth century B.C. when the Pentateuch was canonized, religious practice required that the Torah be read publicly every Sabbath, Monday, and Thursday. In order to make the Biblical story more meaningful to the listeners and to fill the obvious gaps in the Biblical narrative, the expounders of the Torah developed aggadic explanations.

---

[1] In modern usage, the term *midrash,* by itself, almost always refers to aggadic material in separate collections; *aggadah* refers to the same type of material interwoven with the halachic material in the Talmud.

On hearing the story of Adam and Eve read from Genesis, a Palestinian countryman would immediately wonder where the boys, Cain and Abel, could have found wives, since Adam and Eve were the sole human inhabitants of the earth. A *midrash* answered the countryman's bewilderment. It said that each of the two first sons of Adam and Eve were born with twin sisters destined to be their brothers' wives. Abel's wife was particularly beautiful, and Cain desired her. (Marriage to sisters, although prohibited by commandment, was not as revolting or as unusual in the third or fourth century B.C. as it is in twentieth-century Western cultures.) With this *midrash,* the preacher (called *darshan,* from the same root as *midrash*) not only answered the question as to where the boys would find brides but also gave a more plausible reason for the hatred Cain felt for his brother.

As the Jews were conquered and reconquered by successive foreign lords, as they were alternately driven and persecuted, and as Jewish youth was wooed by successively more seductive cultures, there was greater and greater need for folk heroes and glorifying myths. *Aggadah* provided them; it became a form of emotional and spiritual support for the distressed Jews. So every sabbath and holiday the preachers wove wonderful stories and allegories and mystical meanings for the people.

In time a great body of midrashic material grew up, based in part on the expert use of folk myth and in part on the ethical messages woven into the *midrashim* by sages. Some of these *aggadot* were purely ethical and were gathered into collections of ethical sayings. The apocryphal book The Wisdom of Ben Sirach is, in effect, a collection of ethical *aggadot.* So too, is the Mishnah tractate Pirke Aboth—the Wisdom of the Fathers. Other midrashic collections were purely historical, embroidering Biblical and post-Biblical events and biographies. But most of the midrashic material was homiletic, explaining Bible passages.

Leopold Zunz, the father of modern Jewish scholarship, described this material: "The *aggadah,* whose aim is to bring heaven nearer to men and to lift men up to heaven, does so by glorifying God and comforting Israel. Hence religious truths, moral lessons, discourses on rewards and punishments, teaching of the laws by which the uniqueness of Israel is shown, pictures of the past and future greatness of Israel, scenes and stories from Jewish history, parallels between divine institutions and those of Israel, praise of the Holy Land, inspiring narratives and great consolations—these are the chief content of these synagogue homilies."[2]

Illustrative of the ethical *aggadah* to be found in Pirke Aboth is the following seeming paradox: "He used to say: Better one hour of repentance and good works in this world than all the life in the world to

[2] *Zur Geschichte und Literatur,* 1845

come; and better one hour of calmness of spirit in the world to come than all the life in this world."[3]

The following tale is typical of the historical-homiletic *midrashim*. The Torah explicitly forbids using tools of iron in building an altar. As a result, Solomon had great trouble fitting the stones, rough-cut in the quarry, in the building of the Temple.[4] A *midrash* explains how the task was accomplished.

Solomon asked his wise men how he could fit the stones without using iron tools. They could suggest only the *shamir*, the worm that cuts stone, used by Moses to engrave the names of the tribes on the gems that covered the *ephod* [breast plate] worn by the high priest.

"Where can the *shamir* be found?" asked Solomon.

"Ask the woman-demon and her young," the wise men answered.

So Solomon called forth the woman-demon and her young and pressed them for the whereabouts of the *shamir*. They said they did not know, and when pressed further, they said that only Asmodeus, king of demons, knew where the *shamir* was. And when Solomon demanded to know where Asmodeus could be found and the manner of his life, they said:

"Asmodeus lives on a mountain. In the mountain is a pit which he has dug. The pit is filled with water and covered by a stone which is sealed with Asmodeus' seal. Every day, Asmodeus ascends to heaven to hear the lesson for the day; then he descends to earth, to hear that lesson[5]; then he returns to his mountain, examines the seal of the pit, opens the pit, drinks from it, closes and seals it again."

Solomon then sent for Benaiah, son of Jehoiada, his chief chamberlain. Solomon gave Benaiah a chain on which was engraved the Holy Name of God, some pieces of wool, and skins of wine and sent him to capture Asmodeus. Benaiah went to Asmodeus' mountain while the demon was away, bored a hole into the pit from below, drawing off the water; he stopped the hole with the wool and then filled the pit with wine poured through the cracks around the rock covering the pit.

When Asmodeus returned, he examined the seal and seeing that it was not touched, he removed the stone covering the pit and found wine. Asmodeus would not drink the wine and recited Biblical verses that inveigh against wine to help him resist drinking. But his thirst overcame him, and he drank deeply and fell asleep.

Then Benaiah wound the chain about Asmodeus' neck, and when the demon awoke and tried to free himself, Benaiah chanted, "The Name of the Lord is upon thee; the Holy Name is upon thee." So Asmodeus allowed himself to be led to Solomon.

[3] Tractate Pirke Aboth 4:22

[4] "For the house, when it was in building, was built of stone made ready at the quarry; and there was neither hammer nor axe nor any tool of iron heard in the house, while it was in building." I Kings 6:7

[5] Asmodeus and his family were considered Jewish demons; therefore they would follow the same rituals as Jews, including daily attendance at the study sessions.

Solomon said to Asmodeus, "I want to build the House of the Sanctuary and cannot do it without the *shamir*." The demon replied, "It was not given to me but to the Angel of the Sea, and the Angel of the Sea entrusted it to the heath cock under sacred oath. The heath cock uses the *shamir* to make the world more habitable for men. He takes the *shamir* to mountains where nothing grows, lays the *shamir* on the rocks, thus splitting them, and inserts seeds into the crevices which grow and cover the rocks."

Solomon sent men to find the heath cock, and they found his nest, over which they placed a glass. When the heath cock returned to his nest and tried to enter it, he could not, so he took out the *shamir* and placed it on the glass to split it. Whereupon Solomon's messengers grabbed the *shamir* and brought it to the king. But the heath cock was so brokenhearted at having violated his oath to the Angel of the Sea that he committed suicide.

Although Solomon had captured Asmodeus only to get the *shamir,* he kept the demon in chains until after he had finished building the Temple. One day, talking with Asmodeus, Solomon asked the demon: "How is it that you, king of the demons, are no more powerful than I, a man, who can keep you imprisoned?"

Asmodeus replied, "Take off my chains and I will show you." This Solomon did, whereupon Asmodeus swallowed the ring on which was engraved the Holy Name, spread his body so one wing touched heaven and the other touched earth, and flung Solomon four hundred leagues into another country. Solomon, finding himself a begger among strangers, said: "What profit has a man from all the labor he has done under the sun?"

This *midrash*, begun as an explanation of a minor passage—how could Solomon build the sanctuary without using iron tools—was probably embellished many times in the retelling. It ended as the explanation, plus an illustration of Solomon's wisdom, plus a cautionary tale about the evils that befall the greedy and those who break their word, plus a sub-story about how the mountains are broken down to make arable land, and concluded with a quotation from Ecclesiastes which tradition ascribes to Solomon.

The Talmud includes much aggadic material, about one-fifth of the Babylonian Talmud being *aggadah* and four-fifths *halachah*. But as with all the Talmudic material, the *aggadot* are strung here and there, sometimes because a particular *aggadah* has reference to the *mishnah* under discussion, sometimes because the rabbi who had the floor at the moment took off on a flight of fancy. But after the close of the Talmud, the literary spirit that had kept the great academies at work for centuries, as if seeking a new outlet now that its major work was done, turned to the compilation and ordering of *midrashim*.

Palestine, rather than Babylon, was the home of the *midrash*. There the Jews were under constant pressure and in constant danger, so the need for inspiring stories was particularly great. People thronged to the synagogues to hear the aggadist tell them stories of Israel's past—and future—glories, of God's constant concern for Israel. It made the degradations to which the Jews were subjected somehow bearable. But word-of-mouth was not enough. The people wanted the stories in a form which could be kept at home and read whenever their spirits needed uplifting. So the great written compilations of *midrashim* began.

The Talmudic *aggadot* could not, of course, deal only with glories; they had to explain the terrible realities which the Jews witnessed and felt daily. The third and fourth century Palestinian Jews wanted to know why the general whom Rabbi Akiba had hailed as the Messiah—Bar Kochba—had lost the last war with the Romans; why, in effect, God had forsaken Israel and doomed them to a miserable existence. So an *aggadah* in the Palestinian Talmud explained why the Emperor Hadrian could reduce the fortress of Bethar and destroy Bar Kochba and his army:

Bar Kochba had two hundred thousand men around Bethar, and each man had cut off a finger to show his hardihood. But the rabbis remonstrated with Bar Kochba, saying: "How can you allow the men of Israel to mutilate themselves?" Bar Kochba asked the wise men how he could put his men to the test if not by cutting off their fingers, and they said, "Accept in your army only those men who, at a gallop, can tear out by its roots a cedar of Lebanon." Bar Kochba tested his men as the wise men said, and he had two hundred thousand men of each kind. And when he went out to war, he said to God: "Lord of the Universe, be Thou neither against us or for us."

Hadrian laid siege to Bethar for three and a half years, but Bar Kochba and his army held. And Rabbi Eleazar of Modim sat in sackcloth and ashes in the city, praying each day, "Lord of the world, enter Thou not into judgment this day; enter Thou not into judgment today."

Hadrian was about to give up the siege when a Samaritan came to him and said that he could give the city into the emperor's hands. Hadrian agreed to continue the siege, and the Samaritan entered the city of Bethar by a tunnel and sought out Rabbi Eleazar. The Samaritan went to the Rabbi and whispered something in his ear. The Samaritan was seen and brought before Bar Kochba.

"What did you say to Rabbi Eleazar, and what did Rabbi Eleazar say unto you?" Bar Kochba asked the Samaritan.

The Samaritan answered: "If I tell you, the emperor will kill me. If I do not tell you, you will kill me. I would rather Hadrian slew me than you. Rabbi Eleazar told me that he would deliver up the city to Hadrian."

Then Bar Kochba went to Rabbi Eleazar and asked him what the Samaritan had said. And Rabbi Eleazar answered, "Nothing." "And what did you say to the Samaritan?" Bar Kochba asked. "Nothing," answered the Rabbi. So Bar Kochba struck Eleazar and he died.

A heavenly Voice was heard: "You have killed Rabbi Eleazar of Modim, the right hand of Israel, the eye of Israel. Therefore your right hand shall wither and your eye shall be extinguished."

The fortress of Bethar fell, and Bar Kochba was slain. The head of Bar

Kochba was brought to Hadrian, and he asked, "Who killed this man?" The
Samaritan said, "I killed Bar Kochba." "Then show me his body," said the
emperor. And they brought the body, but it was encircled by a serpent. And
Hadrian said, "If God had not killed him, who could have?"

The Romans advanced upon the city and slaughtered the inhabitants,
and their horses marched in blood up to the nostrils. . . .

Individual *midrashim* are not dated. To tie a particular *midrash* to a
particular year or place is as difficult as pinpointing the emergence of a
myth or folk tale in any culture. Even those *midrashim* identified by the
names of the Rabbis who spoke them may have been repetitions of stories heard before, or embellishments on a thread of a story dimly
remembered. But the compilations of *midrashim* can be dated, the major
collections having been put together from the sixth to twelfth centuries.

Most of the *midrashim* were Palestinian—but they were not local.
Just as there was constant cross-fertilization of the halachic material in
the Palestinian and Babylonian Talmuds, a process carried forward by
the constant interchange of scholars among the academies, so aggadic
material developed in many places found its way to Palestine and into
the Palestinian compilations.

Collections of halachic *midrashim* were made even before the compilation of the Mishnah in the year 200. Principal early compilations are
the Mechilta, the Sifra, and the Sifre. Mechilta, from the Aramaic word
for treatise, was originally used to denote any arranged collection of
laws. The word came to mean only the collection of halachic *madrashim*
based on Exodus, prepared by the school of the Tanna Ishmael, in the
second century. But despite its purpose, i.e., to be a compilation of laws,
the extant Mechilta contains more homiletic material than halachic.

Sifra, the Aramaic word for book, is a halachic *midrash* to Leviticus,
compiled by the school of Akiba. Sifre (books) is the halachic *midrash*
to Numbers and Deuteronomy—also with a large amount of aggadic
material. It, too, is ascribed to the school of Akiba.

Perhaps the most important of the collections of *midrashim* is the
Midrash Rabba, or Large Midrashim, which includes compilations of
midrashim on ten Biblical books—the five books of Moses and the five
Scrolls (Ruth, Esther Lamentations, Song of Songs, Ecclesiástes).
The books are identified individually rather than as Midrash Rabba:
thus, Bereshit (Genesis) Rabba, Ruth Rabba, etc. (There are also
smaller collections of *midrashim* on these books of the Bible, not
included in the Midrash Rabba.)

Bereshit Rabba is perhaps the earliest of the Large Midrashim,
having been compiled shortly after 500. The *midrashim* on Leviticus
and the Scrolls were completed later in the sixth century. Exodus
Rabba is dated about 700, Deuteronomy about 900; the last book of the

Midrash Rabba, on Numbers, probably was not completed until the twelfth century.

According to the Biblical story, the penalty for eating of the tree of knowledge was death. "Of every tree of the garden thou mayest freely eat; but of the tree of the knowledge of good and evil, thou shalt not eat of it; for in the day that thou eatest thereof thou shalt surely die."[6] How then did Adam and Eve live to beget the world? Bereshit Rabba explains it:

> As Adam stood naked and ashamed, for he knew his nakedness, God withheld Himself; He would not "strive to see a man in the hour of his disgrace." The Lord waited until Adam and Eve had covered themselves with fig leaves. But even before God announced the sentence, Adam knew what was coming, for he heard the angels speaking among themselves and also speaking to God.
>
> "How is it," the angels asked of the Lord, "that Adam still walks in Paradise, that he is not dead?"
>
> God answered: "I said to him 'that in the day thou eatest of the fruit of the tree of the knowledge of good and evil, thou shalt surely die.' But you did not know of what manner of day I spoke—one of your days from the setting of the sun to the setting of the sun, or one of My days of a thousand years. I will give Adam one of My days—of which he shall have 930 years, and seventy years to leave to his descendants.

One of the favorite folk tales of the Jews for centuries has been the *midrash* on Abraham and the Idols, differing versions of which appear in the different collections. One version says that when Terah the idol-maker, Abraham's father, left him in charge of the shop, a customer entered and asked the price of an idol.

"How old are you?" Abraham asked the man.

"Fifty years old," the customer answered.

"And you, who are fifty years old, would bow down to a thing of clay which we made only yesterday?" said Abraham.

Another version has an old woman come to Terah's shop to buy a good, big idol. "But what happened to the large idol you bought last week?" asked Abraham. "Thieves stole it," the woman answered. "You would pray and entrust yourself to an idol that cannot even save itself from thieves?" Abraham said.

In a third version, Abraham was left in charge of the shop and its idols. He took an axe and cut off the feet of the smallest idol, the hands of the next, put out the eyes of a third, and so on. Then he put the axe in the hands of the largest idol. When Terah returned and found the destruction in his shop, he called out, "Who has done this?" And Abraham said, "The largest idol took the axe and slew all the others. See, he still

[6] Genesis 2:16–17

has the axe in his hand. And if you do not believe me, ask him."

However, the Midrash Rabba, like the other collections of *midrashim,* is not entirely or even largely homiletic mythology. The collections include detailed examinations of the meaning of the Torah. The opening chapter of Exodus Rabba is an example of this literature:

Now these are the names of the sons of Israel, who came into Egypt with Jaçob; every man came with his household (Ex.1:1). Thus we read: "He that spareth his rod hateth his son; but he that loveth him chasteneth him betimes" (Prov. 13:24.) Ordinarily, if a man's friend says to him "So-and-so, smite your son," the man is ready even to deprive his friend of his livelihood. Then why "He that spareth his rod hateth his son"? To teach you that anyone who refrains from chastising his son causes him to fall into evil ways and thus comes to hate him. This is what we find in the case of Ishmael, who behaved wickedly before Abraham his father, but Abraham did not chastise him, with the result that Ishmael fell into evil ways, so that Abraham despised him and cast him forth empty-handed from his house. What did Ishmael do? When he was fifteen years old, he commenced to bring idols from the street, toyed with them and worshiped them as he had seen others do. So "when Sarah saw the son of Hagar the Egyptian, whom she had borne unto Abraham, making sport" (Gen. 21:9) [the word *mezahek* being always used of idolatry as in "And they rose up to make merry" (Ex. 32:6)] she immediately said unto Abraham: "Cast out this bondwoman and her son" (Gen. 22:10) lest my son learn of his ways. Hence "And the thing was very grievous in Abraham's sight on account of his son" because he had become depraved. "And God said unto Abraham: Let it not be grievous in thy sight because of the lad"—a proof that Abraham was subsidiary to Sarah in the matter of prophecy. Presently we read: "And Abraham arose up early in the morning, and took bread and a bottle of water . . . and sent her away," to teach you that he hated Ishmael because of his evil ways and sent him together with his mother Hagar away empty-handed and expelled him from his house on this account. [For otherwise,] do you really think that Abraham, of whom it is written "And Abram was very rich in cattle" (Gen. 13:2), could send away his wife and son from his house empty-handed without clothes or means of livelihood? But this is to teach you that when Ishmael became depraved, he ceased to think about him. What became of him in the end? After he had driven him out, he sat at the crossroads, and robbed and molested passers-by, as it is said: "And he shall be a wild ass of a man: his hand shall be against every man" (Gen. 16:12).

Another example: "Now Isaac loved Esau" (Gen. 25:28); hence because he did not chastise him, he became depraved. As we have learned: On that day, Esau the wicked committed five transgressions. He seduced a betrothed maiden, killed a man, denied resurrection, rejected the fundamental principles of religion, and despised his birthright. Moreover, he longed for the death of his father and sought to slay his brother, as it is said: "Let the days of mourning for my father be at hand; then will I slay my brother Jacob." He caused Jacob to flee from his father's home, and he also went to

Ishmael to learn of him evil ways and to get more wives, as it is said: "So Esau went unto Ishmael, and took unto the wives that he had Mahalath the daughter of Ishmael Abraham's son, the sister of Nebaioth, to be his wife."

Similarly, because David did not rebuke or chastise his son Absalom, he fell into evil ways, seeking to slay his father, sleeping with his concubines, and becoming the cause of his wandering barefooted and weeping, and of the slaughter of many thousands and tens of thousands of Israelites, as well as of other sorrows without end. For it is written: "A Psalm of David, when he fled from Absalom his son" (Ps. 3:1) and is followed by: "Lord, how many are mine adversaries become!" Depravity in a man's family is more grievous even than the war of Gog and Magog; for whereas in reference to the war of Gog and Magog it is written: "Why are the nations in an uproar?" (Ps. 2:1), in the case of Absalom it says: "How many are mine adversaries." David treated Adonijah in a similar fashion, neither rebuking nor punishing him, and therefore he became depraved, as it is written: "And his father had not grieved him all his life in saying: 'Why hast thou done so?' " (I Kings 1:6). "And he was born after Absalom." Was not Absalom the son of Maachah, and Adonijah the son of Haggith? Then why "And he was born after Absalom?" Only to show us that because Absalom had become corrupt on account of his father's failure to chastise him, while in the case of Adonijah we are told: "And his father had not grieved him all his life," therefore he also became corrupt. On this account does it say: "And he was born after Absalom."

"But he that loveth him chasteneth him betimes" (Prov. 13:24). This refers to the Holy One, blessed be He; because of His love for Israel, as it is written: "I have loved you, saith the Lord" (Mal. 1:2), doth He heap upon them chastisements. You will find that the three precious gifts which God gave unto Israel were all given after much suffering: the Torah, Eretz Israel, and the Life to Come. The Torah, for it is written: "Happy is the man whom Thou chastisest (instruct) O Lord, and teachest out of Thy Law" (Ps. 94:12). Eretz Israel, for it is written: "And thou shalt consider in thy heart, that, as a man chasteneth his son, so the Lord thy God chasteneth thee" (Deut. 8:5), and see what is written after this: "For the Lord thy God bringeth thee into a good land." The Life to Come, for it is written: "For the commandment is a lamp, and the teaching is light, and reproofs of instruction are the way of life" (Prov. 6:23).

But a father who chastises his son causes the son to have additional love for him, and he honors him, as it is said: "Correct thy son and he will give thee rest; yea, he will give delight unto thy soul" (Prov. 29:17), and it also says: "Chasten thy son, for there is hope" (Prov. 19:18). He will increase the son's love for him, for it is said: "But he that loveth him chasteneth him betimes" (Prov. 13:24); because he chasteneth him betimes, therefore doth he love him. You will find that Abraham chastened Isaac his son, and taught him Torah and to walk in his ways, for in reference to Abraham, it says: "Because that Abraham hearkened to My voice" (Gen. 26:5), and it is written: "And these are the generations of Isaac, Abraham's son: Abraham begot Isaac" (Gen. 25:19), to teach you that he was like his father in all things: in beauty, wisdom, riches, and good deeds. You must know that

Isaac was thirty-seven years old when his father was about to sacrifice him, yet though it says: "And Abraham was old and advanced in years" (Gen. 24:1), he bound him like a lamb and he did not restrain him; therefore "And Abraham gave all that he had unto Isaac" (Gen. 25:5)—a proof that "He loveth him who chasteneth him betimes." Similarly, Isaac used to chasten Jacob betimes, for Isaac taught him Torah and rebuked him in the schoolhouse, as it is said: "And Jacob was a quiet man, dwelling in tents" (Gen. 25:27). He learned all that his father taught him and then separated from his father, and secluded himself in the house of Eber to study Torah; therefore did he merit the blessing, and inherited the land, as it is said: "And Jacob dwelt in the land of his father's sojournings, in the land of Canaan" (Gen. 37:1).

Also Jacob, our ancestor, chastised his children and taught them of his ways, so that no dross should be in them; for thus it is written: "Now these are the names of the sons of Israel, who came into Egypt with Jacob," comparing them all to Jacob, because all of them were as righteous as he—a proof that "He that loveth him chasteneth him betimes."

A second major cycle of midrashic volumes is the Tanchuma-Yelammedenu Midrashim, ascribed to Tanchuma ben Abba, a famous Palestinian aggadist of the fourth century. These *midrashim* are arranged in the form of a question on *halachah*, a short halachic answer, then a longer homiletic interpretation. The Tanchuma Midrashim are arranged to follow the order of the weekly portions of the Bible read in the synagogue. The second part of the title comes from the opening phrase of many of the *midrashim*: *Yelammedenu Rabenu* (let our Master teach us). This collection dates from the sixth to eighth centuries.

The generation that built the tower of Babel was guilty of a tremendous crime—pridefully challenging God. But the builders of the tower were not put to death for warring against heaven (in the surrounding Hellenic culture, this crime, *hubris*, invariably led to death). Tanchuma explained why not:

The generation of the flood was utterly destroyed because they were guilty of rapine, while the generation of the tower of Babel was preserved despite their blasphemies. God dealt more leniently with the generation of the tower because He places the greatest value on peace and harmony. The generation of the flood hated one another in their hearts, and so were wiped out, root and branch. The generation of the tower, although warring on God, dwelt amicably together, loved one another. So they were punished, but allowed to live.

The Pesikta cycle of *midrashim* was compiled in the eighth and ninth centuries. These *midrashim* deal with the passages of the Bible read on holidays and special sabbaths. They were cut from the larger body of *midrashim,* thus Pesikta, from *pesek,* to divide or cut.

The fast of Tishah B'Ab, the ninth day of the month of Ab, which commemorates the destruction of the Temple by Nebuchadnezzar in 586 B.C., is a day of deep mourning and despair. On that day, the book of Lamentations, ascribed to Jeremiah, is read in the synagogue. A *midrash* in the Pesikta cycle gives the Jeremiah story a message of hope:

Jeremiah saw the smoke of the burning Temple from his village of Anathoth, and he thought that perhaps the children of Israel had repented, that the smoke was from their sacrifices of sin-offerings. But when he drew near and mounted the wall of the city, he saw the stones of the Temple falling. He ran, seeking the road by which the sinners had been taken away. "I will go with them and be lost with them," Jeremiah cried. He saw the path covered with blood and the footprints of the children taken by the Babylonians. And he knelt and kissed the bloody footprints. He came upon the exiles and embraced them and told them of a vision he had seen.

"As I came up to Jerusalem I saw a woman seated on a hill, dressed in black, her hair hanging down, weeping and waiting for someone to comfort her. I came up to her and said: If thou art a spirit, begone, but if thou art a woman, speak. And she answered: Do you not know me? I am she who had seven sons, and they are now dead. And now I do not know for whom to weep and for whom to tear my hair. And I answered her, saying: Art thou better than mother Zion which is become a wilderness for beasts? And she said: I am thy mother, Zion; I am the mother of seven sons, of whom it is written, she is withered, she who bore seven sons. Then speaking in the name of the Eternal, I said to her:

"The evil which has befallen thee is like the evil that befell Job. The sons and daughters of Job were taken away, and your sons and daughters were taken away. The gold and silver of Job were taken away, and your gold and silver were taken away. God threw him upon a dung-heap, and God has thrown thee upon a dung-heap. But the Lord your God prepared consolation for Job; so has He prepared consolation for thee. He doubled the sons and daughters of Job, and He shall double thy sons and daughters. He doubled his gold and silver, and He shall double thine. He cleaned away from Job the filth of the dung-heap, and He shall clean away thy filth. And thy habitation, oh Zion, which men of flesh and bone built, and which men of flesh and blood destroyed, the Lord God will rebuild in time to come, as it is written: He bringeth together the children of Israel."

There are many other collections of *midrashim*, and many more that have disappeared. There must at one time have been midrashic collections on every book of the Bible. The *midrashim* on Psalms, Proverbs, and Samuel are still known. *Midrashim* of Job, Ezra, Chronicles, and Isaiah are mentioned in ancient literature, but cannot be found.

The most complete midrashic collection was unknown until the nineteenth century, when it was found in Yemen. This is the Midrash haGadol, the Great Midrash. It includes *midrashim* on the entire Torah, some very ancient, some from such comparatively late figures as Rashi, Abraham ibn Ezra, and Maimonides. It could not have been compiled before the thirteenth century.

A *midrash* from the Midrash haGadol attempts to explain—or excuse
—some of the bloodthirstiness of the Bible, which casually recounts the
total destruction of cities and the wiping out of entire peoples.

Isaac instituted tithing, giving one-tenth of his produce to the poor, so he
was rewarded with abundant harvests. Even when the land was barren and
the year was without rain, Isaac's fields yielded a hundred times more than
other fields. But Isaac's wealth was the cause of envy among the Philistines.
This people, being wicked, begrudged their fellow man any good and
rejoiced when their fellow man fell upon hard times. So they envied Isaac,
and envy leads to hatred, so they hated him. In this hatred, they stopped up
the wells which Abraham had built, and the land was without water. This
broke the pact which Abraham had made with the Philistines—so they have
only themselves to blame if the Israelites later exterminated them.

Midrashim did not spring full-blown from the minds of inventive
sages, no matter how fertile. Story ideas were taken from folk tales of all
peoples and embellished with legendary material from all the myth-
creating nations. Rabbi Akiba and his disciple Rabbi Meir, both great
aggadists, were acquainted with Aesop's fables, and many of their *midrashim* sound like Jewish adaptations of these, particularly a series
involving a very wise fox. The Bible is remarkably free of demonology;
in fact, the philosopher Philo, first century, who tried to reconcile
Judaism and the logical systems of the Greek philosophers, asserted that
any mythological elements in Jewish thought had crept in from non-
Jewish sources. Yet only a few centuries later, the aggadists were filling
their stories with the Prince of Darkness, anthropomorphic celestial
bodies, and gigantic sea beasts. These could only have been taken over
from Persian and Indian mythology.

Much of this aggadic material was embraced by the church—which
understandably then rejected all halachic literature—during the widen-
ing split between Christianity and Judaism in the first five centuries after
Jesus. Many of the stories told about early Christian saints and martyrs
were retellings of *midrashim*.

For example, a *midrash* tells that when the Temple was completed
by Solomon, the priests gathered to place the Ark in the Holy of Holies.
But as they approached that awesome place, the doors swung shut and
none could open them. Then Solomon stood before the closed doors and
recited from Psalm 24: "Lift up your heads, O ye gates, even lift them
up, ye everlasting doors, and the King of Glory shall come in." Whereupon the gates opened, and the Ark was moved into the holy place.[7]
Thus, although he was born of Bathsheba and David, both guilty of
adultery, Solomon's legitimate right to the throne was demonstrated.

[7] Shemot Rabba

The *Legenda Aurea*—a collection that might be called the Midrash Rabba of the Church—tells much the same story about St. Basilius, an early bishop. The doors of Basilius' church closed when heretics would have entered, and none could open the doors until Basilius recited the passage from Psalm 24. Then the doors of his church opened. The reference to "King of Glory" in this later instance is rather obscure.

However, the debt of Christian legend to Jewish *midrash* was repaid in later centuries. *Midrashim* composed by European rabbis from the twelfth century on tended to draw on the religious and secular folk tales of the majority culture in which they found themselves. Late Jewish *midrashim* tell of men being turned into animals, an adaptation of the werewolf story, and of the coffin of a sage that floated hundreds of miles down a river, an adaptation of the story of St. Emmeran.

By its nature—the explanation of wonders and hidden things through illustrative stories and allegories—and because of its purpose—teaching legal and ethical values through homilies—the creation of midrashic material did not stop at any particular point in history. There was no canon of *midrashim* to be closed. There was no rule that *midrashim* had to be told in a particular language. Nor did they have to be composed by prophets—though ascription to a great sage was a help. So *midrashim* continued to be created into the modern era.

The purest strain of *midrashim* in more recent centuries comes from the eighteenth- and nineteenth-century *Chasidim*. Israel of Medjiboz, 1700–1760, the Baal Shem Tov (Master of the Good Name), founded this Jewish revivalist movement when Eastern European Jewry was at its lowest ebb. The Jews had virtually been wiped out physically by the Cossak Chmielnicki in the middle of the seventeenth century; they were emotionally and spiritually drained by the collapse of the False Messiah, Sabbatai Zevi; and the formerly uneasy tolerance of their regional lords had hardened into active persecution. By stressing the importance of prayer over learning, of joy in God's works and gifts over asceticism, the Baal Shem Tov gave the miserable Jews a religion of song and dancing, of general optimism and ecstatic religious experience. And one of the great joys of the *Chasidim* was to listen to their wonder-working rabbis tell stories that gave light upon—and made light of—their plight. For example, on the dangers of riches and the advantages of poverty:

A rich man—who was, as in most Chasidic tales, also stingy—came to ask a blessing from the Chasidic Rebbe. The Rebbe took him by the hand to the window and asked the rich man what he saw.

"Why, people, a lot of people walking in the street," said the rich man.

Then the Rebbe took the man to the other side of the room and asked him to look in a mirror. "What do you see now?" asked the Rebbe.

"Only myself," said the rich man.

Then the Rebbe explained: "Both the window and the mirror are made of glass. But one is coated with silver. When you look through plain glass, you see people. When your vision is blocked by silver, you see only yourself."

The Chasidic *midrashim* are generally ascribed to specific great teachers or rabbis. Among the most beloved was the saintly Levi Yitzchok of Bereditchev. It is told of him that he was once asked this question:

"Moses was so humble that when God called upon him to go to Egypt to deliver the Children of Israel, Moses implored God to send someone more worthy. But when God called upon Moses to accept the Torah, why did he accept without hesitation?"

Levi Yitzchok answered: "Moses had seen the tall mountains come before God, and each begged for the privilege of being the one on which the revelation would be given. But God chose that little mountain, Sinai. That's why, when Moses was called to come up to that mountain, he did not resist."

Levi Yitzchok was also a great arguer with God. In the middle of a prayer, the Rebbe of Bereditchev stopped and said to God:

"Lord of the World, You must forgive Israel their sins. If You do this—good. But if You do not do this, I shall tell all the world that the phylacteries You wear are invalid. For what is the verse enclosed in Your phylacteries? It is a verse of David's, Your annointed: "Who is like Thy people Israel, a unique nation on earth!' But if You do not forgive Israel their sins, then they are no longer a 'unique nation on earth'; the verse contained in Your phylacteries is untrue, and they are become invalid.

"Lord of the world, Your people Israel are Your head-phylacteries. When a simple Jew drops his phylacteries, he picks them up carefully, cleans them, and kisses them. Lord, Your phylacteries have fallen to the ground."[8]

The *Masseh* books, written from the fifteenth century on in contemporary Yiddish, mainly for women, are also a form of *midrash*. The first Jewish novel, *Ahabat Zion* (The Love of Zion) by Abraham Mapu, is a romance of the days of Isaiah and King Hezekiah. It is also in the midrashic strain, albeit longer-winded than the rabbis ever would. have dared to be. I. L. Peretz, greatest of nineteenth century Jewish storytellers, was in the direct midrashic line when he wrote *Bonche Schweig* and a hundred other tales. So, too, are Sholom Aleichem in "Tit for Tat" and many others, S. Y. Agnon in his Jerusalem stories, and I. J. Singer, as well as his brother, the seemingly avant-grade I. Bashevis Singer. Among the distinctly native American writers are many who—

---

[8] Adapted from Martin Buber, *Tales of the Chasidim*, Farrar, Straus and Young, 1947.

admittedly or not—carry forward the great stream of *midrash*. Isaac Rosenfeld in his stories of King Solomon may be called an aggadist; half the stories in Bernard Malamud's collections would fit into a twentieth-century Midrash haGadol; and Philip Roth's "Eli the Fanatic" and "The Conversion of the Jews" have the same tone and purpose as the great *midrashim*.

Aggadah and *midrash* served one more purpose for the Jews. In most other religions, challengers of God (or gods) are blasphemers who are put to death, or they are founders of schismatic sects. The Jews have a tradition of challenging God—and they revere the great challengers. The *midrashim* enunciated this tradition and gave support to those who would publicly call God to account. The following *midrash*, from the Tanchuma cycle and other compilations, illustrates this tradition:

When God commanded Abraham to withhold his hand from sacrificing Isaac, the distraught father cried, "And man may tempt another because he does not know what is in his heart, but Thou knowest all things and surely knew that I was ready to sacrifice my son."

God said, "I knew it before it happened, that you would withhold nothing from me, not even your soul."

"Then why did You cause me to suffer so?" Abraham asked.

God answered, "It was My wish that the world should know what I know, that I chose you from among the nations with good reason. Now it has been shown for all men to see that you fear and love God."

Whereupon, God spoke to the heavens: "By Myself I swear."

Abraham heard God's words and said, "Thou swearest; but I swear that I shall not leave this altar until I have had my say."

So God told Abraham to voice whatever he had to say.

Then Abraham recalled to God His promise that out of Abraham's loins would come a seed that would fill all the world. "Who was that seed?" Abraham asked. And God answered, "Isaac."

Then Abraham recalled to God His promise that Abraham's seed would be as numerous as the sands of the seashore. "Through which of my children would these sands descend?" Abraham asked. And God answered, "Isaac."

Then Abraham said, "When You called upon me to take my son, my only son, Isaac, and to sacrifice him, I might have reproached You with Your own promises. But I did not. I said nothing. Now I call upon You, when the children of Isaac fall upon evil times and trespass upon Your Law, be mindful of the offering of their father Isaac and withhold Your reproaches, forgive their sins."

God said, "I have heard what you have said; now listen to My words. Your children will sin before Me in time to come and I will judge them on New Year's Day [Rosh Hashanah]. If they desire pardon for their sin, let them blow the ram's horn, and I will recall the ram that was substituted for Isaac. And I will not reproach them."

TEN

Commentaries and Codes

FOR ALMOST TWO CENTURIES after the closing of the Babylonian Talmud in 500, there were no important literary additions to the main body of Jewish learning. The academies continued as before; the subject matter continued the same: the Talmud. And the methods of teaching were the same, the methods which had previously produced the Talmud. But students and teachers were so steeped in the language and tradition of the Talmud, so enveloped by the physical and intellectual walls that had sheltered the Rabbis of the Talmud, that no additional written texts were necessary.

However, in these centuries the Talmud had moved beyond Babylon, had become known to the other communities of the Diaspora. Copies of the work had been brought into the synagogues and study houses of the dispersed communities of the Jews. The rabbis and scholars of these distant communities were not as thoroughly grounded, not as enveloped in the language and meaning of the Talmud as the Babylonian teachers. They could not so easily relate the *halachot*, the rulings on law, discussed in the Talmud to the practical questions that came before them. Letters were sent from the distant communities to the heads of the academies at Sura and Pumbeditha in Babylonia, seeking explanations of Talmudic statements and their application to specific local problems. The answers they received, called Responsa, were only opinion, but they had great authority. (The first recorded responsum was from Shishna Gaon,[1] whose term as head of the academy of Sura was from 670 to 689.)

Thus the first written commentaries on the Talmud, sporadic and unrelated to each other, were in the Responsa of the *Geonim*. There was

[1] The heads of the Babylonia academies were called *Gaon* (plural, *Geonim*), a title best translated as Excellency.

no effort during the centuries immediately following the closing of the Talmud to write down a commentary that would guide a student or a rabbi. But as the centuries lengthened, language changed and methods of study changed. Even the students in the Babylonian academies needed some explanations, some help with the already archaic language of the Talmud. So, about 900, Zemach Gaon wrote a dictionary of Talmudic words and phrases in which the explanations were of necessity a commentary on the original material.

The first connected commentary on the Talmud was the work of the most illustrious of the *Geonim,* Saadia Gaon, head of the academy of Sura from 928 to 942. A scholar of tremendous brilliance and breadth of intellect, Saadia was named head of the academy despite what the book-proud Babylonian Jews considered a most significant drawback—he was a foreigner, a native of Egypt. Although the academies were already declining—they were to close a few decades after Saadia's death—his contributions to every branch of Jewish learning brought Sura to a new pinnacle of authority. Saadia's commentary on the Talmud was lost, but it is known by references to it in the work of other scholars.[2] The last of the *Geonim,* Hai (969–1038), also wrote a commentary, of which fragments are known.

The Babylonian academies had been declining for generations; with the death of Hai Gaon, Babylon lost its position of centrality in Jewish scholarship, and therefore in law and authority. By the year 1000 there were strong centers of Jewish scholarship, and consequent authority, in Palestine, North Africa, Spain, France, Italy, and Germany. These centers differed as to their scholarly source: the North African and Spanish centers were, in effect, dependencies of the Babylonian schools; the French, Italian, and German schools were the intellectual inheritors of the Palestinian schools. The Babylonian *Geonim* were authority for all Islamic Jewry; the Jews of Christian lands looked more to the Palestinian authorities.

The advantage was with the European Jews; they had readier access to Palestine than did the Islamic Jews to Babylon. Travel between Spain and North Africa and Babylon was arduous and infrequent, so contact was mainly by letter. But the European Jews regularly sent pilgrims by ship from Italy to Palestine, and Rashi, for example, mentions the visits of Palestinian scholars to Northern France. Italy's position as the crossroads between Europe and Palestine led to its development as a particularly strong center of Jewish learning. In fact, Charlemagne,[3] who ruled

---

[2] Fragments of Saadia's Arabic commentary on the Talmud were found in the Genizah at Cairo in 1897 by Dr. Solomon Schechter.

[3] Some scholars hold that the French King involved was Charles the Bald, who ruled from 840 to 875.

from 768 to 814, had so high a regard for Jews and their learning that he moved a family of Italian scholars—Rabbi Kalonymos of Lucca—from Italy to Mainz to strengthen Jewish education in Germany.

But neither Asiatic center, Babylonia or Palestine, could maintain its dominance over the European and North African schools. In a tremendous burst of intellectual vigor, the Jewish scholars of Europe and North Africa produced during a three-century period—roughly, the eleventh, twelfth, and thirteenth centuries—a literature that rivaled in depth and importance that of the Rabbinic period.

A legend with strong historical evidence to back it gives another reason for the loosening of the intellectual bonds between Babylon and Islamic Jewry. In 960 four great rabbis set out from Bari, in southern Italy, to visit the European communities and to collect funds for the support of the Italian academies. The ship on which they had taken passage was captured by the fleet of the Caliph of Córdoba, and the rabbis were taken as slaves.The Islamic Jewish communities heard of the capture, and in fulfillment of the commandment which requires Jews to ransom Jewish slaves, they raised money to buy back the rabbis. Rabbi Moses and his son Chanoch were sold to the Jews of Córdoba, who immediately set them up in their own academy. Rabbi Chusiel was sold to the Jews of Kairouan in North Africa and similarly installed. Rabbi Shmariah was sold to the Jews of Alexandria and became head of their academy. Now, with great rabbis and flourishing academies, these centers of Islamic Jewry no longer needed Responsa from Babylon to chart courses through the sea of the Talmud.

The North African academies west of Egypt were very active for a period, producing commentaries and other works of exegesis. But toward the end of the eleventh century, and particularly after the rise of the fanatic Almohades sect among the Muslims, the Jews of North Africa had to take up the wanderer's pack again. Many moved to Spain and added luster to that country's Golden Age.

The Talmud was the same for all Jews, and the purpose of scholarship was the same—namely, to know and follow the Law. So the results of that scholarship were almost the same, with some significant differences growing out of different environments, different traditions of study, and different surrounding cultures. In addition, although the Babylonian Talmud was *the* Talmud for both groups, the European Jews also had a good knowledge of the Palestinian Talmud, adding to their scholarship a dimension that was largely missing from the scholarship of the Islamic Jews.

But more than geography divided the North African-Spanish Jewish scholars from the French-German-Italian scholars, more than the distance between their native lands and the distance between the academies in which they had their intellectual roots.

> In general . . . the Halachic literature of the Jewries under Mohammedan rules is distinguished by its simplicity, clearness, and systematization. That of the West European Jewries, on the other hand, is distinguished by mental acumen and scholastic analysis but lacks the above-named qualities. It is for this reason that the Halachic activity of the former Jewries (Spanish-African) was developed more along the lines of code making and Responsa, giving plain decisions on legal matters, while that of the latter Jewries (West European) followed more in the line of commentaries and *novellae* where mental acumen can be displayed. That there were scholars in both Jewries engaged in all lines of Halachic literature is needless to say.[4]

The two major figures of the period appear to bear out Dr. Waxman's thesis. The Spanish-African Maimonides is *the* codifier of the Talmud; Rabbi Solomon ben Isaac, called Rashi, a Frenchman educated in Germany, was the ultimate commentator on the Talmud.

The Spanish commentators on the Talmud, including Maimonides, attempted to bring order, to systematize the vast "ocean of Talmud." For example, the commentary of Rabbi Chanannel of the Spanish-African school summarizes the contents of the Talmudic passages, extracting the legal opinions imbedded therein. The French-German commentators, on the other hand, did not systematize. They stuck closely to the text, explaining words, expressions, and subsections of subsections.

The Spanish commentaries were generally the work of individual scholars. The French-German commentaries were generally the work of schools. The Spanish commentaries were generally intended as guides for rabbinical courts and for ordinary Jews who did not study Talmud every day but needed immediate decisions on law. The French-German commentaries were generally intended as aids to students and scholars. Rather than offer quick answers, as did the southern commentaries, the works of the northern schools were incentives to further study that might lead to answers.

The French-German school of Talmudic commentators was founded by Gershom ben Jehudah (960–1028). A native of France, Rabbi Gershom studied in Mainz, Germany, and established an academy to which came students from throughout the continent. When these students returned to their homes, the authority of their great teacher went with them. As a result, the opinions on law given by Rabbi Gershom were decisive, not only in the community in which he had authority, but

---

[4] Meyer Waxman, *History of Jewish Literature,* Vol. II, Bloch, 1938.

everywhere in Europe. Thus he was called the "Light of the Exile." And thus it was that Rabbi Gershom's ban on polygamy, a practice sanctioned by the Torah and the Talmud but not practiced for centuries, was universally accepted by western Jews.

Rabbi Gershom's major contribution to Talmudic exegesis was to do the groundwork necessary to the later commentators: he prepared the definitive copy of the Talmud. Since this many-volume work had been reproduced only by hand copy, done in many communities and countries over five centuries, sometimes under the most trying circumstances, it had suffered many errors and excisions. The books studied in the *Beth haMidrash* in Worms may have been sufficiently different from those studies in Córdoba or Lucca or Troyes to have caused substantial differences in interpretation. Rabbi Gershom obtained copies of the Talmud from all over the world, compared them, and through great scholarship and an intuitive sense of rightness, re-created the correct text.

There is a commentary ascribed to Rabbi Gershom, but this was the work, not of the Rabbi himself, but of generations of scholars at his school. According to scholars, this commentary is more properly titled the Mayence (Mainz) Commentary.

Much like modern students, the pupils at the academies in France and Germany kept notebooks on the comments and explanations offered by their teachers. And, again much like their modern counterparts, the eleventh- and twelfth-century students at the Talmudic academies handed down their notebooks from generation to generation of pupils. The notebooks of the students of a particular teacher tended to be much the same, differing only according to the ability of the individual student to abstract and generalize from what he had heard. Students also added notes they read in their fellow students' notebooks and, if they were bright enough, included their own thoughts on the passages under discussion in class. These notebooks were called *kuntres*, from the Latin *commentarius*, a notebook or commentary. (Despite its Latin derivation, the word was given a Hebrew plural ending—*kuntresim*.)

Rabbi Solomon ben Isaac—called Rashi from *RA*bbi *SH*lomo ben *I*saac—was born in 1040. He began his monumental commentary on the Talmud in the *kuntres* he kept and copied as a student in the academies at Worms and Mainz. Rashi's notebook therefore included many of the *kuntresim* popular during his student days, and much of the Mayence Commentary. On his return home to Troyes, where he kept vineyards and made wine, Rashi completely rewrote his notebook, extending it, adding to it as his studies took him deeper and deeper into the ocean of the Talmud. When Rashi became head of his own academy, he used his *kuntres* as the classroom text and tested it against the intellectual needs and ambitions and searchings of his students. Every sentence and expression was put before generations of students, reworded if the students found that a particular commentary lacked clarity, expanded if the students found it insufficient. This great commentary on the Talmud of Rabbi Solomon ben Isaac became the commentary that is published as an integral part of the printed Talmud.

Rashi's genius lay in his encyclopedic knowledge of the subject, in his love of the Torah and the Talmud, in his intuitive sense of both scholarly and stylistic rightness. He had, in memory, the entire body of both Talmuds, of all the Geonic literature, of the *Midrashim* known to that time, and all the books written on the Talmud. When a passage of the Talmud was under discussion, Rashi could offer his students all the explanations, all the various versions, all the illustrative comments made on the passage during half a millennium. Since the Talmud has no punctuation marks, Rashi's commentary generally indicates whether a sentence ends in a period or should be read as a question. Where the dialogue of the Rabbis made identification of the speakers difficult, Rashi indicated who was speaking. Where necessary for complete understanding, Rashi gave historical notes, described the customs of the times, and located geographical places. And since his students were French-speaking, Rashi used French words when he wasn't sure that a Hebrew or Aramaic explanation would suffice.

At the time of his death, Rashi had about completed the third draft of his commentary. After his death his students lovingly made a complete fourth draft, using the best versions of the third and filling in the lapses from Rashi's own notes. Completion of Rashi's work and its adoption as the definitive commentary had a very positive effect upon future students, but a negative effect on historical scholarship. Rashi's work was so complete and satisfactory that it was no longer necessary to study the other works of Talmudic exegesis that had had authority before his time. Unused by students, these earlier works disappeared.

Rashi's studies were not limited to the Talmud. He also wrote a commentary on the Pentateuch which was even more widely used for several centuries than his commentary on the Talmud. Rashi on the Torah was translated into Latin, German, and English and was a major sourcebook for Church scholars. The monk Nicholas of Lyra quoted Rashi so often that he was called Rashi's Ape. When Martin Luther translated the Bible from the original Hebrew, he leaned heavily on Nicholas of Lyra—so the German Lutheran Bible reflects much of Rashi's commentary on the Pentateuch.

An example of Rashi's method is seen in the following portion of his commentary on Deuteronomy. The comment is on two phrases from the Shema, the sole creedal statement of the Jew: "Hear, O Israel, The Lord our God, the Lord is One," and "thou shalt love the Lord thy God with all thy heart, and with all thy soul, and with all thy might." Rashi explains:

"The Lord our God, the Lord is One" means the Lord who is our God is not at present the God of the other peoples of the world. But He will eventually be the One sole God of all the world, as it is said in Zechariah 14:9, "In that day shall the Lord our God be One and His name One."

"Thou shalt love the Lord thy God" means to fulfill his commandments out of love (rather than fear) because one who acts out of love acts from a higher motive than one who acts out of fear. One who acts out of fear of his master may run off when his master troubles him too much, while one who acts out of love will endure all for his beloved.

After Rashi, and the acceptance of his commentary, the tremendous intellectual ferment and energy that had previously gone into direct Talmudic exegesis had to find a new outlet. The scholars of the French and German academies found this outlet in the production of *Tosaphot*, additions. For 150 years after Rashi's death, the scholars turned out comments, comments on comments, fine distinctions on points of law, discussions, and analyses—all based on the Talmud. In effect, it was as if the great days of the Talmud had been reborn. Just as the Rabbis of the Talmud produced the Gemarah, a commentary on and expansion of the Mishnah, so the Tosaphists produced a commentary on the Gemarah. Great scholars rivaled each other in the depth and brilliance and vivacity of their discussions of the Gemarah, even resurrecting the method of the Rabbis: *pilpul*. In style and method and field of study, the Tosaphists were akin to the Scholastics in the Christian universities of the time.

Commentary was one method of explicating the Talmud, but it was primarily a tool for the scholar; it was not suited to the needs of the ordinary worker or man of affairs. The Mishnah may have been deliberately constructed without apparent logical form or system so that those who sought knowledge would have to study deeply. But the non-student, the businessman, the farmer, or the artisan also needed to know—and he didn't have the background or the time to search the commentaries. What was needed was a code, a rearrangement, a listing, even an index by which the ordinary man could find what he needed to know.

During the centuries after the completion of the Talmud, some of the *Geonim* attempted to write codes. Impetus to the writing of codes came from the development of the anti-Rabbinic Jewish sect of Karaites. Since the Karaites challenged the Talmud, and Talmudic decisions were often a mystery to the ordinary Jew, the *Geonim* had to develop quick references that would tell the ordinary Jew what was Law and what was not. The most important of the codes of the Geonic period was the *Halachot Gedolot*—the large collection of *halachot*. Saadia Gaon and the last of the *Geonim*, Hai, also wrote small codes of laws covering specific problems in daily life. Saadia's codes, for example, included "On

Inheritance," "On Pledges," and "On Testimony and Contracts."

The leaders of the North African academies also attempted to codify portions of the Talmud, but it was left to the greatest of these African sages to produce the first comprehensive code. He was Isaac Alfasi, Rabbi of Fez. Alfasi had to flee from the Almohades to Spain when he was seventy-five years old. But having found sanctuary, he did not seek an old man's peace in retirement. He established a new academy and wrote his great code—which he also called the Halachot, patterned after the earlier Gaonic Halachot Gedolot. But Rabbi Isaac's code has always been called simply the Alfasi. The Alfasi is essentially an abridgment of the Talmud; it is important because of Alfasi's manner of abridging. The Rabbis of the Talmud often differed and frequently could not arrive at a unanimous decision on what was Law. Alfasi, following rules of his own devising, determined which decisions were authoritative; he excluded from his code those decisions he considered invalid. Although a member of the African-Spanish school, he knew the Palestinian Talmud and was the first codifier to use it as a check on the Babylonian sages.

An epigram that has been repeated by Jews for eight centuries says, "From Moses to Moses there was none like Moses"—meaning, between the Biblical Moses of Pharaoh's Egypt and the twelfth-century Moses ben Maimon of Saladin's Egypt, there was no rival to the latter. Moses ben Maimon, a genius of law and logic, a seminal philosopher, and an innovative physician, was born in 1135 in Córdoba. Son of the *dayan,* or judge, of the Jewish community of that city, Moses and his family had to flee the Almohades when he was fifteen. After years of wandering in Spain, North Africa, and Palestine, the Maimon family finally reached Egypt in 1165. And during fifteen years of wandering, Moses studied and wrote. His first work, a treatise on the calendar, was published when he was twenty-three; his second, *Logical Terms,* was published a few years later. These, like most of his later works, were written in Arabic and had to be translated into Hebrew for European Jews.

In 1168, when Maimonides[5] was thirty-three years old and already court physician to the Sultan Saladin, he published the first of his great works, his commentary on the Mishnah. Twelve years later, in 1180, he published his second enduring monument, a codification of the Talmud the *Mishneh Torah,* and in 1190, one of the western world's great works of philosophy, *The Guide of the Perplexed.*

In the introduction to his code, Maimonides gives his reasons for undertaking the monumental task of arranging the entire Oral Law in

---

[5] Some Jewish scholars of the period had the Greek "son of" suffix, —*ides,* affixed to their names rather than the Hebrew "ben": Moses ben Maimon equals Moses Maimonides. The reason is obscure; the suffix may have come from Christian scholars, or may have been a mark of respect for great scholarship.

more systematic, understandable, and useful form.

At this time, when the trials of our people have grown, and wisdom is diminished, all the Responsa, commentaries, and Halachot of the *Geonim* are becoming difficult for many people to understand. So, too, are the Talmuds themselves, the Babylonian and the Palestinian, each so deep and complex that only men with trained minds can find in them proper decisions. Therefore, I, Moses ben Maimon, the Sephardi [Spanish Jew], girded my loins, and relying on the help of God, devoted myself to all the books and wrote this work. In it I have given the answers to all matters, defining what is permitted and what is not permitted, what is clean and what is unclean, and all other laws. Thus the Oral Law will be clearly arranged, for everyone to see without question and without differences of opinion. Briefly, the purpose of this work is to eliminate the need for other books on Jewish law. In it is collected the entire Oral Law, together with customs, decrees, and proclamations that were made from the time of Moses our teacher to the close of the Talmud, including the opinion and decrees of the *Geonim*. Therefore I call this work Mishneh Torah [Retelling of the Law], for a man should first read the Written Law [The Pentateuch], and then read this book, and he will know the Oral Law and will not need any other book.

The form of the Mishneh Torah demonstrates Maimonides' mastery of order and logic. He follows neither the haphazard arrangement of the law in the Bible nor the involved arrangement in the Talmud. Maimonides abstracted the 613 commandments or precepts scattered through the Pentateuch and used these as the skeleton of his work. He divided the commandments into fourteen categories, each a book, and grouped these into four major divisions: laws on the relationship between God and man; laws concerning the life of the individual—holy days, women and marriage, dietary laws, and vows; civil and criminal laws; and laws operable only when the Jews held Palestine—sacrifices, tithes, sabbatical years. Appended is a book Maimonides titled "Precepts for the Children of Noah," enumerating laws covering Gentiles living in a state governed by Jewish law. The code closes with a few chapters on the Messianic Age:

The prophets and sages looked forward to the coming of the Messiah, not so that Jews would rule the world, nor that the Jews should have dominion over Gentiles, nor that Gentiles should bow down to Jews, nor that Jews should eat, drink, and take pleasure, but that the Jews should be free of oppression and should have time to study Torah and gain wisdom, so that they may deserve the world-to-come. At the time of the coming of the Messiah there will be no war, no hunger, no jealousy or competition, and the sole occupation of the peoples of the world will be to know God. Therefore, the Jews who will be great in wisdom will conceive of their Creator in the highest manner possible to man, as it is written, "For the earth shall be full of the knowledge of the Lord as the waters cover the sea [Isaiah 11:9]."

In twentieth-century terms, the arrangement of the Mishneh Torah may lack systematic logic. But this fault, if it exists, is not Maimonides'. For example, Maimonides places the rules governing burials in the section of his code dealing with criminal law. This, in Maimonides' terms, is logical, since interment is rarely mentioned in the Bible, one of the few citations being in the passage dealing with disposal of the corpses of those executed by a court order. In general, any seeming illogic is due to the nature of Jewish law: there is no division between sacred and profane, between religion and reality, between sin and crime. Murder, incest, and desecrating the sabbath are all capital violations of the Law for which the Biblical punishment is the same.

The language of the Mishneh Torah is Hebrew, with some Aramaic words. Maimonides explains in his preface that he did not use the *style* of the Bible, because its usage was not sufficiently detailed for a legal code; and he did not use the *language* of the Talmud (Aramaic), because it was little known to the people. Instead, he used the language and the style known to the people.

Publication of the Mishneh Torah was widely—but not universally—hailed. Some rabbis, in those years of Almohades and Crusader persecutions, were repelled by Maimonides' ecumenism: "The teachings of him of Nazareth [Jesus] and of the man of Ishmael [Mohammed] help to bring mankind to perfection." Other rabbis saw in the code of Maimonides a threat. They feared that this book which simplified the Talmud would, in time, supplant the Talmud as the text for scholars. And in some places, this did happen. Perhaps the greatest antagonist of Maimonides' code was Abraham ben David of Posquiers, France. This scholar wrote learned refutations of Maimonides' choice of decisions in the code—and in that peculiar Rabbinic acceptance of contrary opinion, these refutations were published as an appendix to later editions of the Mishneh Torah.

Illustrative of Maimonides' style and method are the following passages from the Mishneh Torah:

There are eight degrees of charity. The highest is to give assistance to a neighbor who has fallen on hard times by making him self-supporting through a gift, a loan, by making him a partner, or by finding him a job.

The second degree is to give charity so that the giver does not know who received his charity, and the recipient does not know the giver. This is in fulfillment of the commandment of disinterested giving exemplified by the Room of Secret Charity which existed in the Temple, where the righteous deposited their alms and the poor were secretly aided.

Third is when the giver knows who receives his charity, but the receiver does not know from whom the aid came. Thus our sages went about secretly throwing money into the doorways of the poor. This is a proper course to pursue, particularly where the administrators of the community charity fund are not fair.

The next lower degree is when the recipient of charity knows the giver, but the giver does not know to whom he gave. Thus our great sages used to tie money in bags and throw the bags over their shoulders for the poor to pick up, so they would not feel shame.

The fifth degree is when a man puts alms into the hands of the poor before he is asked.

The sixth degree is when a man gives alms to the poor after he is asked.

The seventh degree of charity is when a man gives less than he should, but does so cheerfully.

And the lowest degree of charity is when a man gives grudgingly.

Every Jew is required to offer up his life for the sanctification of the name of God. But this applies only to the capital crimes of idolatry, unchastity [adultery and incest], and murder. One must choose death rather than commit these crimes. Anyone who does so has sanctified the name of God.

But if a Jew has a choice between breaking some other commandment and losing his life, he should yield to the sin rather than give up his life, for the Torah says that man is to *live* by God's commandments, not to *die* by them. A Jew who sacrifices his life by refusing to violate a divine commandment (other than idolatry, unchastity, and murder) is guilty of suicide.

If a person is critically ill, it is permitted to do everything possible (even violate commandments) to restore him to health, except to break the commandments against idolatry, unchastity, and murder. Where life can be saved, any remedy prescribed by a physician may be used, even though the remedy may be otherwise prohibited by the Torah.

Eight hours of sleep, being one-third of the whole day, is enough. One should not go to bed immediately after eating, but wait three or four hours. Heavier food should be eaten after the lighter food. Thus, if fowl and meat are served at the same meal, the meat should be eaten after the fowl. Some foods, are exteremly harmful, namely stale fish, stale meat, stale cheese, mushrooms, and wine fresh from the press.

Unripe fruits are to be avoided for they will spoil the body. Sour fruits are not good; they may be eaten sparingly only in summer and in hot climates. Figs, grapes, and almonds are always edible, either fresh or dried. Honey and wine are good for the old, particularly in winter, but bad for the young. In summer, a person should eat only two-thirds of what he eats in winter.

Wise men first learn a trade, then acquire a home, then marry. Fools marry first, then acquire a home if they have the money, then seek means of earning a living—or else seek charity.

A teacher must not be angry or upset when his pupil fails to understand what is being taught; he should go over it many times until the pupil finally understands. Neither should a pupil hesitate to ask questions of his teacher.

If the teacher loses patience, the pupil should say: "Rabbi, this is the Torah. I must learn it, even though I do not have the capacity for scholarship."

Just as a pupil must respect his teacher, so the teacher must respect his pupils. The sages said: "Let the honor of the students be to you as your own." Pupils increase the knowledge of the teacher and broaden his understanding. A sage said: "I have learned much from my teachers, more from my fellow rabbis, but most from my students."

A synagogue may be turned into a house of study, but a house of study may not be turned into a synagogue, because the holiness of a house of study is greater than that of a synagogue: objects may be raised to holier use but not lowered to less holy use.

We have never heard of a Jewish community without a communal charity fund. Anyone who spends thirty days or more in a town is compelled to contribute toward the public charity. No one ever becomes impoverished by giving charity.

Beginning about the twelfth century, Jews were forced to withdraw from intellectual, and finally even from physical, contact with their European neighbors. They were expelled first from England, then France, the Rhineland, Spain, and Portugal. They were decimated, some communities totally destroyed, by Crusader armies, by mobs whipped into religious frenzy, or simply by legal proscriptions against their usual means of earning their livelihood. As persecutions increased and daily life become burdensome, the Jews turned inward. The great minds among them gave up wide-ranging cultural pursuits—philosophy and poetry, science and mathematics, grammar and lexicography—and restricted themselves to the Torah and the Talmud. In searching for and solving the intricate problems in these books, the Jews found outlet for their spiritual needs and intellectual vigor.

Nor was this merely an exercise in mental acrobatics. Piety increased as persecution increased. Ritual and ceremony and tradition were a blessing rather than a burden, for they gave form and meaning to life in what seemed a formless and senseless world. If they were to be killed for the manner of their worship, reasoned the Jews, they wanted to be sure that every jot and tittle of that practice was faithfully observed.

The rabbis and scholars searched and commented and codified so that every Jew would know exactly what was required of him, and when, and the manner of fulfilling the requirement. Every scholar compiled his own code, often without adding anything to the great codes, but translating the general code to the specifics of his own community and his own generation.

One important code was produced during this period. About two centuries after Maimonides, Rabbi Jacob ben Asher produced a code he called the *Sefer ha Turim*, the Book of Rows, so-called after the four rows of gems on the breastplate of the Biblical High Priest. This code, and Rabbi Jacob himself, became known as the Tur. Although a Spanish Jew, the Tur was completely familiar with both Spanish and French-German schools of Talmudic exegesis, and his code was an excellent synthesis of the content and methods of both schools. This quality and the Tur's light, crisp style caused his code to be accepted as authoritative for the next two centuries.

By the sixteenth century, the Jews of Europe were so scattered that the unifying strength of local custom, of "how our fathers used to do it," called *minhag* in Hebrew, had almost disappeared. In communities where refugee Jews from Spain, France, Germany, and Italy each tried to hold on to the past, fierce quarrels broke out as to which *minhag* would obtain. In some places a formal community—meaning a community with a synagogue, a school, and a community charitable fund— could not be organized because of these divisions. It was time for a definitive, universal, and authoritarian code. This was provided by the *Shulchan Aruch* of Joseph Caro.

Caro was a Spanish Jew until the expulsion in 1492. Thereafter he lived in Bulgaria, in Adrianople, coming finally to Safed in Palestine, where he became head of the Kabbalist community. After twenty-five years of work, Caro produced what he hoped would be his great work, his monument, a codification of the law he called the *Beth Joseph*, the House of Joseph. But the Beth Joseph was a very large and complex work, and students did not take to it easily. So Caro wrote a digest which he called the *Shulchan Aruch,* the Prepared Table, meaning it to serve as a study guide to the larger work.

The Shulchan Aruch was based on the codes of Maimonides, Alfasi, and the Tur—in part because these were the definitive works of codification of the law, and in part because although Caro was known as a great scholar, he did not have the authority necessary to put his work on a plane with the others. In choosing among the three prior codes, Caro accepted as definitive any opinion which was held by at least two of the three older codes. Where there was no majority opinion among the three, Caro drew his own from the basic source, the Talmud.

This was his method of work; as to presentation, the Shulchan Aruch stated decisions flatly, without question, and with absolute authority—unlike the "on the one hand and on the other hand" pattern of earlier sources. The weary, wandering, and dispirited Jews grabbed at this law which was easy to understand and didn't trouble them with if's, and's, and but's. The Sephardic Jews accepted it almost immediately as *the* authority. The Ashkenazic Jews accepted it as completely, after it was amended by Rabbi Moses Isserles of Poland.

The accidents of history helped a great deal in placing the Shulchan Aruch in this powerful position. For one thing, it was the first code written after the invention of the printing press and so was immediately and widely distributed. It didn't have to wait for slow, laborious, and expensive copying. Second, most exiled Jews—and half the Jews of the world were exiled—were not yet settled in their new homes; they had not yet established new academies; their rabbis were too busy with practical matters to immerse themselves in study. Everyone welcomed the easy-to-use, authoritative list of do's and don't's in the Shulchan Aruch. This was also the period of greatest activity and influence of the mystic Kabbalist, who were too busy attempting to plumb the mysteries of acrostics and numerology to study the Talmud. They, too, grabbed at the easy answers in the Shulchan Aruch.

So Caro's code, which, as just another code, however scholarly, might have served a positive purpose in the continuing development of Judaism, became a strait jacket and eventually a dead hand on what was until then a moving, progressing religion. The Shulchan Aruch tended to stifle scholarship rather than stimulate it as earlier codes had done. It tended to freeze sixteenth-century concepts on future generations of Jews.

The great work of codifying the Law was ended. Maimonides had made a system of it; the Tur had sifted it critically; Caro had unified and frozen it.

ELEVEN

The Responsa: The Living Law

IF ONE OF THE DISTINGUISHING MARKS of a nation is that the people within it are governed by the same legal code, the Jews are, in that one sense, what their detractors have claimed: a supranational nation. Jewish law has governed Jews in Asia, Africa, Europe, and the Americas. It has governed not only their religion but also their family affairs and commercial life, and has even regulated internal taxation. The only area in which Jewish law was not operative during the last millennium was in criminal law (although Jewish criminal law was applied in Spain as recently as the fifteenth century). The usual forms of legal punishment for crime—imprisonment, corporal and capital punishment—belonged to the civil authorities. This Jewish law was not intended to supersede local law; Jews obeyed the King's (or the Parliament's) law at least to the extent that other residents of the state did. But the Jews superimposed on local law their stricter code. They paid taxes to the king, to the baron, and also to the Jewish community fund. They paid to king and baron because local law demanded it, they paid into the community fund because Jewish law required it.

A body of law that has to cover simultaneously the Jews of Italy, France, Germany, and England has to be extremely resilient; it has to have the ability to adapt quickly to the many different conditions prevailing in the many kingdoms in which Jews lived. The mechanism that made Jewish law so adaptable was the system of Responsa.

Despite its many codes and codifiers, Jewish law is more case law than code or statute law; within broad limits, the decisions of judges establish, and sometimes change, the meaning of the statue. Because of the peculiar nature of the Jews' dispersed condition, a case sometimes had to be decided by judges several thousand miles from the place where the question arose. Sometimes the questions raised were hypothetical rather than specific to an individual case. The Responsa—the judgments on the cases, the answers to the questions—were generally in the form of letters and represented the learned opinion of the rabbi rather than judicial dicta.

The Responsa literature, however, is much more than a record of case law. Because a responsum often dealt with a particular problem of a particular Jew or Jewish community in a particular time and place, these legal opinions and essays are a documentary history of the Jews. Often, they provide the only contemporary record of their life and times and conditions.

For example, an eyewitness description of the destruction of the Jewish community of Polni exists only because it is recorded in a responsum of Rabbi Menachem-Mendel Krochman of Nikolsburg (died 1661). The community of Polni was wiped out in the Chmielnicki massacres of 1648. A married woman of the community escaped and eventually sought a legal opinion from Rabbi Menachem-Mendel as to her status. There were no living witnesses to the death of her husband; was she a widow under Jewish law and permitted to remarry? In his responsum, the rabbi includes the entire petition—and the only record of a historical event.

The manner of living of Jews in Poland is described in a responsum by Rabbi Moses Isserles to a question that would appear, on its face, to be quite narrow. Rabbi Moses was asked whether it is required or permitted to affix a *mezuzah*[1] to the entrance posts of a Jewish street, or was it enough to place one on each individual house? The responsum includes a dissertation on how Jews lived in a Polish province—quite different from the enclosed ghettos of the West.

That Jews were smiths and ironmongers in Eastern Europe is shown in a responsum dealing with whether smelting fires can be kept burning through the sabbath. And the only historical source of an episode in the history of Silesia comes from a responsum of Rabbi Meir of Lublin. The Jews of that province were under edict of expulsion, but bought revocation of the edict for two thousand pieces of gold. The responsum adapted the law on redemption of slaves to the more modern threat of expulsion.

The Responsa form is not unique to Jews. Early Roman law leaned heavily on "answers of the learned," *responsa prudentium*. The Emperor Augustus gave certain learned men the right to issue Responsa which had the force of imperial edicts. The Moslem *mufti* is also the author of

---

[1] The *mezuzah* is a metal case, containing a passage from the Torah, affixed to the doorpost of a Jewish home. It is done in accordance with the Biblical injunction, "And thou shalt write them [the commandments] upon the door-posts of thy house, and upon thy gates. . . ." (Deuteronomy 11:20)

Responsa; the mufti advises the *cadi,* the judge, on the interpretation of the Koran. And the Attorney General of the United States, like the attorneys general of many states, can issue opinions on the meaning of statutes. While these opinions—or Responsa—are not binding on American judges, they certainly determine whether or not the Justice Department will view a particular action as a violation of law.

The Responsa on Jewish law go back to the period before the basic law was codified, that is, before the Pentateuch was canonized in the fifth century B.C. Malachi 2:7 gives the authority: "For the priest's lips should keep knowledge, and they [the people] should seek the law at his mouth. . . ." Since that time there have been periods in which there was a great deal of Responsa activity and periods when very few Responsa were issued. But at no time, including the present, has this form of law-making died out; Responsa are still sought and are still being used to determine the Law.

Early Responsa were oral; they identified or interpreted the Oral Law before that tradition was permitted to be written. But an oral responsum had limited use even in a geographically united nation. It could not travel very far without being garbled in the retelling. And oral Responsa were of even less use to a dispersed nation. So Responsa were written even before the ban on writing the Oral Law was lifted by the Rabbis. The Talmud deals with this question, and an early responsum on Responsa says that *new* interpretations could be written even if the older basic Oral Law could not. In any case, said another Rabbi, better that one article of the Law (barring writing the Oral Law) be broken rather than that the entire Law be forgotten or violated through lack of knowledge.

Once the Talmud was completed, a stream of letters poured into Babylonia, to the *Geonim* of the academies, asking for clarifications and interpretations. And an answering stream of Responsa poured out. This was the beginning of the Responsa literature that adapted Jewish law to the changing conditions of the world. From that beginning, the Responsa literature can be divided into five broad time periods:

1. Gaonic Responsa from the sixth through the tenth centuries.
2. Responsa of the pre-code era, eleventh and twelfth centuries.
3. Responsa of the twelfth through fifteenth centuries, mainly in the West.
4. Responsa of the sixteenth through eighteenth centuries, mainly in Eastern Europe.
5. Modern Responsa dealing with the changes brought about by political and scientific revolutions.

Even more broadly, the Responsa can be divided by type into those written before codes were widely used and those written after codes were universal. Most of the questions asked in the earlier, pre-code period were simply, "What is the law?" Many of these questions would not have required Responsa if an adequate code had been available. But the deliberate lack of organization of the Mishnah and the Gemarah, their unsystematic nature, made it difficult for any but the most learned scholars to find answers. So questions were addressed to the learned rabbis and answered in Responsa.

Once codes were written and distributed, particularly the universally accepted codes of the Tur and the Shulchan Aruch, there were readily available answers to these simple questions. The later, post-code Responsa dealt with far more complicated issues, with questions that were not explicit in the codes, or with questions on which the codes differed.

Responsa differed also between East and West, reflecting the differing life situations of the Jews in the two areas. The early Spanish and French-German Responsa reflected the more open life of these communities. Living in comparative freedom, the intellectual horizons of western Jews could expand, so their questions dealt with history and philosophy and theology as well as with the specifics of the Law. The later East European Responsa dealt mainly with narrow legal matters, reflecting the persecution and resulting seclusion of these communities.

The Responsa of the Gaonic period dealt mainly with questions of worship. The dispersed Jews tended to develop their own local customs and rituals—which were inevitably questioned by someone who remembered the "old ways." If the questioner created division, authority was invoked, and that authority generally was the head of an academy in Babylonia.

Language is often the first casualty of transplanting a people, and the Jews of the West tended to forget the second language of worship, Aramaic. So traditionalists fought modernists on the validity of Jewish ritual without Aramaic. One such quarrel was referred to Hai Gaon in the tenth century. A Spanish community asked Hai whether the custom of reading the Bible three times on the sabbath, twice in Hebrew and once in the Targum (Aramaic translation) was still necessary.

Hai Gaon's responsum said that the requirement to read in both languages was stated in both Mishnah and Gemarah. He ended his responsum, "Are we to say that this statement is no longer important? God forbid! . . . We did not know until now that they were neglecting the Targum in Spain."

The *Geonim* themselves seemed to place little historical importance on their Responsa. Questions were posed and answered as succinctly as possible, with a short "yes" or "no" if that would do, at length if required. But the *Geonim* didn't think highly enough of this literature to keep copies. Whatever Gaonic Responsa exist—there are twelve major collections—are from the copies kept by the recipients or from copies made in Cairo, the distribution point for mail between Asia and Africa and Europe.

African and European Responsa of the immediate post-Gaonic period had much the same character as the Gaonic Responsa. In fact, the Responsa of Rabbi Chananel and Rabbi Nissim of Kairouan are included in collections of Gaonic Responsa. And despite the proliferation of academies in North Africa, Spain, France, Germany, and Italy, the Responsa of the heads of these academies had almost the same authority as those of the Babylonian *Geonim*. But whether these Responsa became part of the permanent literature depended as much on accident as on the dedication of disciples. Alfasi and Maimonides wrote many hundreds of Responsa; they are known because they were collected by their disciples. But Rashi's Responsa, which may have totaled thousands, were not collected; the only ones known are those woven into commentaries.

Perhaps the most important responsum of the period was Maimonides' "Letter to Yemen." This long essay was written in response to an appeal from the Jews of Yemen, asking for guidance. The community was in danger of dissolution because the Jews of Yemen were being offered the choice of death or renouncing Judaism. Many Jews, particularly the young men, were accepting the religion of Mohammed; others were turning to astrology, to Messianism, or to Greek philosophy.

Maimonides answered the appeal in a letter to a head of the Yemenite community, Jacob Alfayumi, asking that the letter be read to every Jewish congregation. So successful was Maimonides' responsum in stiffening Jewish resistance to conversion that Yemenite Jews included a reference to Maimonides in their daily prayers from that day on. The "Letter to Yemen" said, in part:

My fellow Jews, it is important that you consider what I say here. Impress it upon the minds of your children and women so their faith will be strengthened. May the Lord keep us from doubt of His purpose. . . .

Ever since Moses received the Law on Mount Sinai, despots have made it their first duty and final aim to destroy our Torah by violence. These are the first of two groups who seek to challenge the Divine Order. The second group includes the most educated members of the nations against us. These attempt to destroy our Torah, not be violence, but by false logic and controversy. They use writings as the despots use the sword. But neither shall succeed. The God of truth will not permit it, because they seek an end beyond the power of man. . . .

My brothers, in the time of Nebuchadnezzar, Jews were forced to worship idols. And God destroyed Nebuchadnezzar. . . .

The Greeks tried to abolish the Torah in the time of the Second Temple.
. . . And God destroyed their empire and their laws. . . .

Do not be dismayed by persecutions, for these are trials to test and purify
us. Hearten one another; let the elders guide the youth and the leaders guide
the people. Accept these principles of our faith, for they shall not fail:

God is one, and Moses is his prophet. The Torah was divinely revealed
to Moses. The Torah cannot be changed or repealed. It cannot be supplanted
by another revelation. . . .

I see that you are inclined to astrology. Dismiss such thoughts from
your minds. In Moses' time astrologers predicted that our people would
never reach freedom. But Egypt was smitten by plagues. . . .

Those among you who predict the coming of the Messiah are wrong.
God will prove them wrong and will send His Messiah in His own good
time. . . .

May God grant that we behold the return of the exiles. May He take us
out of the dark in which He has placed us. May He remove the shadow
from our eyes and from our hearts. Peace, peace, much peace to you. Amen.

The nature of Responsa changed toward the end of the twelfth century. Until that time, intimate knowledge of the Talmud was limited to
the students in the Babylonian academies and the scholars in the West,
but by the middle of the twelfth century there were thousands of scholars and rabbis in Europe who were competent to pass upon the simple
questions, to say "yes" or "no," "permitted" or "prohibited." When
these students and scholars, well-grounded in the Talmud, asked questions of the heads of their academies, simple answers were not sufficient.
So Responsa tended to lengthen, to become legal essays with footnotes
and references to buttress the respondent's answers. Copies of these Responsa, which took a great deal of work and time, were kept by the writers and often published. The two most important writers of Responsa of
this period—important both in the kinds of questions put before them
and in the authority given their opinions long after their deaths—were
Rashi's grandson, Rabbi Jacob ben Meir, called Rabbenu Tam
(1100–1171), and Rabbi Solomon ben Adret (1235–1310).

Illustrative of the period and of the problems is a responsum from
Solomon ben Adret to Abba Mari ben Moses of Montpelier. The latter
had written about a recurrent Jewish problem, one that had plagued
Jewish communities from the days of Alexander the Great: the young
men were spending more and more time studying the Greek philosophers and less and less time studying the Torah and Talmud. Rabbi
Solomon laid down the law (as of the thirteenth century, of course):

You say in your letter: "I am not angry about one who possesses books
of Greek philosophers, for if there is something of good in them, it may justify the entire book. And even an unlearned person will not be misled, for
the names of the authors indicate that they are gentiles. . . ." But the reason

for our outcry is that study of these books supplants study of the Law. . . .

In truth, he who devotes all his time to the Greek books is unprotected from the danger that is in them. These books make the bitter sweet and the sweet bitter; the words of these books appeal at first to the heart, but in the end they cause dissension and disagreement with the True Law. . . . In fact, it is impossible for these opposites—Greek philosophy and Hebrew tradition—to come together. Can a man believe the Biblical miracles, while holding to the belief that it is impossible for a rock to give water? . . . In so far as the philosophers are concerned, he who believes in anything that cannot be deduced from their logic is an ignorant man who will believe everything. They alone are wise and we are animals. . . .

We are servants of God. He has made us, not we ourselves. We have decreed, therefore, for ourselves and our children and all who follow us, by the power of the rabbinic ban, that for a period of fifty years no member of our congregation shall study the books of the Greeks on natural philosophy and metaphysics, whether in their language or another, before he reaches his twenty-fifth year; that no member of our congregation teach anyone these philosophies until he has reached his twenty-fifth year, lest they follow these studies and turn away from the Torah of Israel which is above these wisdoms. . . . We exclude from this ban the study of medicine. Although this study, too, is based on the study of natural philosophy, the Torah itself accords the physician the right to heal.

This we have decreed as a ban over the Scroll of the Torah, in the presence of the congregation, in the year sixty-five of the fifth thousand."[2]

Evident in this responsum is the conflict within Rabbi Solomon between the scholar and the leader of a community responsible for its continuance. So he put three limits on his rabbinic ban: not all Greek books were included—the study of medicine was approved; the ban was limited to fifty years, after which another rabbi would have to judge in light of the situation at that time; the ban was limited to youths—mature men (those over twenty-five) who had established strong scholarly habits were excluded from the ban.

In terms of the number written, the greatest period of Responsa literature was from the twelfth to the sixteenth century. Almost every scholar and rabbi wrote Responsa. Two leading authorities alone composed a total of more than ten thousand Responsa: ben Adret is reputed to have written more than seven thousand; Rabbi Meir of Rothenburg wrote more than three thousand.

These were the centuries of almost universal persecution of Jews in Europe. The Crusades, the Black Death, religious fanaticism, and expulsions from England, France, Spain, and Germany resulted in the breakup of communities, in the movement of hundreds of thousands of expellees, in forced conversions. Each of these raised innumerable prob-

[2] The year 5065 of the Hebrew calendar, or 1305.

lems. Was the child of a forcibly converted (Marrano) father, whose mother escaped and returned to Judaism, a Jew? What was the situation of the mother? Thousands of Jews accepted death rather than conversion; at what point should resistance cease? Was a man who accepted conversion rather than death guilty of idolatry? These were problems involving not only life, but life in the hereafter. Added to these were thousands and thousands of minor problems (though major to the Jews seeking answers) in the communities into which the Jews fled. These were particularly numerous in the North African and Eastern Mediterranean communities in which the Spanish Jews found refuge. There bitter quarrels broke out between the "wearers of the turban" (Jews from Moslem countries) and the "wearers of the skullcap" (Jews from Spain).

In every litigation there is a winner and a loser. In a national court system, the loser can appeal to a higher court. But the rabbi's authority is limited to his own congregation; for the rest, only his scholarly attainments and reputation clothe his Responsa with authority. So it was inevitable that the very system of Responsa was questioned—and answered in a responsum. One of the great scholars of the period, Rabbi Jacob Moellin, wrote:

You say that one should not rely upon Responsa; on the contrary, I say they are good law and should be relied on more than the law given by the codifiers. For the codifiers were not present at the time the decision was made, whereas the writers of Responsa dealt with the realities of the case.

Illustrative of the way in which Talmudic law was adapted to meet the special needs of the day is the responsum of Rabbi Meir of Rothenburg on the purity—i.e., the right to return to marriage—of women captured by Crusaders.

The question concerns the *anussim* [literally, those under duress, in this case, the prisoners] of Dukenhausen. I am asked whether the women are permitted to return to their husbands. The Talmud says that a woman captured by the Gentiles for the purpose of killing [not for ransom and therefore who might have been molested] is not permitted to return to her husband, but that a woman captured for ransom [who would not usually be harmed] is permitted to return to her husband. But this is so only where the Jews are dominant. Here, the Gentiles are dominant, so even if the woman was captured only for ransom, she would not be permitted to her husband.

But in this case, there were other Jewish captives present [who can testify to her purity]. For the Talmud says that anyone is eligible to testify in her favor except her husband and her own slave. . . .

Therefore, in my opinion, these women, even if there were only one witness to testify . . . that they were not violated, are permitted to their husbands.

By the end of the fifteenth century, not a single known Jew remained in the entire Iberian peninsula, and the seats of Jewish learning in France and Germany had been effectively destroyed. Yet within a generation a tremendous volume of rabbinic literature began to pour out of new communities of Jews in Eastern Europe and the Turkish Empire.

Poland was a new place for the far-ranging Jews. There were no old communities of Jews into which the refugees had to fit. And, during their first two centuries in this land, the Jews were allowed to develop relatively freely; they were permitted to create their own institutions and government. So the rabbis had to create a new legal system, based on their ancient codes, of course, to meet the requirements of the new homeland. This legal system developed out of the Responsa of the rabbis of that time and place, particularly those of Solomon Luria of Lublin, Meir of Lublin, and Moses Isserles of Cracow.

Issues like the acceptance of women released from captivity were of tremendous personal importance, but they may not have been as significant in forming the culture of the Jews of Eastern Europe as seemingly less important questions. For example, covering the head: this was a long-held tradition among Jews in Moslem countries, but a comparatively new custom among northern Jews. However, since covering the head was a mark of piety (and perhaps of difference from the Christian), it caught on quickly and strongly. As always, there were nonconformists who insisted on going bareheaded. The question was put to Moses Isserles. He responded:

I do not know of any prohibition against pronouncing blessings with the head uncovered. To some scholars it is evident that one is forbidden to mention God without covering the head.[3] But I do not know the source of this procription. I even find disagreement on this question in the Talmud. . . . [Isserles cites the Talmudic passages]. . . . It is clear from this that there is no real prohibition against reciting the *Shema* [the basic creedal statement] with head uncovered, and that God did not burden the Jews with such a requirement.

But what can I do, since other rabbis have said that the head must be covered when reciting a blessing? I am surprised to learn that they even prohibit an uncovered head when not at prayer. I do not know where this prohibition came from. . . .

But I cannot be lenient in this matter. . . . Even without a prohibition, even were piety not involved . . . a scholar ought to follow the custom, since people consider an uncovered head a violation of Jewish law.

[3] Since a pious Jew would recite scores of blessings every day, each including God's name, he would tend to keep his head covered all the time if it was required to cover the head when saying a blessing.

So pervasive was the custom and the authority of Responsa that even the non-Jewish world had recourse to it in dealing with Jews. In the mid-eighteenth century the royal Austrian government asked a responsum of Rabbi Ezekiel Landau of Prague. The issue was the sanctity of a Jew's oath. The specific issue was whether a Jew would consider an oath binding if he took the oath on a Torah that was unfit for synagogue use because it was imperfect. (A Torah is imperfect if some of the letters are worn away or if it was incorrectly copied, even by a letter.) But behind this specific case was a much larger issue: the widespread Christian doubt about the validity of a Jew's oath to a Christian. This doubt, and the libel based on it, was first written into law by Emperor Justinian in the sixth century. And anti-Semites used the *Kol Nidre* prayer as proof of their contention that the Jews' religion permitted them to violate any oath involving Gentiles.

Kol Nidre (All Vows) is the opening statement at services on the eve of the holiest day in the Jewish calendar, Yom Kippur, the Day of Atonement. This prayer became part of Jewish ritual during the Gaonic period and has always referred to only two types of oaths: those forgotten and thus violated, and those taken under duress. Oaths violated because of forgetfulness had to be forgiven before the Day of Atonement, because the Jews hold that to break one's word profanes the soul, and atonement cannot be asked in this state. The oaths taken under duress were often oaths of acceptance of another faith, e.g., forced conversion. Recitation of the *Kol Nidre* prayer permitted Jews who had violated these two types of oaths to pray in the congregation of Israel. The prayer says:

By authority of the heavenly tribunal, and of the court below, with divine sanction and with the sanction of this holy congregation, we declare it lawful to pray together with those who have transgressed.

All vows, bonds, promises, obligations, and oaths wherewith we have vowed, sworn, and bound ourselves from this Day of Atonement unto the next Day of Atonement—may it come unto us for good—lo, of all these, we repent us in them. They shall be absolved, released, annulled, made void, and of no effect; they shall not be binding, nor shall they have any power. Our vows shall not be vows; our bonds shall not be bonds; and our oaths shall not be oaths.

And the congregation of Israel shall be forgiven, as well as the stranger that dwells among them, since the people have transgressed unwittingly. . . .[4]

The question of taking an oath on an unfit Torah was put to Rabbi

---

[4] Rabbis of all rites and divisions have tried to remove the *Kol Nidre* statement from the service, but it has so strong a hold on the deepest emotional well-springs of the Jews, it represents so much that was terrible and so much that was glorious in their past, that all demands to eliminate it have failed.

Ezekiel by an officer of the Imperial Court. Rabbi Ezekiel's responsum said:

> We Jews are commanded not to swear falsely even if we do not hold a Torah in our hand. Holding the Book is not pertinent to the taking of an oath. In essence, an oath consists of saying "I swear. . . ." This in itself is a valid oath. This is upheld in the Torah itself many times, in the Talmud, in Maimonides, in the Shulchan Aruch.

The responsum then cited the relevant passages from these books, explained their meaning, and continued:

> These explain clearly that the oath is valid without holding any object in the hands. Now we shall explain the Law in the case of someone who takes an oath on the Torah; and the case of one who takes an oath on an unfit Torah. . . .
>
> The custom of placing a book in the hands of one who takes an oath, or of having him place his hands upon the Book, is not to make the oath valid. It is to remind him who takes an oath of the punishments recorded in the Torah for taking a false oath. . . .
>
> Even if the Torah on which one takes an oath is unfit [for use in the synagogue], yet it retains its sanctity. For we are permitted to correct imperfections in the written Torah and read it again in the synagogue. . . . The Talmud says that if all the letters of a Torah were worn away except for eighty-five, we would still be permitted to violate the sabbath to rescue that volume from a fire. . . .
>
> All that I have written above is clear as to law and to practice. . . . The truth testifieth unto itself. . . .

Rabbi Ezekiel's responsum of oaths was part of the pre-modern world and dealt with an ancient problem. But Rabbi Ezekiel lived during the political and intellectual revolution when ideas of freedom, of modern science, of modern scholarship were already breaking the mold of the past. So among Rabbi Ezekiel's Responsa were some dealing with issues undreamed of by the earlier generations of rabbis. For example, he was asked whether the ancient injunction against cutting the corners of the beard—as a result of which traditional Jews go bearded—also barred use of a depilatory. Rabbi Ezekiel, a modernist, said depilatories were permitted.

The nineteenth century brought whole new areas of problems requiring new volumes of Responsa. Democratic revolutions brought open societies in which increasing contact between Jew and Gentile raised questions. New inventions and new methods of production raised questions. New ideas of worship raised questions. These questions were raised mainly in the West; progress and new ideas stopped at the Russian border, behind which lived millions of Jews. Many volumes of Responsa came out of Austrian Galicia and Hungary and Germany and

Western Europe; few came from the Pale of Settlement.[5] But beginning in 1881, Jews from Russia began streaking west, driven by the anti-Jewish May Laws of 1881. They moved to France and England, but mainly to America. In these new cultures, expressed in unknown languages, the Jews faced more thousands of questions. They sought answers to these questions from the religious authorities they accepted, those in the old country. Questions flowed out of America to Kovno and Vilna and Minsk and Pinsk and Kishinev—and Responsa flowed back.

Among the nineteenth- and twentieth-century Responsa that helped adapt Jewish law, and the Jews, to the modern era in Europe and America were these:

On using a church building as a synagogue: while Jewish law says that neither Christians nor Mohammedans are idolators, Jews have always worried about the Christian use of pictures, statues, and the crucifix as objects of worship. In 1858, a Jewish congregation in New York had the opportunity of buying a Protestant church and converting it into a synagogue. But had its former use spoiled it for use as a synagogue? The rabbi of the New York congregation wrote to Rabbi Joseph Saul Nathanson of Lemberg. Rabbi Nathanson's responsum said:

There is in New York a house of prayer, a Lutheran church. This was built as a private house and later turned into a church. . . . Over the lintel of the gate of the house is written in English "Welsh-Scotch Methodist Church" and the interpretation of these words is "Lutheran church of the descendants of the land of Wales and the descendants of Scotland." They pray and sing songs to "that man" [Jesus]. Then one man rises and preaches to the people about the greatness of "that man." These people are Protestants without any images or likenesses in the church. . . .

The law seems to me to be that, since the building does not include any likeness or image, it is permitted to turn it into a house of study and prayer, in fact it is in fulfillment of the commandment to thus sanctify God's name.

On eating sturgeon: in order for a fish or other creature of the water to be kosher (fit for food under Jewish dietary law), it must have fins and scales. Late in the eighteenth century, Rabbi Ezekiel of Prague, who had never before seen a sturgeon, was asked whether this fish was kosher. The correspondent sent a sample of the fish along with the request. Rabbi Ezekiel claimed to discern scales on the sturgeon and declared it kosher. For more than a generation the dispute raged. Counter-Responsa were written; booklets were published. After Rabbi Ezekiel's death, the combined rabbinate of Prague reaffirmed Rabbi Ezekiel's

[5] The Pale of Settlement was established by Catherine the Great to accommodate Jews absorbed into the Russian Empire after the Partition of Poland. At the time the Pale was created, Jews were not permitted in Russia.

decision. But the issue was never really settled; sturgeon is still suspect by ultra-orthodox Jews.

On music in the synagogue: the first Reform congregation of Jews was established in 1810 in Germany. The major difference between this and the traditional synagogue was that it had an organ, whereas tradition barred music in the synagogue. A storm of controversy arose. Rabbi Shem-Tov of Leghorn, Italy, was asked about the use of music. His responsum said:

> I have been asked by my brothers from a distant country what is my unworthy opinion as to the use in the synagogue of a musical instrument known as an organ. Those who favor it say it is the same instrument cited in Psalms [92:4]. Those who oppose it say it is a Christian custom, and that the use of music is barred by Talmudic law. What is the law on this matter?
>
> It appears obvious, in my humble opinion, that the organ is permitted. . . . The Rabbis of the Talmud who forbade instrumental music did so only in connection with wine, with levity. . . . [Rabbi Shem-Tov then cites the Talmudic passages.]
>
> But in the case of worship, where levity is not involved, music serves a good purpose. It gladdens the hearts of men, women, and children who come to hear, causing them to rejoice in the commandments of God—which is the essence of worship, since the Bible says, "Serve the Lord with gladness" [Psalm 100:2]. It is clear then that the use of instrumental and vocal music is both good and according to law.

On electricity: the widespread use of electricity created as many problems for legalistic Jews as any other invention of the modern world. Is electricity fire in the sense that a candle or an oil lamp is fire? Is work involved in closing a switch? Does picking up a telephone, operated by electricity, cause work to be done? And a hundred others. The first Responsa on electricity were quite liberal. Rabbi Isaac Shmelkes of Lemberg held that electricity was fire like other fires and that the sabbath blessings could be said over an electric light. Later Responsa denied that electric candles could be used as sabbath candles. Some rabbis held that so little actual work was involved in turning a switch that it did not violate the injunction against work on the sabbath. Later rabbis took cognizance of the tremendous work involved in creating the electricity, and the work it did, and forbade using electrical current in any manner on the sabbath.

On automation: a twentieth-century responsum dealt with a very modern question, the self-winding watch. It was, of course, asked of a rabbi in Switzerland. A watch may not be wound on the sabbath; is it permitted to wear a self-winding watch on that day since the normal activity of the body serves to activate the winding mechanism? The rabbi's responsum held that if the watch was running when it was put on, it could be worn; but if it had run down, it could not be put on—and thus started—on the sabbath.

None of the Responsa dealing with electricity and other twentieth-century marvels resolve the problems, for each day brings new inventions and new problems. Radio and television bring the problem of joining in prayers with a distant rabbi or cantor. The automatic switch brings the question of setting an automatic timer before the sabbath which will activate a kitchen range during the sabbath. No definitive answers have been given yet. And the answers are becoming increasingly academic for a growing majority of Jews.

But against this record of modern Responsa to relatively unimportant ritual questions are the Responsa of the Nazi period. Few documents in Jewish history describe as pointedly the history of an era, the sense of tradition, and the unquenchable hope intrinsic in Jewish literature.

In the period 1941–43, Abraham Kahana Shapiro was chief rabbi of Kovno, the major Jewish center of Lithuania. Into his office came hundreds of questions from the ghetto into which the Nazis had herded the Lithuanian Jews. Old and feeble, Rabbi Shapiro could not deal with all these questions, and they were given to Rabbi Ephraim Oshry to formulate Responsa. Among the questions asked and the responses given[6] were the following:

Question: Every day the Nazis force one thousand Jewish slave laborers to work at building an airport. The only food given these laborers is one bowl of soup. Many of the workers will not eat the soup because it is not kosher, thus endangering their lives. Is it permitted to eat the soup?
Response: Yes. . . . "The principle of lifting the ban on non-kosher food in order to save an endangered life may be applied in this case."

Question: Is it permissible for a man to save his life, so that he may join the partisans, by purchasing a certificate of baptism?
Response: Such an act is forbidden "although the purchaser of the certificate does so with definite mental reservations, believing still in the God of the Jews. In any event, it is our duty and privilege to suffer martyrdom, our duty and privilege to invite death rather than deceive the Gentiles into thinking that we have denied the God of Israel."

Question: A Jewish family had given up all practice of Judaism, including circumcision. The head of the family was killed by the Nazis as a Jew and the mother and children forced into the ghetto. The son wants to die as a Jew, and seeks circumcision. There are no pious circumcisers left alive in Kovno. Is it permitted by a non-practicing Jewish doctor?
Response: The doctor is permitted to perform the circumcision.

Question: The Germans have published an edict ordering death for any

---

[6] Translation by Jacob Sloan in *The Reconstructionist*, May 1, 1959.

Jewish woman who becomes pregnant. Is it permitted to use contraceptives, and abortion if necessary?

Response: Both are permitted.

Question: "On the sixth day of Marheshvan 5701 (October 28, 1941), two days before the destruction of the Kovno ghetto, one of the chief men of the city came to see me. This was a time when tens of thousands of men, women, and children were being slaughtered before our very eyes, and every resident of the ghetto lived in daily expectation of the same bitter end. My visitor told me that he could not bear to see the killing of his wife, children, and grandchildren—it was the German practice to force parents to witness the death of their children, husbands the death of their wives, and then to kill the horror-struck witness in his turn. Unable to bear the prospect of witnessing the suffering of his beloved ones, certain that his heart would break at the sight, my petitioner asked: would it be permissible for him to hasten his own end through suicide, though against our religion? In addition, he pleaded, he would escape a horrible death and ensure a Jewish burial in one of the graveyards in Kovno."

Response: "It is forbidden to us to publish any ruling permitting an individual to commit suicide under these circumstances. By so doing, we would be giving aid and comfort to the vile enemy. The Nazis have frequently complained that the Jews of Poland, unlike those of Berlin, refuse to commit suicide. Suicide at such a moment as this smacks of sacrilege, because it seems to indicate failure on the part of the Jews to place themselves in God's hands. Besides, the Nazi murderers are intent on throwing us into such despair that we shall cease to hope to be rescued through Divine intervention.

"Be it noted at this point that in all the Kovno ghetto there were only three cases of suicide. The rest of the ghetto continued to believe that God would not abandon His people. . . ."

Question: "Immediately after we were liberated from the ghetto, I was asked an important question, which touched not only the person who came before me but many other Jewish women as well who had survived humiliation and physical abuse by German officers. The specific question was this: A young woman of good family came to me crying that . . . she was one of our poor sisters who had been humiliated by the Germans. Besides abusing her body, the Germans had tattooed on her arm the legend: *Whore for Hitler's Troops*. After liberation, she had succeeded in finding her husband, and they hoped to resume their marriage and set up a proper Jewish home. They had lost all their children at the hands of the Germans. But, seeing the fearful tattoo on her arm, the husband was taken aback . . . before living together as man and wife they had first to clarify whether she was permitted to him. . . ."

Response: "Far be it from any man to cast aspersions on pious Jewish women in such a plight as this. Rather, it is our duty to proclaim the reward they will receive for their suffering. We must avoid causing them any unnecessary anguish. Certainly, husbands who have divorced their wives under similar circumstances have acted reprehensibly. We live in terrible times when such things are possible. Nor, in my opinion, need husband and wife in this case make any effort to remove the cursed legend on the wife's arm. Rather, let it be preserved and exhibited—not as a sign of disgrace and humiliation, but as the symbol of honor and courage, in behalf of those who were slaughtered. Let it be a reminder to us and to the world that God has taken and will take His revenge on His people's oppressors."

TWELVE

The Challenge of Philosophy —
The Guide of the Perplexed

PHILOSOPHY GENERALLY BEGINS in the questioning mind of an individual. It begins when one man, exercising his most human attribute, asks himself, "What is the true meaning of—," and realizes he must first ask, "What is truth?" and then, "What is meaning?"

On the other hand, religious philosophy, or a philosophy that seeks answers to questions raised by religiously revealed truth, is generally a group development rather than that of an individual. It evolves out of the confrontation of groups with differing cultures based on competing revealed truths.

During the ten centuries in which Judaism developed from the broad, unstructured monotheism (often denied in practice) of the tribes and the first kingdoms to the highly structured religion of the Second Temple, Judaism not faced by serious intellectual challenge. Intellectually isolated and insulated, tradition, custom, and the powerful hold of the prophetic revelation served as a substitute for philosophy. The continuing development of the Written and Oral Laws resolved competing ideas and took care of the intellectual doubts that arose in individual Jews.

But when Alexander the Great marched through Palestine on his way to Egypt, Jew and Greek met. After Alexander's death his empire split between Seleucid and Ptolemaic empires, and the only overland communication between the capital cities of Antioch and Alexandria was through the Jewish heartland. Hellenism confronted Judaism on every side; it challenged the style of Jewish life, the arts and crafts of the Jews, and the intellectual concepts of the Jews.

Living in a dominantly Hellenic world, the Jew had to become Hellenized; he had to become acculturated, particularly if he lived outside Palestine, and by the first century B.C. more than a million Jews lived in Egypt alone. Increasingly the Jews felt the need to reconcile their Jewish and Hellenic patterns of life and thought. A philosophic defense of Judaism became necessary. It was first offered by the aptly named Philo Judaeus of Alexandria (born 25 B.C.), the "first theologian, first psychologist of faith, first mystic among believers in monotheism, and first systematizer of Biblical allegory."[1]

The Bible is not a book of philosophy and could not in itself serve as the answer to the questions raised by Greek thought. The Bible did not systematically define the human condition, nor did it offer philosophical guides, other than ethical, to the solution of the problem of human existence. The Scriptures did not even recast the questions that should be asked, a proper function of philosophy.

Two books of the Bible did attempt philosophical treatment of at least one major area in philosophy—ethics. Job raised the question of whether man's ethical and moral conduct bore any relation to his earthly situation: in effect, whether there is any logic in the good life. Ecclesiastes questioned whether there is any purpose in life itself: in effect, whether living is worth while. But neither book came to grips with the problems in ways that would satisfy philosophers schooled in Greek rationalism.

One of the methods used by Jewish thinkers to reconcile revelation and reason was to redefine the philosophical problem and then show how Scripture could be used to provide the same answers as those arrived at through logic. Often this involved composing the differences between conflicting Biblical passages.

This was Philo's method in the first century. He attempted, sometimes with indifferent success, to show the Jews the kinship between their tradition and the wisdom of the Greek philosophers; he attempted to show the Hellenic intellectuals that the Scriptures were valid according to the systems of Aristotle and Plato. In so doing, Philo tried to combine two contradictory concepts of God: the Greek concept of God as First Cause or Prime Mover, the initiator of the universe utterly removed from man and incomprehensible to man; and the Jewish concept of the God, both initiator and continuing Creator of the universe and all within it, a personal God both incomprehensible and ever-known.

Philo's method was mainly to reinterpret the Bible through allegory and *aggadah*. The divine origin of the Bible could not be denied by a Jew, so Philo could not deny the often contradictory statements in the

[1] Hans Lewy, *Three Jewish Philosophers,* Meridan Books and Jewish Publication Society, 1960.

Bible. He therefore reinterpreted the statements in terms of allegory and extended them through *aggadah*. For example, there are statements in the very first pages of the Torah that bring any rationalist to a halt. Adam and Eve, having eaten of the forbidden fruit, attempt to hide from God. And God says, "Where art thou?" But God is all-seeing; no one can hide from Him. Why then does He ask where Adam and Eve are hiding? Philo explains this apparent irrationality as an allegory; it shows a wicked man attempting to hide his evil thoughts from the voice of reason within him.

Philo's psychology drew a picture of man constantly torn between two poles, each pole a part of his inner self. At one pole is the remote God, source of pure intellect; at the other pole is matter, source of passion and sin. Man stands between the poles. He is connected to the upper pole by his intellect, his reason—the higher part of his soul; he is tied to the lower pole by his body, by its needs and desires—the lower half of his soul. Following Greek philosophy rather than Jewish concepts, Philo held that man's highest perfection is achieved when he overcomes his body, his passions and desires, and rises through wisdom toward the God-pole. At that point, man's soul touches God and achieves immortality.

As a philosopher, the highest level of occupational attainment in the ancient world, Philo was also an excellent apologist for the Jews—using the same method of allegory. The Hellenic world sneered at the Jewish proscription against work on the sabbath. Romans, for example, initiated the idea (echoed by anti-Semites for two thousand years after) that Jews despised work and looked down upon workmen. Philo answered that the Jews hold labor in the highest regard, but also revere wisdom as did the Greek philosophers, and study is the path to wisdom. So work was denied on the sabbath in order that Jews would have one day in the week devoted only to study and spiritual development.

Philo's apologetics and interpretations of the Bible were convincing to the intellectuals of Rome and were a factor in the philo-Semitism, often leading to conversion, that was fashionable in upper-class Rome during that period. But he had no continuing influence upon philosophy among the Jews. He was rejected by the Rabbis of the Talmud and forgotten by Jews until the modern era. Medieval Jewish thinkers did not know him. But he was accepted by the early Christian theologians and exerted serious influence on their thinking.

The Romans were condescending to Greek philosophy but were unable to produce anything to equal it. Thus, Greek thought in philosophy, medicine, mathematics, and natural philosophy was dominant in the Mediterranean world. Even when Rome declined in worldly strength and intellectual vigor and finally succumbed to the barbarians, Greek thought did not die. That it did not die was not because of the Romans, but in spite of them. The Emperor Justinian attempted to wipe out Greek philosophy and forced the closing of the Athenian schools in 529. But by that time schools of Greek philosophy had already been established in the Middle East. These schools, maintained by Syrian Christians, taught Aristotle in philosophy, Hippocrates and Galen in medicine, Euclid and Archimedes in mathematics. The language of these schools, Syriac, became the intellectual tongue of the Middle Eastern world.

In the seventh century this world became Muslim. But this was a vital, vigorous, intellectually curious Islam, and Greek thought was stimulated rather than suppressed. The Muslims accepted the Syriac Christians as teachers and soon surpassed their instructors. They developed their own important schools of philosophy, always based on the philosophical systems they learned from their Syriac teachers—on Aristotle and the followers of Plato. The Jews studied in the Muslim schools of philosophy and became, in turn, Aristotelian philosophers. In their turn, they surpassed *their* teachers, and for a period Jewish philosophers dominated the world of pure thought. And in the later Middle Ages, Christian Europe relearned Greek philosophy from the Jews.[2] Thus this system of thought, one of the major roots of Western culture, came full circle: suppressed by the Christian East, it was transmitted by Syriac teachers to the Muslims, who transmitted it to the Jews, who gave it back to the Christian West.

In the centuries between Philo and Mohammed, the period after the destruction of the Second Temple and the end of the Jewish commonwealth, the time of the development of the Talmud, the Jewish gaze was turned inward. Jews had little contact with other cultures of a philosophical bent. The Jewish center was in Babylonia, but the Babylonians did not offer an intellectual challenge. So there were few pressures which might have caused the authority of revelation to be called into question. As a result, the Talmud is not a philosophical work. It includes much speculation about the nature of God and man, but this speculation is neither consistent nor philosophic nor rationalistic. Whatever philosophic questions arose in Talmudic times were answered by *midrashim*. However, in the ninth and tenth centuries, when the Jews were chal-

[2] *Mekor Chaim* (Fountain of Life), written in Arabic by the poet-philospher Solomon ibn Gabirol (1021–1067), was translated into Spanish and Latin shortly after its publication. Its Latin title was a direct translation: *Fons Vitae*. In this form, the work had great influence on the thought of the Scholastics and later Churchmen. The name of its author was forgotten in the Christian academies, and the work was ascribed to a monk called Avicebrol or Avicebron. In the nineteenth century, the scholar Salomon Munk discovered that this Church classic was the creation of an eleventh-century Spanish Jew.

lenged internally by the Karaites and externally by the vigorous Moslem philosophers, a strongly intellectual culture again impinged on Jewish scholarship. Philosophy was necessary once more; the Jews had to extract from the Bible substantive statements as to the nature of God, the nature of man, the nature of his soul, and the manner of creation.

The most important philosopher to answer this challenge was Saadia Gaon (tenth century), head of the Academy of Sura in Babylonia, the first major Jewish philosopher after Philo. And like Philo, Saadia turned to philosophy to defend traditional Jewish concepts against the questions raised by internal and external doubters. Internally, the Karaite sect held that the Written Law, the Torah, was valid, but that everything added by the Rabbis of the Mishnah and the Talmud was without validity. Externally, one school of Muslim philosophers even raised doubts about the validity of revelation itself.

In his major philosophical work, *The Book of Doctrines and Beliefs,* Saadia explains why he undertook to answer these challenges:

> Some people have found truth and rejoice in the knowledge that they have. . . . Others have arrived at truth, but doubt it. They do not know it with certainty and fail to hold on to it. . . . Still others affirm with confidence that which is untrue. . . . Others follow a certain belief for a time, reject it for another belief, give that up for still a third belief. . . .
>
> . . . I saw men sunk in a sea of doubt, covered by the waters of confusion. . . . But as my Lord granted me some knowledge that can be of help to them, and gave me some ability which I could employ for their benefit, I felt it my duty to help them. . . .

Then, using the methods developed out of Aristotle by the Muslim philosophers, Saadia interpreted Judaism in the light of reason. He held that nothing taught in the Bible or the Talmud violated the laws of logic and that the basic concepts of Judaism—absolute monotheism, creation by God, free will, the hereafter, and the logic of the Law—could be demonstrated through contemplation. Any conflict that appeared to arise was not between faith and reason but between faith and faulty reason. That is, if contemplation (intellectual speculation) did not eventually give the same conclusion as that given by faith, the fault must lie in the process of reasoning; a false conclusion must have been drawn at one point. Extended to their ultimate logical ends, reason and faith had to meet.

In this reasoning, Saadia was in the direct line of Aristotle. Both believed that error came not from faults in perception but from inability to use the reasoning powers fully. Thus, heresy could come as easily from insufficient knowedlge as from faith without reason.

Using classic Aristotelian logic, with one difference, Saadia offered proof that the world was created by God. He disagreed with Aristotle's idea that the world was eternal, without beginning and end. Saadia posited a finite world and finite time; therefore the world had to have had a beginning, and it had to have been created. Nor could it have been created out of primal matter, as Plato thought. If the world had been created, it had had a creator—who was God.

Saadia concluded that God has only four attributes: oneness, existence, power, and wisdom. Any passage in the Bible or the Talmud that might be read to impute other attributes must be read figuratively. His rule was: "An expression in the Bible or anywhere else concerning God and His actions which differs from what is acceptable to true philosophy must be explained figuratively."

God, according to the logic of *Doctrines and Beliefs,* created the world out of his infinite goodness, for existence is in itself good. In order to make man's existence still better, God gave him the Torah. But God did not make man naturally good—that is, without the ability to do evil—because a higher goodness is achieved when man struggles against his ability to do evil in order to arrive at goodness.

The Torah, according to Saadia, includes laws that can be derived through reason and laws whose reasonable basis may not be evident to the imperfect logic of man. Both must be obeyed. The Law is revealed by God through His prophets—but the prophecies have authority because they are logical, not because of the miracles that may have attended their revelation.

In dealing with the problem of reward and punishment raised in the book of Job, Saadia concluded that earthly rewards and punishment are only part of a total scheme; the rest is hidden from man by time and the hereafter. And if man is to fulfill this scheme, part of which unfolds in the hereafter, he must have a quality that lives into the hereafter, that is immortal—the soul.

Saadia accepted the three-part soul of Aristotle and Plato. One part represents the elemental needs of man such as food and procreation; a second part represents emotion; the third part represents reason. And he showed how this three-part view of the soul was also the Biblical view, which uses three different words to designate these various aspects of the soul: *nefesh, ruach, neshameh.*

The one important Jewish philosopher of the medieval period who refused to follow the strict Aristotelian line and who did not fall into the trap of pure logic was not a philosopher. He was, as could be expected, a poet. He was Judah Halevi (1080–1140), a Spanish Jew and according to Jewish legend the greatest poet since David. Halevi's philosophical work, the *Kuzari,* is the only book of Jewish philosophy written in the classic form of the dialogue. The book is in the form of a letter from

Joseph, king of the Chazars, to Chasdai ibn Shaprut of Córdoba, diplomatic counselor to the Caliph. It tells of the conversion to Judaism of the Chazars, a tribe living in what is now southern Russia. King Bulan of the Chazars sought for the true God and summoned Christian, Muslim, and Jewish philosophers to tell him of their God. After listening to their arguments and after lengthy questioning of each representative of the major faiths, Bulan chose Judaism for his nation. The major fact—the conversion of the Chazars in the eighth century—is a historical truth, even if the dialogues leading up to it were a poet's invention.

In the *Kuzari*, Halevi maintained that God cannot be adduced through logic and that all philosophical proofs of the existence of God fail. God can be perceived, finally, only by the "inward eye of the soul." The modern concept of the "leap of faith" is much like Halevi's intuitive knowledge of God. Halevi also developed a theory of history in the *Kuzari,* using it as the base for his arguments for Judaism over the daughter religions. When Bulan asks the Jewish scholar in what he believes, the scholar says he believes in God as He is revealed through Jewish history—the Bible. And as proof of the Bible's validity, he points to its acceptance as revealed truth by both Christian and Muslim.

When King Bulan counters by pointing to the historic and continuing low estate of the Jews, persecuted and enslaved everywhere, the Jewish scholar answers that suffering is not necessarily an indication of error or of evil. Moreover, the Jews can liberate themselves from their low estate and from suffering merely by a simple declaration of conversion to Christianity or Islam. Yet they do not and have not done so. If an entire people accept their suffering century after century, which is against human nature, there must be a divine force at work and an ultimate glory in clinging to that faith.

Halevi's ideal man, much like Plato's, is ethical and pious. And like Plato, Halevi conceived of him as a just ruler. But in Halevi's ideal, man is ruler over his soul and his body, seeing to it that neither is denied its proper function and that neither invades the other's domain. Thus this ideal man is neither ascetic—denying justice to the body and its passions—nor glutton and libertine—denying justice to the soul. Instead, he lives a moderate life, half of the body, half of the soul. Here, of course, Halevi parts company both with Plato and with earlier Jewish philosophers who saw the ideal man as a pure passionless soul, a pure intellect which has overcome the desires of the flesh.

Medieval Jewish philosophy, in general, was a much more intense and much more intellectual attempt to do what Philo and Saadia tried to do: to reconcile two independent sources of truth—revelation and reason. The Bible and the sacred books based on it were beyond challenge to the medieval mind, whether Christian, Muslim, or Jewish.

Equally unchallenged by scholars of all theologies were the truths arrived at through rational reflection. Yet these two accepted sources of truth appeared at times to contradict each other.

The Jewish philosophers held that religion and philosophy were essentially identical; only the methods used were different. Philosophy taught by rational projection from sensory perceptions; religion taught by authoritative statements based on divine revelation. But the content taught by both methods was essentially the same; it remained merely to reconcile the language.

Efforts at reconciliation required that specific problems be enunciated and parallel answers to these problems be found in revelation and reason. The problems involved the existence of God, His unity, His attributes, the creation of the universe, providence, free will, rewards and punishment, the authority of the Law, the validity of phophecy, the uniqueness of Moses as prophet, the soul and immortality, and the question of ethics—why should a man be good? and what is good?

For the most part, these questions could not be answered singly. Consideration of one question required a preceding proof of another. For example, consideration of the problem of ethics in Judaism and in ethical systems stemming from Plato requires prior resolution of the problem of free will. And none of these questions could be considered without prior knowledge in all the basic disciplines known in the medieval world: the principles of logic, natural philosophy or the nature of the physical world, moral philosophy or the understanding of human conduct (which is called psychology in the modern world). Of course the philosopher also had to have an exhaustive knowledge of the Bible and the Talmud, or else what revelation could he examine?

Maimonides' genius was based on his total mastery of each of these disciplines. He began his career as a philosopher; his second book, *Logical Terms*, was an introduction to philosophy. He was a great physician and author of many treatises on medicine (on drugs, asthma, fits, coitus, hemorrhoids, poisons, Galen, Hippocrates, etc.). He was the preeminent codifier of the Talmud. And with the writing of the *Moreh Nebukim, The Guide of the Perplexed,* he established a watershed in Jewish philosophy.

After publication of this work, earlier books of Jewish philosophy were mainly of historical interest; every book that came afterward was influenced by him. The struggle for philosophy as a discipline in Jewish scholarship was carried forward in the centuries after Maimonides mainly as a struggle between Maimonists and anti-Maimonists. The influence of Jewish philosophy on Christian thought stemmed mainly from Maimonides—the greatest of the Scholastics, Thomas Aquinas and Albertus Magnus, quoted extensively from Maimonides—and his influence on Jewish thought extended through the centuries to Spinoza in the seventeenth and to Herman Cohen, leader of the modern Neo-Kantian school, in the twentieth.

The Guide of the Perplexed was written in 1190, when Maimonides was a mature man of fifty-five. It was composed in Arabic, translated into Hebrew in 1200, into Latin a few years later, into Spanish by 1419, and into Italian in 1591. Few books in that pre-printing era were as widely distributed.

Maimonides did not write the *Guide* for other philosophers, nor was it addressed to laymen; it was written for students with a background in philosophy who were troubled by the seeming contradiction between what they had learned from the philosophers and what they had been taught by the Rabbis. For this informed audience Maimonides could write a learned book using the technical terms of philosophy that were part of the intellectual currency of the educated men of the twelfth century. He did not bother to explain them, just as a modern writer would not bother to explain terms like id, superego, transcendentalism, or $E=MC^2$ for a modern intellectual audience. The fact that the language of medieval philosophy is not part of the cultural armament of the twentieth-century intellectual makes the *Guide* difficult to follow.

Unlike other medieval philosophers, Maimonides did not begin his proof of the existence of God with a proof of the creation of the universe, thus positing the existence of a creator, who was *the* Creator, who was God. Maimonides held that the existence of God was independent of the creation of the universe. Creation was one problem; the existence of God required other proofs. Maimonides' proofs of His existence—he offered four—were based on twenty-six propositions in logic which the philosopher derived from Aristotle's physics and metaphysics.

These proofs—again Maimonides diers from other philosophers of the period—did not constitute the first section of the *Guide*. Maimonides' student audience was not as troubled about the existence of God as they were about the anthropomorphisms which gave God physical attributes in the Bible. So in the first of the three books of the *Guide,* Maimonides lists and discusses every word and phrase in the Bible which could imply some corporeal or earthly attribute for God.

The only real knowledge of God available to us, he says, is that He exists. After that we know only what He is not, the negative attributes, not what He is, the positive attributes. We know that He has no physical characteristics, no injustice, no blindness to any thing or any action, etc.

After attempting to satisfy the students' first worries (the primary perplexities of the perplexed), Maimonides turned in Book II of the *Guide* to proofs of the creation of the world. He used Aristotle's logic to disprove Aristotle's contention that the universe is eternal. Here Maimonides could not bring himself to break totally with the Father of Logic;

instead, he offered the proposition that where conclusive proofs are not forthcoming, reasonable men should choose those conclusions that satisfy most of the evident conditions. And since Aristotle could not actually prove the eternality of the universe—Maimonides suggests that Aristotle put forward this idea only tentatively—Maimonides accepted the Biblical version of creation allegorically. This in turn raised the question of the validity of prophecy, since the Biblical story was revealed through prophecy.

Maimonides exhibited great psychological insight in explaining the nature of prophecy. He said that the prophet is, first, a man of perfect ethical conduct; second, of great intellectual attainment; and third, blessed with tremendous fantasy. But even these attributes do not by themselves make the prophet; this imaginative, ethically perfect, intellectual giant must also be touched by the spirit of God. He then becomes a prophet of one of eleven degrees of prophecy, depending on how the spirit of God manifested itself to him.

The lowest degrees of prophets were those who merely felt the need to speak out; the Judges and the writers of the Hagiographa were in this group. The next levels included those who received their prophecies in dreams, such as Zechariah, the early Samuel, and Isaiah. On the highest level were those like Abraham who saw visions while awake. These classifications cover all prophets except *the* Prophet, Moses. He was alone in having direct communication with God, which allowed him to bring the Torah to man.

In Book III of the *Guide,* Maimonides deals with the problem of theodicy, the paradox of the existence of evil in a universe created by the God of all mercy and all justice. He does this in much the same way as he dealt with the attributes of God—in negatives. Evil is not a thing, says Maimonides, but a non-thing; it is the absence of good. (A parallel in the physical world would be the definition of cold as the absence of heat.) Evil is made possible by the imperfection of matter; this lack does not permit matter, animate and inanimate, to receive or to perceive the divine good. However, since evil does exist in God's creation, it also has a positive aspect; it serves some good purpose. For example, sickness and death are evils, but they are also necessary in a finite universe peopled with finite beings. The very process of continuing creation requires these evils; creation is birth and growth, which imply decay and death.

There are three types or qualities of evil, says Maimonides. The evil caused by nature (storms, earthquakes, or drought), the evil caused by one man to another (war and violence), and the evil man does to himself. On balance, these evils do not diminish God's perfection. The first quality of evil occurs so infrequently (if man does not cause it himself) that the steady courses of the seasons, the regularity of seed and fruit, and the abundant flow of water far outweigh the occasional lapses in nature. The other two qualities of evil are caused by men to whom God has given free will. Why blame them on God?

The *Guide* describes two kinds of divine providence: that extended to man, and that extended to all other living things. The providence God extends to the nonhuman world is directed only to the type, to the genus: to the race of dogs, not to any individual dog; to the fish of the sea, not to any particular fish. The providence extended to man, on the other hand, is directed to each individual, who is then left free to follow God's providence or not.

Every medieval philosopher dealt with proofs of the existence of God. Maimonides built his proofs on Aristotelian logic, the foundation of Western philosophy, as did almost all other philosophers, regardless of theology. But Maimonides' proofs illustrate his differences with other philosophers—Jewish, Christian, and Muslim—and his philosophical method.

In his first proof of the existence of God, Maimonides compared the three views of the creation of the world current in the twelfth century:

The Biblical view: God created everything out of nothing. Time is also a divine creation, since without a moving thing there cannot be motion, and without motion there is no time.

The Platonic view: the world is subject to birth and decay; therefore it originated in time. But it could not have been made out of nothing, because this is like saying that being and not being are possible at the same time. Matter both was created by God and is co-eternal with God.

The Aristotelian view: time and motion are eternal; the heavens and the spheres are also eternal and not subject to creation and decay. Matter in our world is also not subject to creation and decay; it merely changes form, a process that has been going on eternally.

Maimonides attempted to disprove the Greek philosophers on both scientific and philosophic grounds. Scientifically, he disproved Aristotle's explanation of the eternal, infinite movement of the heavens by citing discrepancies in the Greek philosopher's explanations of the direction and speed of motion of the stars. Philosophically, Maimonides disproved the possibility of the creation of a complex, composite world by a simple mechanical Intelligence. He accepted the oneness of the Intelligence, but posited a Supreme Intelligence with will, purpose, and design. Essentially, Maimonides was rejecting both Greek philosophers' concepts of a universe governed by impersonal, mechanical laws.

In any case, said Maimonides, all three (Biblical, Aristotelian, and Platonic) explanations of the creation of the world have logical flaws. However, there is a philosophical rule to take care of such a contingency: where no theory answers all objections, the one that leaves fewest logical flaws, he holds, is of a universe created out of nothing by an eternal, incorporeal, unitary God—Who is, of course, expressed in allegory and symbol in the Torah.

Maimonides' other proofs were not as detailed, but they were, in the logician's phrase, more elegant. The second proof developed in four steps:

1. If in a thing made up of two elements one element is sometimes found by itself, the second element must also have the property of existing by itself.

2. Some things have the properties of causing motion and of being moved, such as a hand. Other things have only the property of being moved, such as a stone.

3. Therefore, if some things have the two elements of causing motion and of being moved, and we find some things that have only the element of being moved, it follows that there must be a thing that has only the property of causing motion without being moved (see step 1 above).

4. This thing having the ability to move without being itself subject to motion must be indivisible, incorporeal, and not subject to time. This is God.

The third proof was based on the Aristotelian concept of necessary existence; the fourth paralleled the third, using actuality and potentiality instead of the mover and the object being moved as in the second proof.

In all his philosophical work Maimonides had a single goal: to show that the teachings of the Torah were consistent with basic philosophical truths. Where contradictions appear, they are only on the surface and are due to insistence on reading Scripture literally, thus denying its real meaning. Instead, logical analysis shows that the Torah is the highest form of philosophical truth. And this truth should be sought by scholars for two reasons: the welfare of the soul, and the welfare of the body.

Welfare of the soul is achieved by communicating to the people those correct beliefs that are within their intellectual ability to understand. Some [beliefs] have to be communicated by direct statements, others by parables, since the multitude, on the whole, cannot understand the statements as they are. The welfare of the body is achieved by setting right the way people live together. This is done by removing injustice; this means that no man is permitted whatever he may want and have the power to do, but must do those things that will benefit the people. It is also done by training every person in socially useful habits so that affairs in the community run smoothly.[3]

Although the *Guide* was written in Arabic, Maimonides closed it

[3] *The Guide of the Perplexed*, Chapter 27.

with a poem in Hebrew, apparently composed by himself:

> To each who calls Him, God is near indeed,
> If he but call in truth nor turn away.
> By each who seeks Him He is found with ease,
> If straight to Him he strives and does not stray.[4]

[4] Translated by Chaim Rabin, *The Guide of the Perplexed*, East and West Library, London, 1952.

THIRTEEN

Mysticism:
The Kabbalah and the Zohar

ALL RELIGIONS BEGIN IN MYSTICISM, in man's sense of his own inadequacy in the face of the enormous forces determining his existence and in man's desire to overcome this earthly limitation by direct communion with the Supreme Being. While at times this mystic element in Judaism was strong enough to be dominant, the mainstream of Jewish religious thought was rationalistic. The prophets and the Rabbis, for the most part, frowned on mysticism. They accepted the premise that the goal of man was communion with God, but they held that this communion could be achieved mainly through proper communion (love) with fellow man—a very practical and non-mystical concept. Still, the mystic component was present at every stage in Judaism's growth—an inevitable development, since the very opening chapters of the Torah, the story of creation, rouse mystic speculations.

The philosophical basis of Jewish mysticism may be stated thus: God cannot be perceived by the senses, and only dimly, if at all, by the intellect; He can be experienced only through a mystic unity between man and the heavens. In attempting to achieve this unity, man does more than fulfill his personal need and purpose; he also brings closer the End of Days, the World to Come, and the Time of the Messiah.

Physical man, said the mystics, cannot have communion with God. Only his immaterial essence, his soul, can achieve this communion. So methods had to be developed by which the soul could be freed from its earthly, sensory ties. However, even when the soul is freed to climb to heaven, there are evil spirits that will try to hinder this communion. So the mystics developed secret magics that would gain mastery over the evil spirits. And once having gained power over these spirits, the mystic could force them into the service of man.

Mysticism also attempted to resolve those questions, central to

Jewish philosophy, that were inadequately answered by the philosophers, at least for the common man: how can the inconceivable, purely spiritual God have a direct relationship with the gross, materialistic world? How could the incorporeal, totally exalted Being create this base world, and out of what matter?

The answer offered by the mystics to these questions was that God did not and does not act directly upon matter; He acts through mediators. This concept was accepted by almost all mystics from the earliest days; they differed, however, on the nature of the mediators. Were these mediators creations of God? In which case the original question remained unanswered: created out of what? Or were they part of the Eternal? This latter idea was generally accepted by Jewish mystics.

Since everything in Judaism must be rooted in the Torah, and the teachings of mysticism were not specifically mentioned in the canon, the mystics called their teachings *Kabbalah*, from the Hebrew word for tradition, or transmitted teachings: in effect, ancient wisdom handed down. The secret mystic teachings were to be found in the Torah, said the Kabbalists, if one knew where and how to find them.

Rabbi Simeon said: If a man looks upon the Torah as merely a book presenting narratives and everyday maters, alas for him. . . . The Torah, in all its words, holds supernal truths and sublime secrets.

. . . When the angels descend to earth they don earthly garments, else they could neither abide in the world, nor could it bear to have them. But if this is so for angels, then how much more so it must be with the Torah. . . . The world could not endure the Torah if she had not garbed herself in garments of this world.

Thus the tales related in the Torah are simply her outer garments, and woe to the man who regards the outer garb as the Torah itself, for such a man will be deprived of his portion in the next world. Thus David said: "Open Thou mine eyes, that I may behold wondrous things out of Thy law" [Psalms 119:18], that is to say, the things that are underneath. See now. The most visible part of man is the clothes that he has on, and they who lack understanding, when they look at the man, are apt not to see more in him than these clothes. In reality, however, it is the body of the man that constitutes the pride of his clothes, and his soul constitutes the pride of his body.

So it is with the Torah. Its narrations which relate to the things of the world constitute the garments which clothe the body of the Torah; and that body is composed of the Torah's precepts. People without understanding see only the narrations, the garment; those somewhat more penetrating see also the body. But the truly wise . . . pierce all the way through to the soul, to the true Torah which is the root principle of all. These same will in the future be vouchsafed to penetrate to the very soul of the soul of the Torah. . . .

Woe to the sinners who look upon the Torah as simply tales pertaining to things of the world, seeing thus only the outer garment. But the righteous whose gaze penetrates to the very Torah, happy are they. Just as the wine must be in a jar to keep, so the Torah must be contained in an outer garment. The garment is made up of tales and stories; but we, we are bound to penetrate beyond.[1]

The secrets of Kabbalah are not arrived at through contemplation, logical deduction, or rational speculation. Nor, except in one aspect, are they found through revelation. The secrets come out of the psychic experiences of those who attempt to pierce the mysteries. And like any other psychic experiences, they are very hard to communicate, even harder to understand at second hand. As a result, those who share the mysteries are a small, elect group. They are initiates specially favored to join in the mystic experiences.

The one aspect of revelation in Kabbalah has to do with the prophet Elijah, somehow transmuted to a supernatural messenger of God.[2] Elijah keeps cropping up in Kabbalistic literature and is held by some Kabbalists to be the angel who reveals to the elect the Kabbalistic teachings and mysteries.

In time, the term Kabbalah came to refer to the entire body of Jewish mysticism concerned with the mystic manifestations of God and His powers and conceived as a sacred ancient tradition rather than as the product of human intellect. Where the Rabbis of the Talmud and their followers in later centuries saw the study of the Torah as the maximum form of piety, the Kabbalists gave first place to prayer in a state of ecstasy, believing that this opened the way to direct knowledge of God. But Kabbalah was not all ecstatic prayer and mystical experience; it also had a strong rationalistic side. Even its magic was rooted in the Kabbalists' attempts to answer those questions the logicians and rationalists could not answer. As part of its rationalism, Kabbalah laid great stress upon ethical conduct.

This remarkable product of Jewish intellectual activity cannot be satisfactorily estimated as a whole unless the religio-ethical side of Kabbalah is more strongly emphasized. . . . It constantly falls back upon Scripture for its origin and authenticity. . . . While mysticism itself is the expression of the intensest religious feeling, where reason lies dormant, Jewish mysticism is essentially an attempt to harmonize universal reason with the Scriptures; and the allegorical interpretation of the Biblical writings by the [philosophical] Aristotelians as well as the [symbolic] Palestinians may justly be regarded as its starting point. These interpretations had their origin in the conviction that

---

[1] *Zohar: The Book of Splendor*, Gershom G. Scholem, ed., Schocken Books, New York, 1949.

[2] This concept of Elijah has become part of Jewish belief and ritual. Even in modern times Jews place a special cup of wine on the Seder table (the ceremony, including the evening meal, opening the celebration of the Passover) and open the door of the house so that Elijah may come in and partake of the Seder.

the truths of Greek philosophy were already contained in Scripture, although given only to the select few to lift the veil and discern beneath the letter of the Bible.[3]

Jewish mysticism began in Biblical days, long before the term Kabbalah was invented.[4] By the first century it had become a proper subject for scholarly study. Philo Judaeus speculated on the Platonic idea of emanations as intermediaries between God and the physical world. The Roman philosopher Plotinus (205–270) traveled in the East and returned to combine Indian, Persian, Greek, and Jewish mystic theories into a systematic structure of these emanations. The Rabbis of the Talmud speculated on these mysteries, particularly when they were commenting on Genesis and the visions of Ezekiel. The speculations were later embroidered by new ideas that entered Jewish thought from the Syriac Greeks, the Zoroastrian Babylonians, and the Gnostic sect of the Byzantium Christians. From these foreign and domestic concepts and myths, the Jews wove into their mysticism ideas of upper and nether worlds, angels and demons, ghosts and spirits—ideas that had been unknown or of little importance to the Jews until then.

But the Rabbis of the Talmud, while fascinated by these speculations, distrusted them as much as had Ben Sirach five or six centuries earlier. A warning legend from the Talmud tells what happened to four of the greatest scholars of their time when they dared to look too deeply into God's mysteries: Rabbi ben Zoma went mad; Rabbi ben Azzai died shortly after he had returned from his journey into the world of the spirit; Elisha ben Abuyah became an apostate and wandered the world seeking peace for his inner torment (Ben Abuyah, called Acher, became a curse word to the Jews); only the fourth scholar, the sainted Rabbi Akiba, survived the experience and found peace and grace, but this was possible only because of Akiba's great virtue. The lesson of the parable is clear: don't attempt to touch the heavenly mysteries unless you are Akiba's peer in saintliness, goodness, and scholarship.

Such warnings did not end mystical speculation, in that or any age. After the close of the Talmud in the Gaonic period, books of mysticism began to appear. Some were so widely known and respected that the *Geonim* wrote commentaries on them. Perhaps the two most influential mystical books of this five-century period were *Hekalot* (Halls) and the *Sefer Yetzirah* (Book of Formations or Creation). Hekalot purports to tell of the experiences of Rabbi Ishmael in heaven and describes the

---

[3] Louis Ginzberg, *Jewish Law and Lore,* Jewish Publication Society, 1955.

[4] It was also distrusted from the earliest days. The apocryphal book of Ben Sirach (second century B.C.) warns, "Thou shalt have no business with secret things" (Ben Sirach 3:22).

ecstatic mysteries to be seen and experienced in the Halls of Heaven. (Ishmael was martyred during the persecutions of the reign of Emperor Hadrian.) Sefer Yetzirah was ascribed to the Patriarch Abraham (it was actually written in the eighth century) and developed a basic philosophical system combining Jewish mysticism, the Platonic emanations, and a system of magic consisting of magical arrangements of letters and numbers. Adepts of this early mysticism (before the invention of the term Kabbalah) were called *Yordeh Merkabah,* Riders of the Chariot [of Ezekiel], and followers of the *Razeh Torah,* the Hidden Torah.

From Babylonia and Palestine, Jewish mysticism moved into the Jewish communities of Europe and blossomed there. Every community produced its own mystic literature, mystic belief, and mystic practices. There were distinctive Spanish, French, Italian, and German Kabbalahs. Some were mainly "practical," dealing in magic; others were mainly "speculative," emphasizing philosophical explanations; many combined practical and speculative Kabbalah in equal parts. The German Jews, oppressed and persecuted, sought hope and revenge and a happy ending through magical Kabbalah. On the other hand, the rationalistic Spanish Jews turned to speculative Kabbalah to find the answers their philosophers could not give them. For them Kabbalah succeeded in rationalizing revelation and logic much better than Maimonides' *Guide.*[5]

In fact it was the great intellectual triumph of the Jewish Aristotelian philosophers in the eleventh, twelfth, and thirteenth centuries that gave Kabbalah its greatest impetus. Maimonides' explanations were addressed to and understood by only a few scholars and students. The mass of Jews could fathom neither the arguments nor the proofs. Yet they too had the same doubts as the scholars. They too wanted proofs that the revealed truths did not violate reason. Mysticism, which suspends logic or substitutes its own logical system, offered more acceptable answers. And Kabbalah offered deep religious emotion instead of the dry intellectualism of the philosophers.

But mysticism and mystery were not limited to the unlearned. Physical oppression and persecution, and intellectual dead ends, made the real world so unacceptable to even intellectually trained minds that they too turned to the bright promise of Kabbalah. Some of the greatest and most learned scholars became adepts of the Kabbalah. It was into this atmosphere that the bible of the Kabbalah, the Zohar, was introduced.

The expulsion of the Jews from Spain and Portugal in 1492, follow-

---

[5] In the modern period Kabbalah had its greatest influence on the Chasidic movement which began in the middle of the eighteenth century and swept East European Jewry. Oddly, it was the ascetic Lurianic Kabbalah (see above) that was adopted by this most unascetic sect.

ing the destruction of the German Jewish communities, was a terrible blow to the Jews of the entire Mediterranean basin. Kabbalah helped ease the pain and offered the possibility of magical intervention. Many of the expelled Iberian Jews found a haven in the Turkish East, including Palestine. There, in the very land God had promised them, in the very place where miracles had been performed, Kabbalah assumed special meaning and importance. In Safed, a town in the Palestinian hills, a group of scholars, mystics, and ascetics came together and formed a new center for the study of Kabbalah. Most important among these extenders of Kabbalah were Isaac Luria, Moses Cordovero, and Chaim Vital.

Chief among them was Luria, known as Ari (*A*shkenazi *R*abbi *I*saac), who developed a complex system of magic words and phrases, amulets and conjurations, ascetic and mystic exercises. Asceticism was foreign to the mainstream of Jewish thought and practice, since Judaism holds that the denial of God's gifts—which include the pleasures of the senses—is, in effect, a denial of God. But Luria managed to blend asceticism and piety into an acceptable amalgam. He claimed that through fasting and denial of the body he purified himself so that the prophet-angel Elijah came to him in a vision and revealed the innermost secrets of the Kabbalah. Luria did not write down his contributions, but his disciple Vital did and published them in a book called *Etz Chaim,* The Tree of Life.

Sefar haZohar, the Book of Splendor, takes its name from a passage in Daniel: "And they that be wise shall shine as the splendor [brightness] of the firmament; and they that turn the many to righteousness as the stars for ever and ever."[6] In the same sense that Maimonides' *Guide* was the watershed for Jewish philosophy, the Zohar was the dividing line for Jewish mysticism. Before the Zohar, mysticism was a disorganized collection of individual ideas; after the Zohar became known, mysticism became a structured, comparatively integrated system.

Like most Kabbalistic books, the Zohar's authority was inflated by ascribing the book to a revered name dead a thousand years. The book was said to have been compiled by Simeon ben Yohai, a Rabbi of the Mishnah (second century), during the thirteen years he and his sons hid from Roman persecution in a cave in Palestine. Simeon was supposed to have buried the manuscript; it was miraculously discovered in the thirteenth century by Moses ben Nachman. Moses sent the book to his son in Catalonia, but while the book was en route on a ship, a great wind came and picked up the manuscript and carried it to Aragon. There it was deposited in the hands of Moses de Leon.

The miraculous discovery and voyage of the book was read as a

---

[6] Daniel 12:3.

parable by the scholars of the time, but they did not doubt Simeon's authorship until about the sixteenth century—despite the obvious discrepancies in language and style. It was written partly in Hebrew and partly in Aramaic—Simeon ben Yohai's natural tongue—and it mentioned some persons who were not even born when Simeon lived. The best judgment is that Moses de Leon compiled the book from many writings, probably including some by Simeon ben Yohai.

The Zohar, which became the canon of the Kabbalists, is more encyclopedia than book; written as a commentary on the Pentateuch, it describes and discusses all the Kabbalistic doctrines and practices. For example, the Kabbalistic interpretation of the character of man as revealed in his physiognomy is part of the Zohar's commentary on a verse from Exodus:

"Moreover, thou shalt look about and choose out all the people, able men." R. Isaac and R. Jose were one day studying the Torah in Tiberias. R. Simeon passed by and asked them what they were engaged upon. They answered him: "The words which we have learned from thee, Master." "Which?" said he. They replied: "It arises out of the verse: 'This is the book of the generations of man; in the day when God created man, in the likeness of God made he him' [Gen. 5:1]. "We were taught," they said, "that this verse indicates that the Holy One showed to the first man all the future generations of mankind: all the leaders, all the sages of each period. We were further taught concerning the mystery contained in the words 'this is the book' that there are two books, an upper and a lower book. The lower book is the 'book of remembrance,' and the upper one is called 'this.' And in order to show that the two are not separated, but form one, it is written 'this is the book.' There are two grades, male and female. For all the souls and spirits that enter human beings are alluded to in the words 'generations of man (Adam),' for they all issue from the 'Righteous One,' and this is the 'watering of the river that went out of Eden to water the garden' [Gen. 2:10]. There is also another, a lower 'Adam,' alluded to in the words, 'on the day that God created man (Adam),' in the same verse. In regard to the upper Adam, the union of male and female is at first only distantly alluded to in the words 'this is the book,' but after they produced offspring, they are called openly 'Adam.' Then it is said that God made man in the 'likeness' of God. By the word 'likeness' we are to understand a kind of mirror in which images appear momentarily and then pass away. According to another explanation, the word 'likeness' refers to the union of male and female organs: and so the Master affirmed. Furthermore: 'This is the book of the generations of Man,' viz., the book which reveals the inner meaning of the features of man, so as to teach the knowledge of human nature. The character of man is revealed in the hair, the forehead, the eyes, the lips, the features of the face, the lines of the hands, and even the ears. By these seven can the different types of men be recognized.

"The Hair. A man with coarse, upstanding, wavy hair is of a truculent disposition. His heart is as stiff as a die. His works are not upright. Have no fellowship with him. A man with very smooth, sleek, and heavy-hanging hair is a good companion, and one benefits from association with him. When left to himself, he is not quite reliable. He cannot keep secrets unless they are of great importance. His actions are sometimes good and sometimes the reverse.

"A man whose hair lies flat, yet is not sleek, is fearless and insolent. He has a strong desire to do good, for he perceives the beauty of goodness, but alas! his good intentions are never realized. In his old age he becomes God-fearing and pious. Great secrets are not to be entrusted to him, but he is safe enough with small ones. He can make much out of little, and his words are listened to with respect. He is under the esoteric sign of the letter Zayin, according to the scheme which our Master has taught us.

"A man whose hair is black and extremely glossy will succeed in all his doings, particularly in secular matters such as commerce, for instance. He is generous. But he prospers only as an individual; anyone associating himself with him will also have success, but not for long. He is also under the letter Zayin.

"One whose hair is black but not glossy is not always successful in mundane affairs. It is good to associate oneself with him for a while in business matters. Should he be a student of the Torah, he will succeed in his studies, and others who will join him will likewise succeed. He is a man who can keep a secret, but not for long. He is of a despondent nature, but will prevail against his enemies. He is under the sign of the letter Yod when it is not included in the letter Zayin, but is numbered independently among the small letters.

"A man who is bald is successful in business, but is not straightforward. There is always a scarcity of food in his house. He is hypocritical; that is, when his baldness begins in youth. If he becomes bald in his old age, he changes and becomes the opposite of what he was before, for good or for ill. This, however, only refers to the baldness which occurs on the forehead, at the spot where the phylactery is put on. Otherwise, it is not so. He is not deceitful, but is given to backbiting and insinuation. He is occasionally sin-fearing. He is under the sign of the letter Zayin when it includes the letter Yod. So much for the mysteries revealed by the different kinds of hair, mysteries revealed and entrusted only to those well versed in holy lore, those who comprehend the ways and mysteries of the Torah, by which they may find out the hidden propensities of men.

"The Forehead. The secret of the forehead belongs under the sign of the letter Nun, which forms the completion of the letter Zayin; sometimes this is included in the symbolism of Zayin and sometimes it stands separately.

"A forehead which rises sharply upward from the nose, being straight and flat without any outward curve or rounding, indicates that its owner is somewhat thoughtless. Such a man will consider himself wise, though in reality he knows little. His temper will be quick, and his tongue like a serpent's. If his forehead has large uneven furrows when he speaks, but other lines on his forehead lie even, he is not a person to associate with save for a brief period. Whatever he plans or does is only for his own advantage; he cares for no one but himself. He is incapable of keeping any secret entrusted to him, and the saying, 'A tale-bearer revealeth secrets' [Prov. 11:13] is true of him; indeed, he cares not what he says. This type of person belongs to the mystery of the letter Nun when it is contained in the letter Zayin. Such a one may be thought of as anything but reliable.

"A fine and rounded forehead indicates a man of great penetration, but whose judgment is sometimes clouded. He loves cheerfulness, and is kind-hearted to all. He has high intellectual interests. Should he study the Torah, he will become very proficient. When he speaks, three large wrinkles appear on his forehead and three smaller ones above each eye. If when he is angry he weeps, he is better than he appears to be. In word and deed he is forth-right and cares nothing for anyone. He will study the Torah with profit. Anyone who allies himself with him will derive benefit from the association and will profit even in secular matters. He is not consistently pious. In legal affairs he will always be unlucky, and should therefore avoid such embroil-ments as far as possible. This type stands in the symbolism of the letter Nun alone when it is not included in the Zayin. It is for this reason that he must shun legal matters, since he does not belong to the region of justice, but to that of love and mercy.

"A person whose forehead is large and yet unrounded—the kind of man who always bends his head, whether he stand or move—this type can be divided into two classes, both witless. The madness of the one is evident, apparent to all; such a person is an acknowledged idiot. On his forehead are four large wrinkles, which usually appear when he speaks. Sometimes, how-ever, the skin of his forehead is stretched and the wrinkles are not evident, but other larger ones appear close to his eyes. He laughs for no reason, and at nothing. His mouth is large and loose. Such a man is of no worth or use. The other kind of madness included in this type is less apparent, and is unnoticeable in common intercourse. Such a man may pursue study with success, even the study of the Torah, though he will not take it up for its own sake, but only to make a show. He makes a great parade of his religion, to give the impression that he is deeply pious, but in reality he has no thought of God, but only of man. The one object of all his thoughts and behavior is to draw attention to himself. This type, with its two distinct var-iants, also stands under the sign of the Nun when it is contained in the Zayin.

"A large rounded forehead indicates one who is open-minded and gener-ally gifted. He can acquire any kind of knowledge, even without a teacher. His undertakings are uniformly successful, except when they are concerned with money matters, in which he sometimes comes to grief. He can infer great things from small; hence he is rightly called discerning. He is detached from the things of this world, and even when he knows that he will suffer by not considering earthly matters, he pays them no heed. He is tenderhearted. His forehead is deeply furrowed by two wrinkles, set high upon his brow, one over each eye. His forehead also has three long lines, and between his eyes is the double vertical furrow which signifies deep thought. He is always concerned with realities and not with appearances, because he does not care what men say about him. He is never afraid for long. He is very concilia-tory. To outsiders his acts appear sometimes childish and sometimes wise.

This type also stands in the sign of the Nun when it is separated and not included in the Zayin. So much for the mystery connected with the study of the forehead.

"The Eyes. The eyes are connected with the symbolism of the letter Samech. These are varieties of color and of form. In the substances which go to compose the visible discernible eye are contained four colors. There is the white of the ball, which is common to all sorts of eyes. Enclosed within this white is the darker hue of the iris—thus white and dark are united. Included in this dark there is yet another shade, a bluish tinge; and the inmost circle of color is black, this being the pupil.

"A man whose eyes are evenly set is straightforward and free from guile. A person with such eyes is always merry and full of jokes. He has good intentions, but seldom carries them out because of his fickleness. His mind is chiefly occupied with worldly things, but he has the capacity for spiritual matters if he should turn his thoughts toward them; therefore he should be encouraged in this direction. His eyebrows are long, slanting downward. In the midst of these several colors of the eye are sundry fine red veins, which are called the 'small letters' of the eyes, because, when the colors shine, their light causes the letters to be revealed in those veins to the initiated, these veins being formed in the shape of the letter Samech when it contains the letter Hey.

"A man who has blue eyes set in white will be of a kindly disposition, but at the same time selfish. If the black is not noticeable in his eyes, he will have strong desires, but not for evil, though he will not resist evil when it approaches. He can be trusted when he speaks of matters within his own knowledge, but not otherwise. He can keep a secret so long as it is a secret, but once it has leaked out he tells everything, since he does nothing perfectly. The colors of such an eye and the type to which its possessor conforms are contained in the mystery of the letter Hey when contained in the letters Zayin and Samech.

"He whose eyes are of a yellowish green color has madness in his veins; he therefore suffers from megalomania and is grandiloquent in his manner and speech. In discussion he is easily defeated. He is not worthy to be instructed in the mystical meanings of the Torah, as he does not accept them meekly but becomes puffed up with his knowledge. This type belongs to the mystery of the letter Hey, which is included in the letter Zayin only, being far removed from the letter Samech on account of his conceit. When such a man speaks, many wrinkles appear on his forehead.

"One whose eyes are pale with a certain admixture of a greenish hue is of an irascible disposition, but is also often kindhearted enough. When angered, however, he becomes cruel. He cannot be entrusted with a secret. He belongs to the sign of the letter Hey when it is included in the letter Samech.

"The man whose eyes are white and blue, with only a spot of black in them, can be trusted with secrets and makes good use of them. If he makes a good beginning in anything, he goes on prospering. His enemies cannot prevail against him; they can do him no evil, and eventually they are entirely subdued by him. Hey is under the sign of the letter Kaph when it is included in the letter Samech.

"So much for the mysteries concerning the eyes, which are revealed unto the wise.

"The Lineaments of the Countenance. For the masters of the inner wisdom the features of the face are not those which appear outwardly, but those within formed by internal forces; for the features of the face are molded by the impress of the inner face which is concealed in the spirit residing within. This spirit produces outward traits which are recognizable to the wise, the true features being discernible from the spirit. Man has a spirit on which the letters of the alphabet are in a way designed. All these letters are enclosed in that spirit, and for a time the designs of those letters enter into the face; and as they enter, the face appears with the design of these letters upon it. But this semblance lasts for a short time only, save upon the faces of adepts in wisdom, on whom it is always visible.

"There is a place which is called 'the world to come,' from whence issues the mystery of the Torah with its alphabet of twenty-two letters, which is the essence of all things. Now that 'river which goes out of Eden' carries all this along with it, so that when the spirits and the souls emerge therefrom, they are all stamped with the imprint of those letters; the which, when the spirit of a man be thus stamped by it, makes also a certain impression on the face." Said R. Simeon to them: "If so, the likeness of the Mother is not impressed upon the form of that spirit."

They replied: "This, Master, is the teaching which we have heard from thine own lips: the design of the letters proceeds from the side which is above, and the image of the Mother is impressed upon the spirit, while below, the form of the letter is hidden in the spirit. The design of the Mother which is outwardly discernible follows the four prototypes—Man, Lion, Bull, and Eagle, in the Supernal Chariot, and the spirit projects the image of them all for a time, because whatsoever belongs to the domain of the spirit thrusts itself forward and is both visible and invisible. All these forms are designed in the shape of the letters, and although they are hidden, they are discerned for a short space by those who have eyes to see, by the wise who can comprehend the mystery of wisdom, to contemplate therein."

Of the two major systems of Kabbalah found in the Zohar, the practical (or magical) and the speculative, the latter is more important. Speculative Kabbalah attempted to define and explain the mystic relationship between the world known to the senses of man and the pure spiritual essence of God. Central to this explanation was the concept of the ten *sephirot* or emanations that mediate between the physical universe and the heavens.

The Roman-Greek philosopher Plotinus had refined the idea of emanations from the ideas of earlier philosophers and other cultures. The Sefer Yetzirah extended this concept. The Spanish-Jewish poet-philosopher Solomon ibn Gabirol (1021–1067) described the creation of the world by emanations that became less spiritual and more material as they receded further and further from the Source. The Zohar brought all these ideas into a single focus.

The basic Kabbalist doctrine of the ten *sephirot* begins with the mystic premise that the idea of God cannot be grasped by the human mind. Yet nothing can exist outside God, Whom the Kabbalists called *En Sof,* Without End, the Boundless One. Philo had put it, "God encloses the world, but is Himself not enclosed by anything." This being so, how could the universe have been created without incorporating part of God within it? This was one paradox—a part of the Boundless One contained within the bounded universe. There was a second paradox: if the universe was created by God, there must have been a time before creation. This supposes that at some moment in time God changed his mind (will) from not creating to creating. But God is changeless, so how could He have changed from non-creating to creating?

Kabbalah begins the explanation by positing a difference between God's will and man's. When a man thinks or creates a thought in his mind, the thought remains an abstraction. But when God thinks, the thought immediately has concrete spiritual existence: thus the *sephirot* which make God's existence known. They are the channels through which God's purely spiritual power became physically creative.

The *sephirot* exist in time and by the will of God—yet they have a kind of potential eternality in them. They are not creations, for created things lose their connection with the Creator, and thus eventually lose their God-given power. But the *sephirot,* as agencies of God's power, must be able to supply sustenance to all things for all times; they cannot lose their power. *Sephirot* are divine manifestations through which God is known. All created things exist only because something of the power of the *sephirot* lives and acts in them.

One of the master Kabbalists of the Safed school explained the eternal simultaneous existence and non-existence of the *sephirot* in a parable: if a stone is struck by iron, sparks fly out. Yet the fire does not exist in the stone or in the iron.[7]

The Kabbalists gave the *sephirot* names, qualities, gender, even color. These masculine and feminine, black, white, blue, and green *sephirot* became as familiar to the Jews as the prophets and heavenly begins; they were addressed, petitioned, and appealed to by their formal and informal names. They were a part of the average Jew's household angelology and demonology.

The ten *sephirot* were arranged in a rigid hierarchy, and each lower *sephirah* grew out of the one immediately above; that is, the second ranking *sephirah* grew out of the first, the third out of the second, etc. Thus the first *sephirah* had all the powers of the *sephirot* under him; the

[7] Moses Cordevero, *Garden of Pomegranates,* sixteenth century.

second had its own power plus all the powers of the succeeding eight, and so on. They were:

1. *Kether* (Crown), also called the Simple Point, because this initial and paramount *sephirah* was unknown and all-embracing. Kether was known familiarly as the Old One, the Ancient of Days (from Daniel 7:9), the White Head, or the Long Face.

2. *Hochmah* (Wisdom) was also known as *Aba* (Father) and was the masculine outgrowth of the Ancient One. This *sephirah* introduced the idea of sexual dualism that runs through the Kabbalah. The Zohar said, "When the Holy One gave definite form to everything that exists, He made things in either masculine or feminine form."

3. *Binah* (Understanding or Intelligence), the highest feminine emanation in the order of *sephirot,* also known as *Ima* (Mother).

4. *Hesed* (Kindness) is also called *Gedulah* (Greatness) and is masculine.

5. *Geburah* (Power) is also called *Din* (Justice) and is feminine.

6. *Tipheret* (Glory or Beauty) is both masculine and feminine because it is a combination of Hesed and Geburah.

7. *Netzah* (Firmness, Might, Victory) is masculine.

8. *Hod* (Splendor) is feminine.

9. *Yesod* (Foundation) combines Netzah and Hod.

10. *Malkut* (Kingdom) has no special attributes but is a kind of funnel through which the qualities of the upper nine *sephirot* are transmitted to the physical world. It is therefore also called *Shechinah,* the Spirit of God.

There were several systems of ascribing color to the *sephirot,* the major one being that of Moses Cordovero. He said Kether was totally black, Hochmah light blue, Binah grass-green, Hesed white, Geburah red, Tipheret light yellow, Netzah white tinged with red, Hod red tinged with white, Yesod reddish yellow; Malkut, representing all the *sephirot,* is all colors.

The first nine *sephirot* were grouped in threes, each triad including a masculine element, a feminine element, and a combining element. The first three *sephirot* represented the world of thought; the second, the world of emotions and morals; the third, the world of nature. The tenth *sephirah,* Malkut, existed alone as the harmony of the other nine.

This triune was paralleled by the Kabbalists' version of the three-part soul—an idea expressed earlier by Plato, Aristotle, the Bible, and the Talmud. The soul called *Neshamah* represented the intellect and corresponded to the first three *sephirot*. The soul called *Ruah* represented the emotion and corresponded to the Hesed-Geburah-Tipheret triad. The soul called *Nefesh* represented man's animal nature and corresponded to the lowest triad of *sephirot*.

Another central concept of the Kabbalah was of *Adam Kadmon*, the Ancient Adam or Primordial Man. Although the writings of Philo were not known to the creators of the Kabbalah, they were familiar with the concept expressed in Philo's idea of Man-before-man—that before man existed, the idea of man existed—and this was the Primordial Man. This highest form of creation reflected in his being and form all that was in creation. Thus the Ancient Adam had within him representations of the ten *sephirot*. The Zohar said: "Before the Holy One, Blessed be He, created any form in the universe, He was without form. But after He made this form . . . of the Heavenly Man, He Himself was expressed in that form."

According to the major system of Kabbalah, the first *sephirah,* Kether, was represented by the head of *Adam Kadmon*, Hochmah was the brain, Binah was the heart, Hesed was the right arm, Geburah was the left arm, Tipheret was the chest, Netzah and Hod were the right and left legs, Yesod was the genital organs, and Malkut was the soles of the feet.[8]

Even this involved system of *sephirot* and the Primordial Man did not quite answer the problem of the connection between the ultimate spirituality and goodness of *En Sof,* the Infinite, and the base matter of the sensory world. So the early Kabbalists pictured intervening worlds. There were two groups of such worlds. The first group of four included the world of emanations; *Beriah,* the world of creative ideas in which is the Throne of God and the heavenly halls, and where the souls of the pious dwell; *Yetzirah,* the world of creative formations, the home of the ten orders of angels and the spirits of man; and *Asiyah,* the world of matter and action, where the Prince of Darkness and the heavenly hosts wage an unending battle.

There was a second group of dead worlds. According to Kabbalistic doctrine, the world of man was not the first world created by God; he created several earlier worlds, but they were imperfect because they lacked some essential qualities, mainly the male-female element, and so were discarded by God. A *midrash* says: "God created worlds after worlds, and destroyed them, until He finally made one of which He

---

[8] The physician and alchemist Paracelsus (sixteenth century), forerunner of modern medicine, was a Kabbalist and used this Kabbalistic representation of man in his medical theories.

could say, 'This one pleases Me, but the others did not please Me.' " [9] However, they could not be totally destroyed because nothing created by God (Who created everything) can be destroyed; things can only be changed. (Here the Kabbalists anticipated the modern physical law of the conservation of matter.)

These imperfect dead worlds are the source of evil, and the worlds of evil are mirror images of the worlds in which goodness exists. For every good thing in this world, there is an evil thing in the dead worlds; these evils seek constant entry into this world and are too often successful in establishing themselves here.

The Kabbalah held that evil is the reverse of divine. Where the divine is real, evil is unreal; where the divine is infinite, evil is finite. Evil occurs in man when he accepts the semblance of reality for reality itself; by so doing, man moves away from the divine source rather than trying to unite himself with it. But the Kabbalists also accepted the idea, although grudgingly, that evil was somehow necessary. One master compared evil with the shell of a nut—useless but necessary.

The soul of man, said the Kabbalists, pre-exists in one of the upper worlds before man is born. The complete, unassigned soul is both masculine and feminine. The two halves are split, the masculine element going to a male child, the feminine to a female child. If the earthly souls are kept from evil, they are united in marriage. Keeping the soul from evil is primarily the responsibility of the male; if he lives an upright life, he will make a proper marriage—that is, he will marry the woman who possesses the other half of his soul. If he lives an improper life, he will make an improper marriage—to a woman whose soul is foreign to his. Obviously, there can be no joy in such a marriage.

Since the soul descends from on high, it must return in time. But the soul, which is given in a pure state, can return only in a similar state. A soul soiled by an unrighteous life cannot return to heaven. Instead, it is given to another body, and another, and another, until it is finally cleansed by a life of goodness.

This idea of the transmigration of souls, widely known in Oriental religions, particularly Hinduism, was rejected by Jews as unworthy of the Torah until the Kabbalah gave it sanction. In a time of persecution and low estate, this concept offered an answer to the Job question: why do the righteous suffer? Obviously, because their souls sinned in previous incarnations and were expiating their sins. Thus ethics became the highest aim of the Kabbalists, for the return of the soul to heaven in a pure state—man's first duty—is accomplished through ethical conduct.

Sometimes, try as they might, souls could not get rid of the burden

[9] Genesis Rabbah

of sin they had accumulated. Then God, in His mercy, might put two souls into a single body, that each might give strength to the other to achieve purification. But sometimes an unclean soul, waiting in nothingness for assignment and another chance to cleanse itself, might enter the body of a good person of its own volition, seeking to rid itself of the accumulation of sin and guilt. This extra, unclean soul was called a *dybbuk,* and later Kabbalists developed elaborate methods of exorcising these evil spirts.

As astrology was more widely known and used than astronomy, alchemy more widely believed than chemistry, so the practical-magical Kabbalah was more widely known than the speculative. But even this part of Kabbalah stemmed quite logically from the intellectual conjectures of the philosophers. Religious philosophy and mysticism both began as a deep interest in the manifestations of God. Since the most awesome—and troublesome—manifestation of God was the creation of the universe, mystics and philosophers were particularly interested in God's creative aspects.

The logical first step in considering the creation was to consider the Torah, for herein is the record of creation and God's role in creation. The Rabbis considered that the idea of the Torah was the very first thing created; it existed before the universe. And since the Torah is the Written Law, the letters that make up the Torah had to be created before the world was created. Thus the letters of the Torah had mystical powers. It followed, then, that special arrangements of letters making special words, and the manipulation of these words, could invoke mystical Godly powers from before the Creation. Naturally, if words have special powers, the most powerful words are those that represent the names of God.

Hebrew, like other early written languages, uses letters for numbers. The first letter, *aleph,* is also one; the second letter, *beth,* is two; *gimel* is three, etc. Thus numbers—which can be manipulated much more easily than letters—can also be put together in magical sequences. This was the background for the magical science called *gematria* in Hebrew, or numerology today.

By this science, Kabbalists created innumerable magic words. The letters making up the names of God were rearranged to form still other words, also magical. Adding up the numerical equivalents of the letters in the names of God gave a magic number, and thousands of other words had the same numerical total. Whole sentences became magic if the first letters of the words spelled—or added up to—one of the magic words derived from the names of God. Then there were special systems of substitutions to create even more magic words. One system substituted the last letter of the alphabet for the first, the next to last for the second, and so on. A second system divided the twenty-two letter Hebrew alphabet into two series of eleven letters each; the first letter of the first series was substituted for the first letter of the second series, and so on until a complete interchange was effected.

By these mystical letter and number games, God's name could be found in almost any passage of the Bible, and that passage became a part of Kabbalistic magic. One scholar, Nachmanides (thirteenth century), held that the entire Torah was composed of the names of God in various combinations.

Angels came late into Jewish theology, generally from the non-Jewish myths of the East. The early books of the Bible speak of some vague heavenly beings called *malochim* (singular, *malach*). Although *malach* is usually translated angel, its literal meaning is messenger. Later Biblical books developed the idea of *malochim,* but it wasn't until the Book of Daniel, written in the second century B.C., that some of these heavenly creatures were given names. Daniel mentions Gabriel (*geber* is man, *El* is God) and Michael. The later non-canonical books built a whole hierarchy of angels, headed by Metatron, prince of the heavenly hosts.

By using the mystical letter and number substitutions on the names of the angels, the Kabbalists came up with still more thousands of magic words. This wasn't merely an exercise, like working out the value of *pi* to a hundred more decimal places; the Kabbalists had a very practical purpose in this multiplication of magic symbols. Knowing an angel's secret name gave the Kabbalist a limited power over that angel. And if the angel had power over the wind or the rain, he could be forced to bring rain during a drought or blow the clouds away during a storm. If the angel had power over the human body or a portion of it, he could be made to cure disease. Almost any angel could be used to guard against evil spirits. From this concept came the idea of amulets and charms. An amulet containing the secret name of the angel with power over cholera would be effective against that disease. A charm with the secret name of the angel of cows would keep the cows from going dry.

In the end, Kabbalah served two major purposes: it elevated prayer, the mystic union of man with God, to a central position in Judaism, when formal Talmudic study tended to de-emphasize it; and it moved Jews away from the dead end of Aristotelianism. But in so doing, Kabbalah also gave to Judaism—particularly to Chasidism—a burden of magic and superstition that was foreign to its ethical-rationalistic base.

FOURTEEN

Liturgy: The Siddur

THE JEWISH BIBLE, developed over a period of fifteen hundred years, was finally closed in the year 90. The Oral Law, which grew for more than a millennium, was effectively enclosed in 500. The codes of law, fluid for more than a thousand years, were frozen in the sixteenth century. Of all the books that determined the daily course of the life of the Jew, only the *Siddur,* the Prayer Book, which began in the period of the Second Temple, remained and remains open.

The Siddur also remains one of the least known of the great works of Jewish religious literature. The Bible has been the subject of intense study by Jewish and non-Jewish scholars. The more parochial books—the Talmud, the commentaries, the Zohar, and the works of philosophy such as *The Guide of the Perplexed*—have also evoked great interest among Christian savants. But Jewish liturgy and its central book, the Siddur, is the one major branch of Jewish religious literature that has not been extensively studied and written about.

Yet "to millions of Jews, every word of [the Siddur] is familiar and loved; and its phrases and responses, especially in the sacred melodies associated with them, can stir them to the depths of their being. No other volume has penetrated the Jewish home as has the Siddur; or has exercised, and continues to exercise, so profound an influence on the life, character, and outlook of the Jewish people, as well in the sphere of personal religion as of moral conduct." [1]

Prayer is as universal and as natural to man as thought. People in all cultures pray, even in those societies in which prayer has been outlawed. "The reason we pray," said William James, "is simply that we cannot

---

[1] Dr. Joseph H. Hertz, *The Daily Prayer Book,* Bloch, 1948.

help praying." The Kabbalists had, as always, a more fanciful and more allegorical explanation. The Zohar says:

As the flame clothes the black, sooty clod in a garment of fire, and releases the heat imprisoned therein, even so does prayer clothe the man in a garment of holiness, evoke the light and fire implanted in him by his Maker, illumine his whole being, and unite the lower and upper worlds.

In ancient cultures, prayer and sacrifice were a single entity. Plato said prayer and sacrifice were inseparable. Among the Jews, too, prayer played a definite role in the Second Temple sacrifice ritual. But the Pentateuch mentions only two specific prayers associated with sacrifice: a prayer when the first fruits are brought to the Temple, and a prayer involving tithing.[2]

There is, however, much more frequent mention in the Torah of prayer not associated with sacrifice. At one of the most agonizing moments in Jewish religious history, when Moses came down from Mt. Sinai with the Tablets of the Law and saw that the Jews had turned from God to the golden calf, Moses did not offer sacrifice to appease God's anger. He interceded for the Jews in prayer unassociated with a material gift.

Biblical Jews appear to have prayed where and when they were moved to do so, without thought of sacrifice. For example, after the battle against the Philistines at Gath, David voices his thanks: "The Lord is my rock, and my fortress, and my deliverer. . . ."[3] The early Psalms were probably sung during ceremonies involving Temple sacrifices, but they were also sung by shepherds alone in the night.

Jewish prayer includes all the forms used by other cultures: adoration, confession, petition, joy, thanksgiving, and declaration. But in its broadest concept, Jewish prayer has a unique quality—if, as modern linguistics holds, the root meanings of words are an indication of deepest communal psychology. The root of the Greek word for prayer is "to wish." The root in German is "to beg." The literal meaning of the Hebrew word *tefillah* (prayer) is "to judge oneself." In effect, when the Jew prays, he calls upon God to render judgment. As Abraham cried out: "Shall not the Judge of all the earth do justly?"[4]

Nor can a Jew shrink from the judgment rendered by God as a result of prayer. This essential feeling about prayer was expressed by Job: "Though He slay me, yet will I trust in Him."[5]

[2] Deuteronomy 26:5–15.
[3] II Samuel 22:2.
[4] Genesis 18:25.
[5] Job 13:15. Marvin H. Pope, ("Job," *The Anchor Bible,* Doubleday, 1965) translates this: "He may slay me, I'll not quaver." Robert Gordis (*The Book of God and Man,* University of Chicago Press, 1966) translates it: "Yes, He may slay me; I have no hope, but I will justify my ways to His face."

Formal congregational prayer not associated with sacrifice is, according to most scholars, a Jewish invention of the sixth century B.C. With the destruction of the First Temple (586 B.C.), sacrifices could no longer be offered. A small, fragmented people was forcibly removed from their land—and from their God for those who held to the idea, universal at the time, that a god belonged to a specific place. Yet this people lived for several generations in a foreign land, in the midst of a powerful culture, without losing their identity or their God. Even after those who had been transported, those who had a memory of the old religion, were dead, their descendants maintained religious unity and cohesiveness. They returned to Palestine with heightened national feeling and stronger religious identity. The synagogue, whose development cannot be divorced from the development of the liturgy, played a major role in this event.

In Babylon, group prayer substituted for the Temple sacrifices. The prophets and priests who had accompanied the Jews to Babylon, particularly Ezekiel, gathered the Jews together on the sabbath and holidays, read the pre-canonical Bible, sang the Psalms, and repeated the prophecies. They composed new prayers for redemption and return that expressed the national rather than the individual soul. In effect, the Jews in Babylon became a body of worshipers—a congregation.

This pattern was not forgotten when the Jews returned to Palestine and built the Second Temple. Sacrifices were begun again once there was a place for sacrifice, but local congregations also continued to function. By the fourth century B.C. there were hundreds of groups of Jews who met on the sabbath to hold religious services in special places designated for this purpose. Another religious practice, which grew up at the same time, combined with the prayer service: in order to make sure that everyone was aware of the contents of the Torah—which had been adopted as a national constitution and religious guide in the middle of the fifth century B.C.—the Torah was read and explained whenever large numbers of people gathered. Since towns were crowded on the sabbath and on the second and fifth days of the week—the farmers' market days—the Torah was read then. Thus Torah reading and instruction on Mondays, Thursdays, sabbaths, and festivals became part of the Jewish religious service.

These new places of congregational worship were not restricted to Palestine. They grew up wherever Jews lived. The first mention of a non-Palestinian Jewish house of worship, in Egypt, is in documents dating from the middle of the third century B.C. The names used in those documents to designate the place are the names still used: in Greek, synagogue; in Hebrew, *Beth haKnesset* (House of Assembly).

The service in the synagogue had nothing to do with sacrifices or priests. Sacrifice was restricted to the Temple in Jerusalem. Thus the men who led the religious devotions and who read and explained the Torah did not have to be drawn from the priestly class. Any person of learning who had the respect of the congregation could do so. The Sacred Word, not the sacrifice, became the core of worship; learning, not priestly inheritance, became the requirement for leadership.

With the synagogue there began a new type of worship in the history of humanity; the type of congregational worship without priest or ritual still maintained substantially in its ancient form in the modern synagogue; and still to be traced in the forms of Christian worship. . . . In their long history, the Jewish people have done scarcely anything more wonderful than to create the synagogue. No human institution has a longer continuing history, and none has done more for the uplifting of the human race."[6]

The destruction of the Second Temple in the year 70, and the almost total destruction of the Jews of Palestine in the Second Roman War, 132–135, might have been fatal to the existence of the Jews as a religious civilization. That it was not may well have been due to the existence of synagogues wherever Jews dwelt.

The development of congregational prayer did not interfere with the parallel development of personal prayer. Jews pray, not only in the synagogue, but everywhere and on all occasions. Every manifestation of the divine wonder brings forth a blessing. The observant Jew recites a blessing, for example, when he sees a rainbow, when he eats, when he comes upon a particularly beautiful or pleasing sight, when he washes his hands—even, in the old days, on moving his bowels. Women, who have a comparatively small part in synagogical prayer, have much to do at home. New dishes are washed before using by the observant housewife. As she puts them into the water, she says: "Blessed art Thou, O Lord our God, who has sanctified us by Thy commandments and commanded us to immerse vessels." Every type of food has its own prayer. On eating bread, the blessing is ". . . who bringest forth bread from the earth"; on eating fruit, the blessing is ". . . who createst the fruit of the tree"; on eating fruit that grows on the earth (strawberries or melons), the blessing is ". . . who createst the fruit of the vine"; on eating grain other than bread, the blessing is ". . . who createst various kinds of good"; and on eating fish, eggs, meat, etc., the blessing is ". . . by whose word all things exist."

The basic Jewish liturgy still used in the synagogues was established by the Men of the Great Assembly (also called the Great Synagogue and the Great Sanhedrin). These were the prophets, scribes, sages, and

⁶ R. T. Herford, *Judaism in the New Testament Period*, Lindsey Press, London, 1928.

teachers who governed Jewish religious and secular life between the time of Ezra (5th century B.C.) and the establishment of the Hasmonean kingdom (middle of the second century B.C.). They established the ancient *Shema* as the basic statement of the liturgy and the *brachah* (plural *berachot*—benediction or blessing) as the basic form of prayer. Every *brachah* began with the same three Hebrew words, and still does: *Baruch atoh Adoney* (Blessed art Thou, O Lord.)

The Men of the Great Assembly also instituted formal home worship as part of the liturgy. Home worship centered around two rituals: *Kiddush* and *Havdalah*. *Kiddush* is said on drinking wine and affirms God's role as Creator, Deliverer, and Lawgiver. *Havdalah* is celebrated at sundown at the close of the sabbath and marks the division between the holy and the secular, the light and the darkness.

Two other concepts of the Men of the Great Assembly permanently marked Jewish worship: the idea of group prayers, and the plural form in prayers. Divine worship became a group function rather than an individual affair; the Jew prayed as a member of a brotherhood rather than as a single person. And his prayers asked or blessed or thanked in the name of "us" and "we": for the community, not for himself alone.

With some few exceptions, the prayers in the service are said in Hebrew rather than Aramaic, the language of the Jews during much of the period of the development of the liturgy. This served to remove the service further from the secular life, to confirm its holiness by the use of the holy tongue. It also made the service universal; wherever Jews lived, whatever their secular language, they all prayed in the same holy language.

The Hellenistic Jews, particularly in Egypt, refused to go along with this use of Hebrew in divine service. They carried on their services in Greek and read the Torah in its Greek translation (the Pentateuch). But these Jews died out—a fact which the later Rabbis offered as a lesson to those who would abandon the holy tongue.

By the end of the first century, the essential order of the service was fixed. The central obligatory rituals were the recitation of the single creedal statement of the Jews, the *Shema*: "Hear, O Israel, the Lord our God, the Lord is One," [7] and eighteen benedictions. There was also a recitation of the Ten Commandments and reading of portions of the Torah.

Other hymns and prayers were added during the Talmudic period. These were often prayers, composed by rabbis or scholars for their personal devotions, which became so popular that they were worked

---

[7] Deuteronomy 6:4.

into the pattern of the congregational service. Great numbers of these prayers, called *piyyutim,* were written then, and in almost every century since. Many became part of the voluntary part of the liturgy, prayers inserted into the service as the individual or congregation pleased or was moved to do.

The *piyyutim* were of particular importance to the Jews in later centuries. In many times and countries the synagogue was the only place in which a Jew could speak freely. It was the only place in which he could express his protests, voice his hopes, and give thanks for his joys. So while many *piyyutim* were in praise of God, many more recited the woes of the people—and demanded justice.

Another form of prayers developed in the Diaspora were the *selichot,* penitential prayers, which became part of the liturgy for fast days and other occasions.

The prayers and the order in which they were recited in the service were not written down during the Talmudic era. However, starting about 500, some forms of prayer books began to appear. Generally, these merely listed the required introductions to prayers and the most important prayer arrangements. For the most part, these early compilations followed a sequence ascribed to Rabbi Meir in the Talmud. Rabbi Meir said every Jew is obliged to recite one hundred benedictions every day. Some of these blessings were contained in the daily services; others were recited on occasions such as arising, breaking the fast, performing any natural bodily function, eating a fruit for the first time that season, or seeing a rainbow or other natural phenomenon.

The best known of these compilations—and the first real Siddur [8] —was by Amram Gaon, head of the academy of Sura in the ninth century. This prayer book, *Compendium of Prayers and Benedictions for the Entire Year,* was arranged and set down by Amram in response to a request from the Jews of Spain. (There did not appear to be any need for such a book in Babylon or Palestine.) A century later, Saadiah Gaon compiled a complete prayer book, *Collection of Prayers and Songs of Prayers,* as a standard text to take the place of the many local prayer books that had grown up.

Prayer books continued to be compiled; in time they developed into encyclopedia covering the entire cycle of Jewish religious life. Maimonides, for example, wrote an authoritative prayer book in the twelfth century which gave the order of prayers for the entire year. These books were called *Machzor,* or repetition. Today, Machzor is

---

[8] From *Siddur Hatefillot,* the order of prayers. *Siddur* is the same word as *Seder,* the name given the ceremonial meal which opens the holiday of Passover. Both mean "order," in the sense of arrangement.

the name given the holiday prayer book; Siddur is the name given the daily and sabbath prayer book.

As the cultural and ritual divisions between Mediterranean and European Jews widened, two major versions of the prayer book developed. The Palestinian Siddur was adopted and adapted by the Ashkenazic Jews of France. Germany, Poland, and Eastern Europe. The Babylonian Siddur grew into the prayer book of the Sephardic Jews of Spain, Turkey, Egypt, and the Mediterranean. While these were the major rites among Jews, they were not the only ones. Minor rites developed their own prayer books, so there were Italian, Byzantine, North African, and Yemenite *siddurim,* as well as local prayer books for the Jews of Avignon, Corfu, and Tripoli.

The publishing of a prayer book, no matter how great the authority of its compiler or editor, did not close the Siddur. Prayers and poems continued to be added with each major revision. The Spanish poets of the eleventh to thirteenth centuries are well represented in almost all prayer books. The Kabbalah and Chasidism were important sources of new *piyyutim* and benedictions. The universally beloved prayer *Lechah Dodi* was written in the sixteenth century. The prayer for the lawful government composed by Joseph Hertz, Chief Rabbi of the British Empire, was written about 1890. And the Orthodox prayer book of Rabbi David de Sola Pool, including many new arrangements and prayers, was published in 1960.

The first Reform prayer book, *The Hamburg Prayer Book,* was published in 1818 and marked a break with all past *siddurim.* This and succeeding Reform prayer books gave the order for a shorter service, one more in keeping with the esthetic and cultural patterns of the countries for which they are written, including many psalms, *piyyutim,* and prayers translated into the local language. *The Union Prayer Book,* the official Reform prayer book for the United States, for example, has more English than Hebrew and eliminates such ancient prayers as those asking for a return to Temple worship. The prayer book of the Conservative congregations, *The Sabbath and Festival Prayer Book,* attempts to "bring tradition into focus with contemporary life." It takes account of the many instances in the Siddur where modern attitudes vary from traditional formulations. It drops passages dealing specifically with animal sacrifices, but includes the prayer for the restoration of Temple worship on Mount Zion. Modern Orthodox prayer books with English translations facing the original Hebrew text have also been published, notably the very scholarly *Daily Prayer Book* of the late Chief Rabbi of the British Empire, Dr. Joseph H. Hertz, and the very beautiful translation in *The Traditional Prayer Book* of Rabbi David De Sola Pool.

The Siddur gives the order of prayer for the three daily services of Jewish worship: the morning service, *Shaharit* (*shahar* means dawn); the afternoon service, *Minchah*, from the word that came to describe the afternoon sacrifice in the Temple; and *Maariv*, the evening service, from *arvit* (of the evening). On sabbaths and holidays there was an additional service in the Temple, so on sabbaths and holidays the synagogue has an additional service, *Musaf* (that which is added).

In the Western world and wherever Jews had to follow the work schedules of the societies in which they lived, it became difficult for a Jew to stop his work in midday to attend afternoon services. So the custom arose of having a combined afternoon and evening service at the end of the day—shortly before the sun went down and shortly after; there were Jews who thought *Minchah-Maariv* was a single word describing a single service.

Despite the many differences in rites and customs, in prayers and the order of prayers, the core of the Jewish service established in the first century remains essentially the same today. Here is the usual order of the modern Ashkenazi morning service (afternoon and evening services are shorter versions of the morning service with some variations; for example, the *Shema* is not said in the *Minchah* service):

1. Preliminary blessings and psalms
2. The *Shema*
3. The *Amidah* (Eighteen Benedictions)
4. The *Tachanun* (petition for pardon)
5. Reading of the Torah on sabbaths, Mondays, and Thursdays (including the *Musaf* addition on sabbaths)
6. The *Ashrei* prayer
7. The *Aleynu* prayer
8. Mourners' *Kaddish*
9. Psalm of the Day and closing hymns.

The opening hymns and blessings begin as the Jew enters the synagogue and recites, "How goodly are thy tents, O Jacob, and thy dwelling places, O Israel . . .," following by selections from the Psalms. In modern synagogues, all this is said congregationally after the people have taken their seats.

The preliminary blessings, each beginning with the six-word formula *"Baruch atoh Adoney, Elohenu Melech ha olam"* (Blessed art Thou, O Lord our God, King of the Universe), give thanks for the ability to distinguish between light and darkness (this is the morning service), for not having been born a heathen, for not having been born a women (women say, "for having made me according to Thy will"), for opening the eyes of the blind, for clothing the naked, for freeing those who are bound, for raising up those who are bowed down, and so on.

Since study is a necessary part of every man's daily service to God and a workman may not have another opportunity for study that day, the preliminary morning service includes a lesson from the Talmud. The usual portion studied at this time explains the thirteen principles of logic by which the Torah is interpreted.

The regular service begins with the singing of the last six psalms in the Book of Psalms—numbers 145 through 150—as well as some composite psalms and the Song of Moses (Exodus 14:30 to 15:18).

In the Temple service the Ten Commandments were recited just before the *Shema,* and this order was followed in the early synagogues. The Rabbis of the Talmud stopped this practice, although the Decalogue is still recited in some Eastern synagogues after the close of the service. Such a drastic and basic change in the order of service needed a powerful reason. It was provided by the early Christians, who held that the only part of the Law that had validity after the coming of Jesus was that contained in the Ten Commandments. So, since the Christians read the Decalogue at their service and taunted the Jews for following the rest of the Law, the Rabbis expunged it from the Jewish service.

The *Shema* is preceded by the formal call to prayer: "Bless ye the Lord Who is to be blessed," to which the congregation responds, "Blessed is the Lord Who is to be blessed for ever and ever." Then follow two traditional benedictions, one giving thanks for the daily renewal of creation, the second for the moral light given through the Torah.

The full *Shema* is then recited congregationally. This includes in addition to the statement of the universality and Oneness of God, Deuteronomy 6:4–9, Deuteronomy 11:13–21, and Numbers 15:37–41. The first paragraph requires the Jew to teach the Law to his children, to bind it upon his arm and forehead (the phylacteries), and to place it on the doorposts of his house (the *mezuzah*). The second paragraph repeats the injunctions for phylacteries and *mezuzah* and lists the earthly and heavenly rewards for those who do so. The third paragraph orders the wearing of fringes (*tsitsit*) on the corners of garments "that ye may look upon it, and remember all the commandments of the Lord, and do them . . . and be holy unto your God."

The benediction recited immediately after the *Shema* is the re-demption prayer opening, "True and certain . . . is this Thy Word for ever and ever," and closing, "O Rock of Israel, arise to the help of Israel, and deliver according to Thy promise. . . ."

The second obligatory section of the service follows the *Shema* and consists of the *Shemonei Esreh,* the Eighteen Benedictions, also called the *Amidah* (Standing) prayer because it is said standing. (The Rabbis also called it simply the Prayer because of its central importance.) Although this series of prayers continues to be called the Eighteen Benedictions, there actually are nineteen, and only seven or eight are pronounced on the sabbath. They fall into three groups: the initial three, the middle thirteen, and the final three. The three final blessings were said by the priests of the Second Temple and are required to be said at all synagogue services. The middle thirteen were written later and are said in their entirety only during weekday morning services.

The three opening benedictions of the *Amidah* are praises and embody the fundamental Jewish beliefs about God, His Covenant, the election of Israel, the promise of the coming of the Messiah, and immortality. The third blessing opens with one of the magnificent outcries repeated in the service: *Kodosh, kodosh, kodosh Adoney tsvahot* (Holy, holy, holy is the Lord of Hosts). The three closing blessings are prayers for the reestablishment of divine service in Jerusalem, for God's daily wonders, and for peace and prosperity.

The thirteen intermediate prayers are petitions. They include six for individual well-being and seven for national well-being. The first six ask for understanding, repentance, forgiveness, deliverance from harm, healing, and deliverance from want. The community petitions ask for the end of the dispersion of the Jews, for the return to a government of judges and counselors under God, for protection against slanderers, for special mercy for the righteous (the leaders of the community, its scholars, and those who have converted to Judaism), for the rebuilding of Jerusalem, for the coming of the Messiah, and for acceptance of these prayers.

The twelfth benediction, asking protection against slanderers, was probably added in the second century and is the one that makes the Eighteen Benedictions actually nineteen. The original language invoked God's protection against sectaries, by which the Jews meant the Christians who were stirring up the Romans against the Jews during that period. But Church pressure in later centuries forced a change in the language of this benediction from "sectaries" to "And for *slanderers* let there be no hope, and let all wickedness perish. . . ."

The form of the *Shemonei Esreh* used on sabbaths includes the opening and closing six benedictions and verses representative of the others. A common middle section is a poem in which each line represents one of the thirteen benedictions. There are also very abbreviated versions to be used in desperate times when the full recitation, or even the shortened form, would imperil the congregation. One of these very short versions, composed by a Rabbi of the Talmud, says: "Let Thy will be done in Heaven above; grant tranquillity of spirit to those who reverence Thee below; and do that which is good in Thy sight. Blessed art Thou, O Lord, Who hearest prayer."

The Eighteen Benedictions are first said standing and silently in order to allow unrestrained confession on the part of the individual praying. After the silent *Amidah*, the reader (the person conducting the service, generally the cantor in the modern synagogue) recites it aloud for those who may not be able to say it themselves.

Following the *Amidah,* and in several other places in various services, is one of the loveliest of prayers:

My God, guard my tongue from evil,
And my lips from speaking with guile.
   Be my soul silent to those who reproach me,
   To all be my soul lowly as the dust.
Open my heart through Thy Torah
That my soul may follow Thy commandments.
   And may all who design evil against me
   Speedily see their design as naught, their purposes defeated.
Do so for the glory of Thy name. Do so for Thy right hand.
Do so for Thy holiness. Do so for Thy Torah,
   That Thy loved ones may be saved.
   Answer my prayer, and save me through Thy right hand.
May the words of my mouth and the meditation of my heart
Find grace before Thee, Lord, my Rock and my Redeemer.
   Creator of harmony of the spheres,
   Mayest Thou create peace for us and for all Israel. Amen.

The *Tachanun* prayers follow the *Amidah* except on sabbaths and festival days. This daily petition for pardon generally includes a silent portion and a portion recited by the reader of the service. It opens with the confession: "O Thou who art merciful and gracious, I have sinned before thee. O Lord, full of mercy, have mercy upon me and receive my supplications." The petition is said with the head bowed, generally resting on the hand, symbolic of prostrating oneself before the altar of the Temple. (Jews do not kneel in prayer.) The choice of prayers and psalms recited during the *Tachanun* is unimportant, as every rite and even locality appears to have its own favorite selections. What is important in this section of the service is the opportunity provided by the silent praying for a full and openhearted dialogue with God.

On Mondays, Thursdays, sabbaths, and holidays the Torah is read after the *Tachanun* prayer, or after the *Amidah* if the *Tachanun* is not said. The portion of the Torah to be read on any day is fixed, and every synagogue in the world following a particular rite reads the same portion on the same day. In ancient Palestine, the Torah was divided so that the three-times-weekly portions would complete the reading of the five books in three years. The more aggressive Babylonian Jews arranged the portions so that the Torah was read within a year. The last verses of the last book, Deuteronomy, and the opening verses of the first book, Genesis, are read on the holiday of *Simchat Torah* (The Rejoicing of the Law) at the close of the autumn harvest festival.

On opening the Ark to remove the Torah for the reading, the following prayers are recited (some parts are not recited on the sabbath): [9]

When the Ark moved forward Moses would say, "Arise, O Lord, and may Thine enemies be dispersed, and they who hate Thee flee before Thee."
For from Zion shall go forth Torah,
And the word of the Lord from Jerusalem
Blessed be He
Who in His holiness has given the Torah
To His people Israel.
The Lord, the Lord, compassionate and gracious God, slow to anger and great in mercy and truth, keeping loving-kindness for thousands, forgiving iniquity, transgression, and sin, and offering absolution.

[This portion is silent prayer.]

Lord of the universe, fulfill the prayers of my heart for good. Respond to my desires and answer my prayerful petition. May it be given to me and to all my family to perform Thy will with a whole heart. Deliver us from evil impulse, and grant our lot in Thy Torah, thus making us worthy of the indwelling of Thy Divine Presence among us. Bestow on us the spirit of wisdom and understanding, the spirit of counsel and might, the spirit of knowledge and reverence for the Lord.

May it be Thy will, Lord our God, God of our fathers, that we be privileged to do deeds that are good in Thy sight, and to walk before Thee in the ways of the upright. Hallow us through Thy commandments that we may be worthy of a happy and long life even unto the world to come. Guard us from evil deeds and from evil times that may come upon this world. For he who trusts in the Lord, loving-kindness shall encompass him. Amen.

May the words of my mouth and the meditation of my heart find grace before Thee, Lord, my Rock and my Redeemer.
Lord, may my prayer to Thee be in a time of grace;
God, in Thine abundant kindness

[9] English versions of these prayers are from *The Traditional Prayer Book*, edited and translated by Dr. David de Sola Pool; Behrman House, N.Y., 1960.

Answer me with Thy saving truth.

Blessed be Thy name, Lord of the universe; blessed be Thy Crown; blessed Thine abiding place.

May Thy favor be with Thy people Israel forever. In Thy Temple reveal to Thy people Thy right hand's redeeming power. Grant us of Thy beneficent light and accept our prayer in mercy. May it be Thy will to prolong our life in goodness. May I also be accounted among the righteous that Thou mayest show me love, and in Thy keeping hold me and all that is mine and that is of Thy people Israel. Thou art He who provides food for all and sustains all. Thou art He who rules over all. Thou art He who rules over monarchs, for dominion is Thine.

I am the servant of the Holy One, blessed be He, before whom and before Whose glorious Torah I bow down at all times. Not on man do I rely, nor do I lean on a son of God, but only on the God of the heavens who is the God of truth, whose Torah is truth and whose prophets were prophets of truth, and who abounds in doing goodness and truth. In Him alone is my trust, and to His holy and glorious name I utter praises.

May it be Thy will to open my heart to Thy Torah, and to fulfill the desires of my heart and the heart of all Thy people Israel for good, for life, and for peace. Amen.

[As the Reader receives the Torah and the Ark is closed:]

> Hear, O Israel, the Lord is our God, the Lord is one.
> One is our God, great is our Lord, holy is His name.
> Proclaim with me the greatness of the Lord,
> And let us extol His name together.

[As the Torah is carried to the reading desk:]

> Thine, O Lord, are greatness, power, glory, victory, and majesty,
> Yea, all that is in the heavens and on earth:
> Thine, O Lord, is dominion, and Thou art exalted supreme over all.
>   Exalt the Lord our God, and worship at His footstool,
>   For He is holy.
> Exalt the Lord our God, and worship at His holy mountain,
> For the Lord our God is holy.

Above all exalted and hallowed, praised and honored, extolled and glorified, be the name of the supreme King of kings, the Holy One, blessed be He, in the worlds He has created, this world and the world to be, in accordance with His will, the will of those who revere Him, and the will of the whole house of Israel. The Rock of the universe, Lord of all creatures, God of all spirits. He who dwells in the infinity of outermost space and the primordial heavens, His holiness crowns His throne of glory and is over the heavenly things.

Now, therefore, Lord our God, may Thy name be hallowed also among us in the sight of all living. May we sing before Thee a new song, even as it is written in Thy Psalms, "Sing to God, sing the praises of His name; extol Him who rides over heaven's vault, whose name is the Lord,

and exult before Him." Yea, may we see eye to eye when He returns to
His dwelling in Zion, even as it is written by His prophet Isaiah, "For
they shall see eye to eye when the Lord returns to Zion." Yea, further it is
said by Isaiah, "The glory of the Lord shall be revealed, and all flesh shall see
it together, for the mouth of the Lord has spoken it."

> Father of mercy,
> Have mercy on us who are held in duress.
> Recall Thy pledged word that forever would bless.
> Deliver our souls from impending distress.
> Withold from us evil; our sins we confess.
> O grant lasting freedom from those who oppress;
> Yea, answer our prayer with Thy saving caress.

[The Torah, splendidly dressed in mantle, breastplate, and crown,
is uncovered and placed on the reading desk. (The mantle is embroidered cloth; the shield and crown are generally silver.) The weekly
portion of the Torah, divided into at least seven sections, is then read.
A different man is called upon to recite the blessing for the reading of
the Torah for each section. (To be called up to the Torah is a signal
honor for a Jew. Central to the ceremony of *Bar Mitzvah* is the first
calling up to the Torah of the thirteen-year-old boy.) When the Torah
is returned to the Ark, after the reading, the following Biblical verses
are recited:]

> And when the Ark rested Moses would say,
> "Dwell, O Lord, among the myriads of families of Israel."
>> Come up, O Lord, to Thy resting place,
>> Thou and the Ark of Thy power.
> May Thy priests be clothed with righteousness,
> And Thy pious sing for joy.
>> For the sake of Thy servant David
>> Turn not back the face of Thine anointed.
> For I have given you a good doctrine,
> My Torah forsake it not.
>> It is the tree of life for those who lay hold of it,
>> And they who uphold it are made happy.
> Its ways are ways of pleasantness,
> And all its paths are peace.
>> Lord, turn us again toward Thee,
>> Yea, we would return;
>> Renew our days as of old."

When the reading of the Torah is completed on sabbaths and
festivals, a portion of the Prophets is read. This part of the service
is the *Haftorah*. The verses from the prophets are also fixed for
the particular part of the Torah they follow and have a thematic
relationship to the Torah portion.

After the *Haftorah*—or after the *Amidah* if the Torah is not read that day—the congregation recites Psalm 145. This is a universalist psalm; it does not mention Israel or indicate any Jewish relationship, but tells of God's goodness to all the beings He created. This part of the service is called the *Ashrei*—a word which has nothing to do with Psalm 145. The name comes from Psalm 84: "Happy are they that dwell in Thy house . . .," a verse of which introduces Psalm 145.

The *Ashrei* is followed by one of the oldest prayers in the Jewish liturgy, the *Aleynu* prayer. Tradition ascribes part of this prayer to Joshua, and some scholars surmise that *Aleynu* dates from before the destruction of the First Temple (585 B.C.), since it does not mention that event nor, a more telling indication, voice hope for the restoration of the kingdom. *Aleynu* gives thanks for the election of Israel and voices the Jews' hope for the day when all idolatry will cease, when those who turn from God shall turn toward Him, and for the coming of the reign of righteousness when all men will share God's grace:

It is for us to praise the Lord of all,
To acclaim the greatness of the God of creation,
    Who has not made us as worldly nations,
    Nor set us up as earthly peoples,
Not making our portion as theirs,
Nor our destiny as that of their multitudes.
    For we bow in worship before the supreme King of kings,
    The Holy One, blessed be He.
He stretched forth the heavens
And laid the foundations of the earth.
    His glorious abode is in the heavens above,
    The domain of His might in exalted heights.
He is our God, there is no other;
In truth our King, there is none else.
    Even thus is it written in His Torah:
    "This day know and lay it to your heart,
That the Lord is God in the heavens above and on the earth below.
There is none else."
We therefore hope in Thee, Lord our God,
Soon to behold the glory of Thy might
    When Thou wilt remove idols from the earth
    And the non-gods shall be wholly destroyed,
When Thou wilt establish the world under Thy rule omnipotent,
And all mankind shall invoke Thy name,
And all the wicked on earth Thou wilt turn to Thee.
    May all earth dwellers perceive and understand
    That to Thee every knee must bend, every tongue vow fealty.

> Before Thee, Lord our God, may all bow down and worship,
> And give honor to Thy glorious name.
> > May they all accept the rule of Thy dominion,
> > And speedily do Thou rule over them forevermore.

For the kingdom is Thine, and to all eternity Thou shalt reign in glory, as it is written in Thy Torah,

> "The Lord shall reign over all the earth;
> > Yea, it is said,
> "The Lord shall reign over all the earth;
> On that day the Lord shall be One and His name One."

Despite its thanks for the election of Israel, this is one of the most non-sectarian, most universalist prayers in the Siddur. Yet it was the special target for medieval persecutors of the Jews. It was specifically suppressed by kings, and those who recited it were killed because the prayer was supposedly anti-Christian. The arguments of Jewish scholars that this prayer was composed centuries before Jesus and thus could not be anti-Christian did not help. Because of its history and because of its great beauty and sense, the *Aleynu* prayer became the special prayer of martyrs.

During the persecution of the Jews of Blois [France] in 1171, where many masters of the Torah were burned at the stake, a witness wrote that the death of the saints was accompanied by a solemn song resounding through the night, causing Churchmen who heard it to wonder at its beauty, the like of which they had never heard before. The death song of the martyred saints was the *Aleynu*.[10]

The mourner's *Kaddish*, which follows the *Aleynu*, is one version of this ancient—and perhaps most widely known—prayer. There are five forms of the *Kaddish*, the Hebrew doxology or formula praise of God. Four of them appear in the service. They are:

The *half-Kaddish*, which is recited between sections of the synagogue service.

The *full Kaddish*, recited between major parts of the service.

The *Rabbis' Kaddish*, recited after study and recitations from the Talmudic literature.

The *orphan's or mourner's Kaddish*, recited during the eleven months of mourning and on the anniversary of the death of parents.

The *burial Kaddish*, recited only at the burial site. (This is not part of the synagogue service.)

The opening paragraph of the *Kaddish* is the basis for the Catholic Church's Magnificat and Pater Noster and the Protestant churches' "Our Father. . .":

---

[10] Joseph haCohen, *Vale of Tears*, sixteenth century.

Magnified and sanctified be His great Name in the world which He hath created according to His will. May He establish His kingdom during your life and during your days, and during the life of all the house of Israel, even speedily and at a near time, and say ye, Amen. . . .

Parts of this prayer were supposed to have been used as a response by worshipers in the Court of the Temple. And it is in this response that the *Kaddish's* early importance lay. Since the earliest days, Jews have responded, *"Yehey Shmey Rabba Mevorach,"* [11] (May His great Name be blessed) [12] whenever—as in the opening phrases of the *Kaddish*—they heard the holiness of God's name proclaimed. The Jews ascribed great virtue to eliciting this blessing response.

When the *Kaddish* assumed its present form is not known, but Jose ben Halaftah, a rabbi of the second century, recorded that it was used in his time, essentially as it is now, at the close of a sermon or lesson. It was through this use, and the fact that Jews used study as a form of worship, that the *Kaddish* prayer became associated with mourning. When a scholar died, other scholars showed respect to his memory by gathering in the deceased's house and conducting a study session in the Torah. The class ended, as was the custom with all classes, with the recitation of the *Kaddish*. But it became embarrassing to choose between scholars and non-scholars; respect for the dead made every Jew a scholar—at least after he died. And since a scholar's son had to be a scholar also, the son of the dead man was given the honor of reciting the *Kaddish* at the close of the memorial study session and of evoking the congregational response: *Yehey Shmey Rabba.* . . .

Thus the custom arose of the son's reciting the Kaddish every day during the eleven months after his father's death, on the anniversary of the death, and at memorial services. This recitation must be done in the presence of a congregation of Jews—at least ten men—in order to evoke the responsive blessing. The best and generally the only place in which to find such a congregation every day is in the synagogue. So the mourner's *Kaddish* became a part of the synagogue service.

Following the mourner's *Kaddish,* the congregation recites the Psalm of the Day and the closing hymns. The Psalm of the Day is fixed in the Siddur, a different psalm for the first day, the second day, etc. This custom was taken from the service in the Second Temple.

The closing hymns include two of the most beloved of Hebrew

[11] This is the Aramaic form used in modern worship.
[12] From Daniel 2:20.

songs: *Yigdal,* sung infrequently now, and *Adon Olam,* almost always sung on almost any occasion. *Yigdal* was written by Daniel ben Judah, religious judge of Rome in the fourteenth century.[13] It opens, "The living God we praise, exalt, adore. . . ." and its theme is Maimonides' thirteen-point Jewish creed. Although this creed has no religious authority among Jews, the beauty and sense of the poem made it a favorite. *Adon Olam* (Lord of the World) was written by Solomon ibn Gabirol, eleventh-century Spanish poet, and is the most popular hymn added to the liturgy in post-Biblical times.

The *Musaf,* or additional part of the service, is recited on sabbaths; it consists mainly of a repetition of the *Amidah.* The *Minchah,* or afternoon service, generally consists of the *Ashrei,* the *Amidah,* the reading of the Torah on the sabbath, the *Aleynu,* and the *Kaddish.* The *Maariv,* or evening service, includes the *Shema,* the *Amidah,* the *Aleynu,* and the *Kaddish.*

The sermon is not an obligatory part of the Jewish service, but it has very ancient precedents. The Levites who went among the people and explained the Law when Ezra put the Torah before them (440 B.C.) were, in effect, giving sermons. The Rabbis of the Talmud, who went before the people on sabbaths and during two special months of the year to explain what they had learned that week, were giving sermons. The custom of rabbinic explanations after the reading of the Torah in the synagogue was not followed during the Middle Ages, but it became very popular again with the rise of Chasidism in the eighteenth century. The stories and parables of the Chasidic preachers were repeated throughout the lands where Jews lived. Today, sermons are as much a part of synagogue services as they are of church services. The sermon is generally delivered at the end of the service.

The Siddur is still in process of change. Prayers for the six million Jews slaughtered by the Nazis are already found in many *siddurim.* New, more colloquial translations are being made; and new, more poetic translations are suggested regularly. The Siddur remains the most open, the least frozen volume in the literature of the Jews. This is a good augury, since the Siddur is today the most known, the most read, the most directly affecting religious book of the Jews.

---

[13] A. Z. Idelsohn, *Jewish Liturgy and its Development,* Henry Holt, 1932. However, this dating is challenged by other scholars.

The Commandments

ALMOST TWO-THIRDS of the 613 commandments deal with religion, with ritual, purification, priests, prophets, form and times of worship, and dietary laws. This leaves about 225 commandments establishing ethical and social standards, regulating family and community life, and protecting the dignity of life. By eliminating duplications, the most significant of these 225 commandments can be reduced to about 100 laws dealing with non-religious matters—plus the commandments in the Decalogue dealing with theft, murder, adultery, false witness, and working a servant or an animal on the sabbath. These are here arbitrarily divided into groups of social and ethical commands, laws on animals, laws on family, business and property law, and laws regulating judicial processes.

SOCIAL AND ETHICAL COMMANDMENTS

1. "Thou shalt love thy neighbor as thyself." Leviticus 19:18
2. "Love ye therefore the stranger. . . ." Deuteronomy 10:19
3. "Thou shalt not abhor an Edomite, for he is thy brother; thou shalt not abhor an Egyptian, because thou wast a stranger in his land." Deuteronomy 23:8
4. "Ye shall not wrong one another. . . ." Leviticus 25:17
5. "Thou shalt rise up before the hoary head, and honor the face of the old man." Leviticus 19:32
6. None shall stand idly by while another's life is in danger. Leviticus 19:16
7. "He that stealeth a man, and selleth him, or if he be found in his hand, he shall surely be put to death." Exodus 21:16
8. "If thy brother, a Hebrew man, or a Hebrew woman, be sold unto thee, he shall serve thee six years, and in the seventh year thou

shalt let him go free from thee. And when thou lettest him go free from thee, thou shalt not let him go empty; thou shalt furnish him liberally out of they flock, and out of thy threshing-floor, and out of thy wine-press. . . ." Deuteronomy 15:12–14

9. "Thou shalt not deliver unto his master a bondman [slave] that is escaped from his master unto thee; he shall dwell with thee, in the midst of thee . . . thou shalt not wrong him." Deuteronomy 23:16–17

10. A female slave cannot be sold. Exodus 21:8

11. Cutting and mutilation in grief are forbidden. Deuteronomy 14:1

12. It is forbidden to punish a woman who has been ravished. Deuteronomy 22:26

13. "There shall not be found among you any one that maketh his son or his daughter to pass through the fire, one that useth divination, a soothsayer, or an enchanter, or a sorcerer, or a charmer, or one that consulteth a ghost or a familiar spirit, or a necromancer." Deuteronomy 18:10–11

14. A woman captured in war must be given a month in which to mourn her dead parents; then she may be taken as a wife. "And . . . if thou have no delight in her, then thou shalt let her go whither she will; but thou shalt not sell her at all for money, thou shalt not deal with her as a slave. . . ." Deuteronomy 21:10–14

15. "At the end of every three years . . . thou shalt bring forth all the tithe of thine increase" for the stranger and the fatherless and the widow and the Levite. Deuteronomy 14:28–29

16. "If there be among you a needy man . . . thou shalt not harden thy heart, nor shut thy hand from thy needy brother; but thou shalt surely open thy hand unto him, and shalt surely lend him sufficient for his need. . . ." Deuteronomy 15:7–8

17. "When thou dost lend thy neighbour any manner of loan, thou shalt not go into his house to fetch his pledge. Thou shalt stand without, and the man to whom thou dost lend shall bring forth the pledge. . . ." Deuteronomy 24:10–11

18. If a poor man pledge something for a loan, "thou shalt not sleep with his pledge; thou shalt surely restore to him the pledge when the sun goeth down, that he may sleep in his garment. . . ." Deuteronomy 24:12–13

19. A day-laborer must be paid on the day in which he performs his labor, "neither shall the sun go down upon" his wages. Deuteronomy 24:15

20. "Thou shalt not oppress a hired servant that is poor and needy, whether he be of thy brethren, or of thy strangers. . . ." Deuteronomy 24:14

21. When you reap a field, and leave a sheaf, "thou shalt not go back to fetch it"; when you harvest the olives, "thou shalt not go over the boughs again"; when you gather the grapes in the vineyard, "thou shalt not glean it after thee; it shall be for the stranger, for the fatherless, and for the widow." Deuteronomy 24:19–21

22. Corners of fields shall not be reaped, nor shall fallen fruit be gathered; "thou shalt leave them for the poor and for the stranger." Leviticus 19:9–10

23. A laborer may eat of the produce of his labor during his work in the field and the vineyard. Deuteronomy 23:25–26

24. It is forbidden to take a pledge from a widow. Deuteronomy 24:17

25. It is forbidden to withhold from the owner anything that is found. Deuteronomy 22:1–3

26. No tools or utensils necessary to a man's work shall be taken in pledge for a loan. Deuteronomy 24:6

27. "Thou shalt not remove thy neighbour's landmark." Deuteronomy 19:14

28. "Thou shalt not have in thy bag diverse weights, a great and a small. Thou shalt not have in thy house diverse measures, a great and a small. A perfect and just weight shalt thou have; a perfect and just measure shalt thou have. . . ." Deuteronomy 25:13–15

29. Gluttony and drunkeness are forbidden. Deuteronomy 21:20

30. The king shall not "multiply horses to himself, nor cause the people to return to Egypt. . . . Neither shall he multiply wives to himself . . . neither shall he greatly multiply to himself silver and gold." Deuteronomy 17:16–17

31. A majority shall decide—but "thou shalt not follow a multitude to do evil. . . ." Exodus 23:2

LAWS ON ANIMALS

1. Mother birds must be allowed to go free when eggs are taken from her nest. Deuteronomy 22:7

2. "Thou shalt not see thy brother's ass or his ox fallen down by the way, and hide thyself from them; thou shalt surely help him to lift them up again." Deuteronomy 22:4

3. "Thou shalt not muzzle the ox when he treadeth out the corn." Deuteronomy 25:4

LAWS ON FAMILY

1. Men and women have an obligation to marry. Genesis 1:28

2. "When a man taketh a wife, and marrieth her, then it cometh to

pass, if she find no favour in his eyes, because he hath found some unseemly thing in her, that he writeth her a bill of divorcement, and giveth it in her hand, and sendeth her out of his house. . . ." Deuteronomy 24:1

3. If a man dies without a child, his brother shall take the widow to wife. Deuteronomy 25:5

4. A father may not put the child of a beloved wife ahead of the child of a hated wife. Deuteronomy 21:15–17

5. A man who falsely accuses his wife of infidelity may not divorce her. Deuteronomy 22:19

6. Marriage is forbidden to a sister, half-sister, niece, aunt, daughter-in-law, sister-in-law, mother and daughter, two sisters. Leviticus 18:7–18

7. Incest is forbidden. Deuteronomy 23:1

8. Both the man and woman guilty of adultery shall be punished by stoning. Deuteronomy 22:22

9. "A bastard shall not enter into the assembly the Lord [Israel]." Deuteronomy 23:3

10. A man who ravishes a virgin shall take her to wife and pay her father; neither can he divorce her in the future. Deuteronomy 22:28–29

11. "There shall be no harlot of the daughters of Israel, neither shall there be a sodomite of the sons of Israel." Deuteronomy 23:18

12. Sexual relations with a woman during menstruation is forbidden. Leviticus 18:19

13. Sodomy and bestiality are forbidden. Leviticus 18:22–23

14. Lewdness that incites to forbidden sex is forbidden. Leviticus 18:6

15. Castration is forbidden. Leviticus 22:24

16. A castrated man shall not marry a daughter of Israel. Deuteronomy 23:2

17. "A woman shall not wear that which pertaineth to a man, neither shall a man put on a woman's garment. . . ." Deuteronomy 22:5

18. Fathers must teach the Law to their children. Deuteronomy 6:7, 11:19

LAWS ON WAR

1. "When thou drawest nigh unto a city to fight against it, then proclaim peace unto it." If the city accepts peace, it shall pay tribute, but its people shall be left unharmed. If the city does not accept the offer of peace, "then shalt thou beseige it." Deuteronomy 20:10–12

2. "When thou shalt beseige a city . . . thou shalt not destroy the

trees thereof by wielding an axe against them; for thou mayest eat of them [the trees], but thou shalt not cut them down. . . . Only the trees of which thou knowest that they are not trees for food, them mayest thou destroy and cut down, that thou mayest build bulwarks against the city. . . ." Deuteronomy 20:19–20

3. When a city is taken in war, all the males shall be killed, "but no women, and the little ones, and the cattle, even all the spoil thereof, shalt thou take for a prey unto thyself" (except for the cities of the Hittites, Amorites, Canaanites, Perizzites, and Jebusites). Deuteronomy 20:13–18

4. "When a man taketh a new wife, he shall not go out in the host [army] . . . he shall be free for his house [from military service] one year. . . ." Deuteronomy 24:5

5. A man who has built a new house, but not dedicated it; a man who has planted a vineyard, but not reaped it; a man who has betrothed a wife, but not "taken her"; a man who is fearful and faint-hearted . . . "let him go and return unto his house." Deuteronomy 20:5–8

6. It is forbidden to be afraid of the enemy. Deuteronomy 20:3

7. "When thou goest forth to battle," a priest shall go before to speak to the warriors. Deuteronomy 20:1–2

8. It is required that latrines be dug outside the camp of the army, and those who do not use the latrines shall be punished. Deuteronomy 23:10–15

LAWS OF BUSINESS AND PROPERTY

1. "If thou sell aught unto thy neighbor, or buy of thy neighbor's hand, ye shall not wrong one another." Leviticus 25:14

2. "At the end of every seven years thou shalt make a release. And this is the manner of the release: every creditor shall release that which he hath lent unto his neighbour; he shall not exact it of his neighbour and his brother. . . ." Deuteronomy 15:1–2

3. Loans made to a stranger (non-Hebrew) may be reclaimed even in the year of release. Deuteronomy 15:3

4. "Thou shalt not lend upon interest to thy brother; interest of money, interest of victuals, interest of anything that is lent upon interest." Deuteronomy 23:20

5. "Unto a foreigner thou mayest lend upon interest. . . ." Deuteronomy 23:21

6. It is forbidden to demand payment of a loan after the year of release. Deuteronomy 15:2

7. It is forbidden to refuse a loan to a needy person because the

year of release is approaching. Deuteronomy 15:9

8. Lines of inheritance are (1) son, (2) daughter, (3) brother, (4) father's brother, etc. Numbers 27:8–11

9. "The priests and the Levites . . . shall have no portion nor inheritance." Deuteronomy 18:1

LAWS ON JUDICIAL PROCESSES

1. It is required to appoint "judges and officers . . . in all thy gates [cities]. . . ." Deuteronomy 16:18

2. "Thou shalt not turn aside from the sentence which they [judges] shall declare unto thee. . . ." Deuteronomy 17:11

3. Criminals shall not be executed without due process of law. Numbers 35:12

4. A man adjudged guilty shall have his case reopened on new evidence. A man declared innocent cannot be retried. Exodus 23:7

5. Circumstantial evidence is not enough in a capital case. Exodus 23:7

6. Judges must judge righteously between a man and his brother, and a stranger. Deuteronomy 1:16

7. Justice must be impartial. "Ye shall do no unrighteousness in judgment; thou shalt not respect the person of the poor, nor favour the person of the mighty; but in righteousness shalt thou judge. . . ." Leviticus 19:15

8. Witnesses are required to testify. Leviticus 5:1

9. Witnesses must be questioned carefully and evidence gathered diligently. Deuteronomy 13:15

10. A vow cannot be broken, and testimony must be truthful. Deuteronomy 23:24

11. False witnesses shall be punished with the same punishment that their false testimony would have visited on the accused. Deuteronomy 19:16–19

12. It is forbidden to curse a judge, a prince, a king—or a teacher. Exodus 22:27

13. Punishment by scourging cannot exceed forty lashes. Deuteronomy 25:3

14. It is forbidden to "pervert the justice due to the stranger, or to the fatherless. . . ." Deuteronomy 24:17

15. The testimony of relatives cannot be used either for or against an accused. Deuteronomy 24:16

16. An accused shall not be condemned on the testimony of a single witness. "At the mouth of two witnesses, or at the mouth of three witnesses, shall a matter be established." Deuteronomy 19:15

17. A lawsuit shall not be heard unless both plaintiff and defendant are present. Exodus 23:1

18. It is forbidden to refuse obedience to the judgment of the court. Deuteronomy 17:11

19. A judge "shalt not wrest judgment; thou shalt not respect persons; neither shalt thou take a gift. . . ." Deuteronomy 16:19

20. A person ignorant of the law shall not be appointed judge. Deuteronomy 1:17

21. Cities of refuge shall be established where those who unintentionally cause death may be safe. Deuteronomy 35:11

22. It is forbidden to allow a murderer to escape to a city of refuge. Deuteronomy 19:11–12

23. It is forbidden to relax the punishment of a murderer or other lawbreaker. Deuteronomy 19:13

24. It is required to build a parapet around the roof of a house "that thou bring not blood upon thy house, if any man fall from thence." Deuteronomy 22:8

25. If a man deal falsely, or rob, or withhold a pledge, or oppress his neighbor, or keep a lost article, or swear falsely, he must make good the loss, plus one-fifth. Leviticus 5:20–24

26. A king shall be set over Israel, but "thou mayest not put a foreigner over thee. . . ." Deuteronomy 17:15

27. You shall hearken unto a prophet, so long as he follows the law. Deuteronomy 18:15–22

28. The king shall write a copy of the law in his own hand, and "he shall read therein all the days of his life. . . ." Deuteronomy 17:18–19

29. It is forbidden to add to or diminish God's Law. Deuteronomy 4:2

30. Punishments and Indemnities:

For smiting father or mother—	death
For cursing father or mother—	death
For stealing a man—	death
For injuring another in a fight—	pay lost time and medical bills
For injuring a woman with child so she loses child—	fine according to husband's demand and judge's decision
For injuring a woman with child so that she has permanent harm—	eye for an eye, etc.
For maiming a slave—	slave goes free
If an ox gores someone—	the ox is killed

If an ox that is known to be dangerous gores someone—	death or ransom for the owner
If an animal falls into a pit—	pit owner pays damage
If animals fight and hurt each other—	animals are sold and money divided between owners
If animals fight and one is known to be dangerous—	owner of dangerous animals pays damages
For stealing an animal—	thief pays five oxen for each ox stolen, four sheep for each sheep
For killing a criminal during the commission of a crime at night—	no penalty
For injuring man committing a crime during daylight—	self-defense cannot be offered
If animal eats in neighbor's fields—	owner of animal must repay from best of his own field
For arson—	arsonist must make full restitution
If man seduces a virgin—	must offer to marry her; if girl's father refuses offer, seducer must pay fifty shekels
For seducing a bethrothed virgin—	death by stoning
For rape—	death by stoning
For harlotry or adultery—	death by stoning

The Tractates of the Mishnah

THE FIRST ORDER OF the Mishnah is *Zeraim* (Seeds); it has eleven tractates:

1. *Berachot* (Blessings) deals with the rules for prayer.
2. *Peah* (Corner), based on Leviticus 19:9–11 and Deuteronomy 24:19–22, deals with the corners of the fields which must be left unharvested for the poor.
3. *Demai* (Doubtful) covers the problem of produce which may be of doubtful purity because it was not properly tithed.
4. *Kilaim* (Mixtures), based on Leviticus 19:19 and Deuteronomy 22:9–12, deals with prohibited mixtures of animals, plants and fibers.
5. *Sheviit* (The Sabbatical Year), based on Exodus 23:10–12, Leviticus 25:2–8, and Deuteronomy 15:1–4, covers the law of the seventh year when the land must lie fallow.
6. *Terumot* (Heave-offerings), based on Numbers 18:8–19 and Deuteronomy 18:4, deals with that portion of the harvest, ranging from one-fortieth to one-sixtieth, which must be given to the priests.
7. *Masserot* (Tithes), based on Leviticus 21:3–23 and Numbers 18:21–26, covers the First Tithe, that belonging to the Levites.
8. *Masser Sheni* (Second Tithe), based on Leviticus 27:30 and Deuteronomy 14:22–29, deals with the tithe which must be taken to Jerusalem or changed into coin and sent to Jerusalem.
9. *Challah* (Dough Offering), based on Numbers 15:18–21, deals with the priests' share of the dough used in baking.
10. *Orlah* (Uncircumcised), based on Leviticus 19:23–25, refers to the fruit of young trees, not to men. This fruit may not be eaten in the first three years, only under special rules during the

second three years.

11. *Bikkurim* (First Fruits), based on Exodus 23:19 and Deuteronomy 26:1–11, deals with rules and ceremonies relating to the bringing of the first fruits [first harvest] to the Temple.

The Second Order is *Moed* (Festivals); it includes twelve tractates:

1. *Shabbat* (Sabbath), based on the Decalogue, deals with observing the sabbath.

2. *Erubin* (Combinations): since a Jew cannot go out of his "place" during the sabbath, this tractate covers the ways and means of defining "place" and enlarging it.

3. *Pesachim* (Passover) deals with the laws of this holiday.

4. *Shekalim* (Shekels), based on Exodus 30:12–16, deals with the Temple tax.

5. *Yoma* (The Day [of Atonement]), based on Leviticus 16:3–34 and Numbers 29:7–11, covers the ceremonies for this holiday as celebrated in the Temple.

6. *Succah* ([Feast of] Booths), based on Leviticus 23:34–43, deals with the rules of celebrating this holiday of the fall harvest.

7. *Behtzah* (Egg), also known as Yom Tov (Holy Day), based on Exodus 12:16 and Leviticus 23:3–36. Work forbidden on the sabbath is also forbidden on the festival holy days, except for the preparation of food. This tractate covers the permitted work. It gets its name from the opening word.

8. *Rosh Hashanah* (New Year), based on Leviticus 23:24 and Numbers 29:1, deals with the calendar generally and the marking of the New Year.

9. *Taanit* (Fasting) covers the rules for fasting.

10. *Megillah* (Scroll [of Esther]) covers the rules for reading the Book of Esther and celebrating the holiday of Purim.

11. *Moed Katan* (Mid-festival Days) deals with the non-sacred days of the eight-day celebrations of the festivals of Passover and Feast of Tabernacles.

12. *Chagigah* (Festival Offering), based on Exodus 23:14 and Deuteronomy 16:16–18, deals with offerings to be made during the three festivals when Palestinian Jews made pilgrimages to the Temple.

The Third Order, *Nashim* (Women), has seven tractates:

1. *Yabamot* (Sisters-in-law) is based on Deuteronomy 25:5–10 and deals with levirate marriage (*levir*—a brother-in-law). The Biblical injunction requires a man to marry his brother's widow (his sister-in-law) if the brother died childless. The man refuses

by going through the ceremony of *halitzah.*

2. *Ketubot* (Marriage Contracts) covers the rules of marriage, settlements, and divorce.

3. *Nedarim* (Vows), based on Numbers 6:2–21, deals with vows and their annulment. This section is put into the order Women because the vows—distinct from oaths—refer mainly to women.

4. *Nazir* (Nazirite Vows), based on Numbers 6:2–21, deals with holy men and women who consecrate themselves to the Lord.

5. *Sotah* (Adulteress), based on Numbers 5:11–31, treats with the procedures in cases where a wife is suspected or has been proven unfaithful.

6. *Gittin* (Bills of Divorce), based on Deuteronomy 24:1–4, includes the rules for preparing, attesting to, and delivering divorce documents.

7. *Kiddushin* (Betrothals) covers the modes of betrothal and the conditions of valid marriage.

The Fourth Order, *Nezikim* (Damages), has ten tractates:

1. *Baba Kamma* (First Gate), based on Exodus 21:28–37 and and 22:1–6, deals with damages to person and property.

2. *Baba Metzia* (Middle Gate), based on Exodus 22:6–14, 24–27, Leviticus 25:14, 35–38, and Deuteronomy 22:1–4, covers found property, buying and selling, trusts, loans, hiring, and renting.

3. *Baba Bathra* (Last Gate), based on Numbers 27:7–11, deals with inheritance, commerce, real estate, and tenants.

4. *Sanhedrin* (Courts) covers the administration of justice.

5. *Makkot* (Stripes) is concerned mainly with crimes whose punishment is flogging; it also deals with cities of refuge.

6. *Shevuot* (Oaths), based on Exodus 22:6–10 and Leviticus 5 and 6, covers the juridical use of oaths.

7. *Eduyot* (Testimony) includes selected laws on unrelated topics, identified by the names of the schools or sages who enunciated them. The name of the tractate comes from the frequent use of "Hillel [or Shammai or whoever] testified that. . . ."

8. *Avodah Zarah* (Idolatry) gives the regulations governing Jews in relation to idols and pagan peoples.

9. *Aboth* (Fathers), better known as "The Sayings of the Fathers," gives philosophical rules for a proper life.

10. *Horayot* (Decisions), based on Leviticus 4 and 5, deals with situations in which a court gives a wrong decision.

The Fifth Order, *Kodashim* (Holy Things), has eleven tractates dealing mainly with matters pertinent only to the time of the Temple.

1. *Zebachin*: sacrifices or animal offerings.
2. *Menachot*: meal offerings.
3. *Chullin*: animals killed for food, ritual slaughter and dietary laws.
4. *Becharot*: first born which are used for sacrifices, the first born son, and inheritance.
5. *Arachin*: valuations, rules for redeeming that which is pledged to God.
6. *Temurah*: substitutes for offerings.
7. *Kerithot*: extirpation, being "cut off" from the Lord or death, offerings to be made if a crime was inadvertent.
8. *Meilah*: the sacrilegious use of Temple property.
9. *Tamid*: daily sacrifice.
10. *Middot*: measurements (the size, shape, and structure) of the Temple.
11. *Kinnim*: birds' nests, bird offerings used by those too poor to afford animal offerings.

The Sixth order, *Tohorot* (Purifications), includes twelve tractates also referring mainly to Temple ceremonies and practices.

1. *Kelim* (Vessels): ritual cleanliness of ordinary objects—beds, clothes, utensils, etc.
2. *Oholot* (Tents): uncleanness associated with corpses of man and animals.
3. *Negaim* (Leprosy).
4. *Parah* (the Red Heifer) used for sacrifices.
5. *Tohorot* (Purifications): lesser uncleanness.
6. *Mikvaot* (Ritual Baths).
7. *Niddah* (the Menstruant).
8. *Machshirin*: things which might make food unclean.
9. *Zabim* (Venereal Disease).
10. *Tebul Yom* (He That Immersed Himself That Day): purification for
11. *Yadaiim* (Hands): washing the hands as a purification.
    minor uncleanness.
12. *Utzkin* (Stalks): uncleanness in plants.

APPENDIX III

The Seven Sections of Proverbs

THE BOOK OF Proverbs is divided into seven major sections:

1. Chapters 1 through 9—an introduction and statement of the theme of the book: The fear of the Lord (the formulation meaning religion) is the essence of wisdom. Wisdom, personified as a female, appeals to the ignorant man, describing the delights of following her way and the penalties of denying her.

> My son, forget not my teaching;
> But let thy heart keep my commandments;
> For length of days, and years of life,
> And peace, will they add to thee.
> Let not kindness and truth forsake thee;
> Bind them about thy neck,
> Write them upon the table of thy heart;
> So shalt thou find grace and good favour
> In the sight of God and man. . . .
>
> The curse of the Lord is in the house of the wicked;
> But He blesseth the habitation of the righteous.
> If it concerneth the scorners, He scorneth them,
> But unto the humble He giveth grace.
> The wise shall inherit honour;
> But as for the fools, they carry away shame.[1]

2. Chapters 10 through 22:16—this part of the book begins with the words "The proverbs of Solomon" and includes 375 sayings marked by great regularity of form and meter; each proverb is made up of two parallel statements. There is much mention of God, more moralizing, much less humor, wit, and sarcasm than in other sections of the book.

[1] Proverbs 3:1–4, 33–35

> The thoughtless believeth every word;
> But the prudent man looketh well to his going.
> A wise man feareth, and departeth from evil;
> But the fool behaveth overbearingly, and is confident.
> He that is soon angry dealeth foolishly;
> And a man of wicked devices is hated.
> The thoughtless come into possession of folly;
> But the prudent are crowned with knowledge.
> The evil bow before the good,
> And the wicked at the gates of the righteous.
> The poor is hated even of his own neighbour;
> But the rich hath many friends. . . .

> In the fear of the Lord a man hath strong confidence;
> And his children shall have a place of refuge.[2]

3. Chapters 22:17 through 24—two collections of "words to the wise" including thirty precepts very close to the thirty precepts in the "instructions of Amen-em-ope," dated variously between 1000 and 600 B.C. For example, Proverbs 22:22 says: "Rob not the weak because he is weak, neither crush the poor in the gate." The Egyptian version says: "Guard thyself against robbing the oppressed and against overbearing the disabled." The whole section appears to be advice to a young man embarking on a civil service career. There are even suggestions on court etiquette.

> When thou sittest to eat with a ruler,
> Consider well him that is before thee;
> And put a knife to thy throat,
> If thou be a man given to appetite
> Be not desirous of his dainties;
> Seeing they are deceitful food.[3]

4. Chapters 25 through 29—these proverbs are introduced by the words, "These are the proverbs of Solomon, which the men of Hezekiah king of Judah copied out." And these sayings may very well have been put together by the scribes of Hezekiah, who ruled in the eighth century B.C. Chapters 25 through 27 are older than Chapters 28 and 29; they are more secular and far less moralizing than the earlier Solomonic proverbs.

5. Chapter 30—the first part of "The words of Agur the son of Jakeh" is a forecast of the later books of wisdom. Agur asks Job-like questions, but gives Ecclesiastes-like answers.

[2] Proverbs 14:15–20, 26
[3] Proverbs 23:1–3

Surely I am brutish, unlike a man,
And have not the understanding of a man;
And I have not learned wisdom,
That I should have the knowledge of the Holy One.
Who hath ascended up into heaven, and descended?
Who hath gathered the wind in his fists?
Who hath bound the waters in his garment?
Who hath established all the ends of the earth?
What is his name, and what is his son's name, if thou knowest?[4]

The second part of this section includes proverbs based on the kind of numerical repetition that Biblical writers and post-Biblical Jewish scholars found fascinating.

There are three things which are too wonderful for me,
Yea, four that say not: "Enough":
The grave; and the barren womb;
The earth that is not satisfied with water;
And the fire that saith not: "Enough."

There are three things which are too wonderful for me,
Yea, four which I know not:
The way of an eagle in the air;
The way of a serpent upon a rock;
The way of a ship in the midst of the sea;
And the way of a man with a young woman.[5]

6. Chapter 31:1–9—"The words of king Lemuel (taught him by his mother)" are a warning against drunkenness and injustice to the poor.

7. Chapter 31:30–31—a poem in acrostic form describing the ideal wife.

A woman of valour who can find?
For her price is far above rubies.
The heart of her husband doth safely trust in her,
And he hath no lack of gain.
She doeth him good and not evil
All the days of her life.
She seeketh wool and flax,
And worketh willingly with her hands.
She is like the merchant-ships;
She bringeth her food from afar.
She riseth also while it is yet night,
And giveth food to her household,
And a portion to her maidens.[6]

---

[4] Proverbs 30:2–4
[5] Proverbs 30:15b–16, 18–19
[6] Proverbs, 31:10–15

An Example of Talmud

MISHNAH. (23a) Civil actions [are to be tried] by three [judges]. Each [litigant] chooses one, and the two jointly choose a third: so holds R. Meir. But the sages rule: the two judges nominate the third. Each party may object to the judge chosen by the other, so holds R. Meir. But the sages say: when is this so? Only if the objector adduces proof that they are either kinsmen or [otherwise] ineligible, but if fit or recognized by the *Beth din,* as *mumhin,*[1] they cannot be disqualified.

Each party may reject the witnesses produced by the other: So holds R. Meir. But the sages say, when is this so? Only when proof is brought that they are either kinsmen or [otherwise] ineligible; but if they are [legally] eligible, no one can disqualify them.

GEMARA. Why should each of the parties choose one [*Beth din*]: do not three [judges] suffice?—The Mishnah is meant thus: If each party chose a different *Beth din* [so that one is not mutually accepted], they must jointly choose a third. Can then the debtor too reject [the *Beth din* chosen by the creditor]? Did not R. Eleazar say: This refers only to the creditor; but the debtor can be compelled to appear for trial in his [the creditor's] town?—It is as R. Johanan said [below]: we learnt this only in reference to Syrian lawcourts [which followed Roman Law]; and so here too; but not *mumhin.* R. Papa said : It may even refer to *mumhin,* e.g., the courts of R. Huna and R. Hisda, for he [the debtor] can say: Am I giving you any trouble?

[1] *Mumhin* (singular, *munheh*): experts; specialists in a field.

We learnt: *The sages rule: the two judges nominate the third.*
Now, should you think it means as we have said, viz., each litigant
chooses a *Beth din;* can a *Beth din,* after being rejected, go and
choose them another? Again, how interpret, each party chooses one?
—But it means thus: Each [litigant] having chosen a judge, these two
[litigants] jointly select a third. Why should they do so?—They
said in "the West" in the name of R. Zera: Since each selects a judge,
and together they [the litigants] select the third, a true judgment
will be rendered.

But the sages rule, etc. Shall we say that they differ in regard to
the law cited by Rab Judah in the name of Rab? For Rab Judah said
in the name of Rab: Witnesses may not sign a deed unless they are
aware who is to sign with them: R. Meir thus disagreeing with the
dictum of Rab Judah given in the name of Rab, while the Rabbis
accept it?—No, all agree with Rab Judah's statement in Rab's name,
and none dispute that the [third judge] must have the consent of
his colleagues; they only differ as to whether the consent of the litigants is necessary. R. Meir maintains that the consent of the litigants
is also required, while the Rabbis hold, only that of the judges is required, but not that of the litigants.

The [above] text [states]: Rab Judah said in Rab's name:
Witnesses may not sign a deed, etc. It has been taught likewise: The
fair minded of the people in Jerusalem used to act thus: They would
not sign a deed without knowing who would sign with them; they
would not sit in judgment unless they knew who was to sit with
them; and they would not sit at table without knowing their fellow
diners.

Each party may object to the judge chosen by the other.
Has then anyone the right to reject judges?—R. Johanan said:
This refers to the Syrian [Roman] courts. But [you say that]
mumhin cannot be rejected? Surely since the last clause states, *but
the sages say: when is this so? Only if the objector adduces proof
that they are either kinsmen or [otherwise] ineligible; but if fit or
recognized by the* Beth din *as* mumhin, *they cannot be disqualified:*
does it not follow that R. Meir refers even to *mumhin!*—It is meant
thus: But if they are fit, they rank as *mumhin* appointed by the
Beth din, and so cannot be disqualified.

Come and hear: "The Rabbis said to R. Meir: It does not rest
with him to reject a judge who is a *mumheh* for the public?—Say
[thus]: It does not rest with him to reject a judge whom the
public has accepted as a *mumheh.* It has been taught likewise: One
may go on rejecting judges until he undertakes [that the action

shall be tried] before a *Beth din* of *mumhin*: this is the view of R. Meir.

But witnesses [when not disqualified] are as *mumhin*, yet R. Meir said: *Each party may reject the witnesses produced by the other*!—Surely it has been stated regarding this: Resh Lakish said: Imagine a holy mouth [R. Meir] uttering such a thing! Read [therefore] the witness [singular]. But for what purpose is a single witness [competent]? Shall we say, for the actual payment of money? then his testimony is Biblically invalid! If for [the administration of] an oath, then his evidence is [legally] as trustworthy as that of two!—In fact, he refers to the payment of money, but it [R. Meir's ruling] arises only where both parties have voluntarily accepted his testimony as equivalent to that of two witnesses. Then what does he thereby teach: that he may retract? But we have already learnt this once. If one says, I accept my father or thy father as trustworthy, or I have confidence in three herdsmen, R. Meir says, He may [subsequently] retract; but the Sages rule, He cannot. (23b) And thereon R. Dimi the son of R. Nahman the son of R. Joseph observed: This means, e.g., that he accepted him as one [of the three judges]!—Both are necessary. Had he stated only the law regarding the "fathers" it might have been assumed that only there do the Rabbis rule that he cannot retract, because "my father" and "thy father" are fit [to act as judges] in other cases; but where one witness is accepted as two, one might have thought that the Rabbis agreed with R. Meir, since he is unfit in general. Whilst had the law been stated in this instance, I might have thought that only here does R. Meir rule thus; but in the other case, he agrees with the Rabbis. Hence both are necessary. But since the first clause mentions, *"Judge"* [singular], whilst the second reads, *"Witnesses"* [plural], it follows that it is to be taught literally?—Said R. Eleazar: This is a case where he [the litigant] together with another come forward to disqualify them. But is he empowered to do this, seeing that he is an interested party?—R. Aha the son of R. Ika said: [Yes], e.g., where he makes public the ground of his objection. What objection is meant? Shall we say, an objection based on a charge of robbery? But does that rest with him, seeing that he is an interested party? Hence it must be an objection on the grounds of family unfitness. Now, R. Meir contends that they [the litigant and his supporter] testify against the man's family, whilst he is automatically disqualified; and the Rabbis hold that after all is said and done, he is an interested party. . . .

Index